[spooks]

Harry's Diary

Also available

Spooks: The Personnel Files

[spooks]

Harry's Diary

headline

Cataloguing in Publication Data is available from the
British Library

Trade paperback ISBN 978 0 7553 3398 1

Typeset in Letter Gothic by Avon DataSet Ltd,
Bidford-on-Avon, Warwickshire

Printed and bound in Great Britain by
Clays Ltd, St Ives plc

Headline's policy is to use papers that are natural,
renewable and recyclable products and made from wood grown
in sustainable forests. The logging and manufacturing
processes are expected to conform to the environmental
regulations of the country of origin.

HEADLINE PUBLISHING GROUP
A division of Hachette Livre UK Ltd
338 Euston Road
London NW1 3BH

www.headline.co.uk
www.hodderheadline.com

1977

[9 June 1977]

There are five reasons, as far as I can see, why a man might choose to keep a diary.

One: as a kind of cheap therapy — a friendly, mute psychologist who offers appointments whenever you want one and never asks the wrong questions. Keeping a diary demarcates your work and home life. Write it all down. Pour it all out. And then shut the covers and shut up about it.

Two: as an aide-memoire for your dotage. A diary written during your working life would act as an interesting retrospective as you slowly slip into the senility of retirement.

Three: for posterity. If you think you have something interesting to say, you might want to pass this on to your children once you're gone. Or your children's children. So they can know what their grandfather was really like.

Four: for publication. As above, but so the whole world can read about you, and not just your family.

Five: for protection. A record of events, as they happen, as viewed by you. A personal, ongoing alibi of minutiae.

1

[spooks]

I have just finished new-recruit training at MI5. I am twenty-three years old. To date, I have no need of therapy. My memory is currently sound. Retirement seems a long way off. And I have absolutely no inclination to turn into some kind of awful hybrid of Ian Fleming and Samuel Pepys. I'd shirk away from anything approaching publicity. It would destroy my career, for one.

I'm not even sure I'm much of a writer. Or rather, I'm not much of a diarist. I enjoy writing. I like to think things through. I enjoyed the philosophy side of my degree as much as the politics. But I distrust amateur psychology. I distrust pouring out one's feelings — whether in public or private.

On the other hand, I can see the advantages of having somewhere to take out my frustrations. I also like the idea that my family might be able to read this one day — long, long after I'm dead — to see what I really did for a living. And in the meantime, I can certainly see the merits of keeping a diary secured away somewhere (somewhere very secure indeed) as a potential defence should the need arise.

It reminds me of a conversation I had with a senior officer during my training.

'You're not as naïve as some of our recruits,' he said. 'You've served in the army. You've seen action. You've seen death. But there will be times here when you long for the moral absolutes of military life: the chain of command; enemies and allies; black and white; right and wrong.

'Let me put it like this,' he continued. 'MI5 is a complex beast. It recruits the brightest and the best. But look at the people at the top. Look at its directors, its executives, its director generals. Are they still the brightest and the best? Or are they the ones who know how to play the game?'

'They're the ones who know how to play the game,' I said. 'But that's obvious. It's the same as any organisation.'

'No,' he said. 'MI5 is different. Here, you'll say black when you mean white, white when you mean black. Everything else is grey. You'll tell your line manager one thing, your agents another and the world outside something else altogether. There are no truths in this job. Only degrees of lying.'

So, I resolved this afternoon, my diary will be where I tell the truth, or at least my perception of the truth. This will be my confessional on the world. It will also be my safety net: a security measure should anything happen to me. If I am blackmailed, here is my defence. If I am sidelined by the service, here is my attack. It is the record of significant events as they happened. Witnessed by me and recorded by me.

Keeping a diary in the security services is a dangerous thing to do. Good men, as well as bad, are killed to protect secrets here. But I think it's worth the risk.

Not that anything of any note has happened since joining. I finished new-recruit training today and was happy with my scores – particularly the five for general attitude. God knows what it would have been a few years ago – 0.1, no doubt. But the army put paid to all that.

I've also cleared the security tests (unsurprising since I was already vetted for Sandhurst). And I did well in the training – although I must admit it was surprisingly simple after two years in the army. There are rumours that I am going to be assigned to A Section – the one that used to be called

Section A, and before that Section F and Section L. Or, in layman's terms, Northern Ireland. But this hasn't been confirmed yet. The bureaucracy here is almost as mind-numbing as the army's.

[16 June 1977]

Yesterday was my wedding. Something happened there which makes it worth noting.

The first bit of the day went very well. The vicar was mercifully brief, my best man, Bill Crombie, didn't forget the rings and I managed not to fluff my lines. Jane looked perfect. I only wish my mother could have been there.

My father gave the reading from Sonnet 138, an MI5 favourite. I reproduce part of it here because it gives the context to what happened next:

> When my love swears that she is made of truth,
> I do believe her, though I know she lies,
> That she might think me some untutor'd youth,
> Unlearned in the world's false subtleties
>
> Therefore I lie with her, and she with me,
> And in our faults by lies we flattered be.

After we'd signed the register, Jane's ghastly mother complained that this was not the most romantic choice for a wedding reading. She was probably right. But I liked the poem. And my father approved of it as well. But then I stupidly compounded the hurt by choosing this moment to tell Jane that I worked for MI5.

An inexplicable decision, perhaps. Why hadn't I told her earlier? She was a friend — at Oxford — before she was a lover. She knows I've been in the army. But I'd let her think that I was applying for the Home Office and not MI5.

Maybe I was worried that I wouldn't make it the whole way through the selection process. Perhaps I wanted to wait until I had concrete good news to give her, and didn't want to share the emotional roller coaster of the journey with her. Or maybe I just wanted to keep this particular secret to myself. I'm not sure.

But I think my main motive was that I was scared of how she would react. I know she likes the fact I used to be in the army. But I think she was secretly hoping for a quiet life once I'd left. Telling her just before we cut the cake that I worked for MI5 might not have been the most sensible decision of my life. But it's good to get these things on paper first, isn't it?

Fortunately, she took it very well. Or at least, she pretended to take it very well.

And so, fully aware of each other's false subtleties, we go out to face the world together.

1978

[10 January 1978]

Feeling quite settled now in Belfast. Jane has got a job teaching English in the local school. And God knows, the kids here could do with learning a little bit of English.

Work so far has been quite boring – just the usual induction seminars. They're reluctant to give you too much responsibility early on. It's the very opposite of the army in some ways. There they throw you into Sandhurst and treat you like muck for a year. You're stripped to the very core of your being, until you barely feel human any more. Idiot Neanderthals with scraping knuckles and an IQ of room temperature shout at you until your ears burst. But then the moment you pass out, you're suddenly in charge of scores of soldiers, many of them older, tougher and more experienced than you are. I don't think anything makes a man grow up faster.

At MI5, it's the opposite, at least in A Section. We've been treated with kid gloves. I long to have a bit of responsibility but spend most of my time doing menial research for my boss, Simon Cooper.

I know exactly how long he likes his tea bag left in for –

Earl Grey, 3 minutes; Twinings ('What's happened to the bloody Earl Grey, Pearce?'), 4 minutes. I know which tie he'll be wearing on any given day — mainly blue, as it 'matches my wife's eyes'. And I know exactly how he answers the phone: 'Cooper, A Section' for internal calls; 'Extension 5070' for external calls.

He's not a bad man. He's a very good man, in fact. But he's just not a patch on my old commanding officer in the Light Blue Dragoons, Colonel Sam Collins.

[18 January 1978]

There was some big news today: the European Court of Human Rights found the UK government guilty of mistreating prisoners in Northern Ireland but cleared us of torture charges. I wonder if the ECHR have seen what the PIRA does to captured British soldiers, or anyone they suspect of being an informer. That might change their mind.

Not sure what the ramifications will be yet. It's a fine line, I suppose, between mistreatment and torture. Where does one end and the other start? Aggressive questioning? Sleep deprivation? Worse?

Not that I've been allowed anywhere near a prisoner. The only thing that's being mistreated in this corner of the office is the kettle.

[2 February 1978]

Jane is really enjoying her work and has finally forgiven me, I

think, for not telling her earlier about my job. I think it helps
that my current work is so tedious and mundane, so she feels I'm
safe at least.

'You're my own little James Bond,' she keeps on teasing me.
'Although slightly shorter and prematurely balding.'

This does not do wonders for my self-esteem.

[5 February 1978]

My childhood friend, Bill Crombie, has just been moved to my
desk, which has made life a whole lot more fun. Bill and I were
at school together and we are still very close.

He is one of the most consummate actors you could ever meet,
but he gave it all up because he wanted to do something 'more
worthwhile' with his time. It's quite humbling when he puts it
like that. I sometimes wonder how many concrete decisions a man
actually takes during the course of his life. Sure, you might
choose one university over another. Or one girl over her friend.
Or one job in preference to an alternative. But how often do you
actually take a leap into the unknown?

Me? School — went there because the law said I had to and
my father had been there too. University — went to Oxford because
Cambridge was full of posh Communist traitors. Army — went there
for my mother's sake. MI5 — came here because I was asked to.

Bill, on the other hand, gave up one of the most promising
stage careers since Gielgud to come and work in a pisspot in
Northern Ireland. He approaches his job with a zeal that is
alien to most people here. It's an enthusiasm I love.

[27 February 1978]

That is not to say that Bill is not above a little light-hearted mischief-making. Similarly frustrated by the lack of opportunities at the moment, he has taken to winding up Simon Cooper whenever possible.

Bill's favourite author is P. G. Wodehouse and he is currently under the impression that he is the debonair, articulate Rupert Psmith, I am his sport-loving friend Mike Jackson, and that between us our job is to bring a bit of sunshine into the life of Mr Bickersdyke (a.k.a. Simon Cooper).

I am playing second fiddle to Bill's little games, but they are fun to observe from the sidelines. To date, they have remained fairly minor — 'accidentally' putting too many sugars in Simon Cooper's tea, telling him Six is on the line when it's actually the Americans and so on. Somehow, he's just managed to stay the right side of the line. The man's so bloody charming he can get away with anything.

Psmith in MI5, as he likes to call it.

[4 March 1978]

Thank God. A vacancy has come up within the office for an agent-handler. This was one of the things that appealed to me most about joining MI5. I've applied. So has Bill.

[6 March 1978]

Slightly against protocol, but Jane has been helping me prepare for the interview in the evenings. She's so intuitive — maybe this comes from being a teacher — that she makes an excellent mock interviewer. It would be horribly lonely having to go through this by yourself. I feel sorry for Bill sometimes, not having anyone permanent around to share things with.

[9 March 1978]

I've been offered the job and Bill is going to work alongside me. Although we're still officially the same rank, he's going to act as my deputy.

He's taken this very well. If it were the other way round, I would hate to work underneath him. A friend whom I've known for almost twenty years bossing me around? But there's very little ego when it comes to Bill. He's happy with whatever comes his way.

'Just don't go shouting at me, Second Lieutenant Pearce,' he warned me this morning. 'I'm not your squaddie.'

We start tomorrow.

[3 April 1978]

Well, I've got what I wished for at last — a serious job. It's almost a month since I started and I've barely had time to reflect at all. I've worked most evenings, and most weekends as well.

Agent-running forms the foundations of our work at MI5 and it is therefore much more vital than the public imagines. The popular perception of espionage is still based around the James Bond model — elite, remarkable individuals doing almost all the work themselves. If the raw material is good enough, runs the argument, you can do almost anything with it. High IQ — absorb any brief. Decent acting skills — pass yourself off as anyone else. Language abilities — gain native fluency with a few months' training. Physical prowess — outrun any bullet and defeat entire armies of ninjas in hand-to-hand combat.

The reality, of course, is very different. If I tried to infiltrate the PIRA, I'd be rumbled within minutes. Even Bill's acting skills wouldn't be sufficient. There would be a slip — a mispronounced word, ignorance of a local football team or a street name, an unfamiliar cultural reference, a common acquaintance who should be known and isn't, and so on.

That is why we run agents. To return to the previous metaphor, the material is already there. We don't have to adopt aliases, create backstories, legends and all the other complex paraphernalia of the undercover officer. We just have to find the material and then mine it. It is the essential difference between an officer and an agent.

In this, my first month, I've been focusing on the existing agent networks. It's a full-time job in its own right and I've had almost no time to concentrate on further recruiting. The previous occupant of my job — George Blair — left Belfast under something of a cloud. Rumour had it that he was running phantom agents and pocketing the proceeds. Gossips say he had too much dirt on Simon Cooper to be sacked and has found himself a nice little sinecure in the press department of the MoD.

The upshot of all this is that Blair has left his desk in a complete mess. His agents are jumpy and suspicious — at least the ones that exist. There is a massive black hole in the accounts. And much of the information flow is spurious or compromised or contradictory.

After a week of investigations, Bill and I concluded that around a fifth of the people on our payroll were double agents. Another fifth (the highest paid) were fictitious. That left just over half actually working for us, and many of these were undermotivated and scared.

Over the last month, Bill and I have spoken face to face with nearly all of them. Everyone has been made aware that there are new brooms in Belfast and we intend to sweep clean.

Most of the double agents are now being fed false information so that they're no use to the PIRA at all. We've also turned a small number by scaring the hell out of them. One method we've used is copied from Mossad, the Israeli intelligence service. Local reporters are paid to print premature obituaries of our target in the paper. Flowers and messages of condolence are sent to his wife. It rarely fails to make someone more receptive to our way of thinking.

You can't always make a rotten apple ripe again, but you can stop it smelling.

Just as importantly, we have taken the time to concentrate on the trustworthy agents we already have in place. In the service, we deploy a combination of carrots and sticks known by the pneumonic MICE — M for money; I for ideology; C for compromise; E for ego. Bribe the greedy, woo the ideologue, blackmail the adulterer and the pervert, flatter the self-obsessed.

This might sound callous, but most of the time it works. Ideological converts are the most effective, but also the trickiest to handle. Often, it is they harassing you for lack of progress and not the other way round. Likewise, compromise works up to a point, but you have to be careful not to push someone too hard or they'll decide that exposure is a better option than the awkward situations you're continuing to put them into.

It's the same for the 'M' and the 'E'. Give someone a bit of money and they'll want more. Give them a bit of praise and they'll get addicted to it.

The balancing act is, therefore, every bit as complicated as it sounds. But it's one I enjoy performing. People interest me. Despite its reassurances to the contrary, MI5 puts these people at great risk. Many of them have families, children and careers to worry about.

As their agent-handler, I am therefore somewhere between boss and brother. Whatever their motivations, all of our agents need reassurance that they are doing the right thing. This involves time as well as money. Time getting to know them, listening to them, understanding them, liking them, even.

There are degrees of loyalty. And nothing exceeds personal loyalty to someone whose opinion you value. It is the art of leadership. It is something I learned in the army and have never forgotten.

[28 April 1978]

Bill and I have done a full audit on the phantom agents run by George Blair and the rumour mill was fairly accurate. Blair must have walked off with hundreds of thousands of unclaimed fees. God knows what he had on Simon Cooper to let him get away with this after he'd been discovered.

On a more positive note, this means that there are now available funds to start recruiting new agents. We have already started to shake the trees of existing networks. Our logic is that every branch can divide into two; every twig into promising, future buds. We tell our current agents that there is safety in numbers (although often the opposite is true). We offer them rewards for every other informer they can bring to the table. And we try to encourage an element of competition between them.

It is here that Bill and I complement each other well. He is the more flamboyant character. It is he who will try the direct approach – the 'accidental' slip of the tongue in the pub; the meaningful look, the dropped, political hints. He is so charming, with a strength of personality that is both gentle and forceful, that few manage to resist him. He is rather less good, however, at the detailed work – the slow build-up, the aftercare, the reassurance. Detail bores him, in fact. And this is where I come in.

In April, we have doubled the size of our network. And all of our agents are genuine. The only problem is that we're beginning to run near our budget limits.

[14 May 1978]

Bill and I had a budgetary meeting with Simon Cooper this morning and he has agreed to double our allowance, calling us the 'best young team he has ever worked with'.

Head Office is delighted with our progress, which they're measuring not only by the size of the network we're running but also by the results it's producing. In the last fortnight, we've prevented at least three attacks on British military personnel and have gained intelligence leading to the arrest and incarceration of ten PIRA members.

[22 June 1978]

On 16 June, I was kidnapped by the Provo's internal security unit – popularly known as the 'Nutting Squad'. It is very rare for this kind of thing to happen to MI5 officers. PIRA go after British soldiers and they go after their own. But we are generally thought of as too shadowy and dangerous to get involved with. My kidnap was a testament to the successes that Bill and I have scored in the last few months. We have ruffled a lot of feathers.

The choice of kidnappers was also significant. As their official name states, the Nutting Squad deals with internal security. The reason for my capture was that PIRA had discovered that many of its double agents had recently been turned back to work for us. I was ambushed at a rendezvous with one of these agents after I'd stupidly let my counter-surveillance instincts slip. They took me along in the hope that it might help them identify their traitors.

It was horrific.

I was mistreated, but not horrendously. I was slapped around a bit, humiliated, that kind of thing. But they knew they were working against the clock. They knew it wouldn't take too long until they were discovered. And they knew the repercussions if they harmed me.

No, the really horrifying thing was what I had to witness.

As I said, the Nutting Squad hoped that my presence might make it more obvious who was who. They were looking for a reaction, a glimpse of recognition, a denunciation. They had rounded up all their suspected informers. But they'd also taken me there to teach me a lesson. There was one man in particular – one of the leaders, Patrick McCann – who meted out the most ferocious beatings to anyone he thought was a traitor.

'You see what you've done to these people,' he'd yell as he pistol-whipped them in front of me. 'You've done this, not me,' he'd shout as he shot people in the back of their kneecaps and they fell, with desperate eyes, at my feet. 'You pulled that trigger.'

The punishments appeared to be quite arbitrary. McCann would walk past some of my best agents and ignore them. Others, whom I'd never seen before in my life, were subjected to the most brutal beatings. I remember watching one man – a tough nut, if ever I've seen one – almost die under the cosh. As far as I could ascertain, he was the victim of a jealous revenge attack from a Provo colleague. Nothing more, nothing less.

There was something in this victim's eyes later that told me he'd flipped. Blind incomprehension had turned to blind hatred. But there was intelligence in those eyes as well. I

17

managed to tell him that there could be a job for him, if he got out alive. I gave him a number and a code word for the Force Research Unit, the army's spy wing.

It was a hunch — and a potentially dangerous one — but we are trained to act on them here. I have a good feeling about this one.

After twenty-four hours of witnessing this carnage, I managed to escape. PIRA's safe-house security was as weak as their network's. In the course of my escape, I had to kill two of McCann's men, which was regrettable and led to an outbreak of shooting between PIRA and the army yesterday. A civilian was killed in the crossfire.

On returning home, I was met by a furious Jane, livid that I'd missed our first wedding anniversary. What kind of excuse did I have? she demanded.

To my shame, I told her exactly what kind of excuse I had. I flipped. I told her what had happened.

'I have married a nightmare,' she said.

Tomorrow I have a debrief with Simon Cooper.

[23 June 1978]

The debrief went very well despite an awful night's sleep.

I was lightly chastised by Simon Cooper for letting my counter-surveillance instincts slip, but nowhere near as badly as I have chastised myself. It was a stupid thing to do — meeting a former double agent by myself, with none of the usual back-up — and I have made a promise to myself that I will never let it happen again. But otherwise, it couldn't have gone more smoothly. Simon is delighted that we've ruffled so many feathers. 'These are the desperate acts of desperate men,' he told me.

But the real coup of the whole incident is the man I saw enduring a ferocious punishment beating.

This morning, he limped into an army barracks and offered his services. We haven't had a 'walk-in' for months and everyone is delighted with me. When asked for his motives, he apparently mentioned 'a hard bastard from MI5 I met last week'.

I'm going to liaise with the Force Research Unit on this one.

The man's code name: Stakeknife.

[25 June 1978]

Surprised Jane with a '374-day anniversary' celebration when she came home from work. She called me a 'soppy old romantic' and I am no longer sleeping on the sofa.

[2 July 1978]

I went down to the Force Research Unit today and met Steak Knife (the correct spelling, I've discovered). He is a remarkable man in many ways.

Our intention is to engineer his promotion to a senior role in the Nutting Squad. This new, centralised security structure is the brainchild of Gerry Adams and a response to its old batallion structures, which made widespread penetration easy.

Fortunately for us, the Nutting Squad have extraordinary access to the entire PIRA structure. They investigate every failed operation. They mete out punishments. They vet potential recruits. There is hardly an activity or an agent not known to them. One of our own agents in there will be worth a hundred elsewhere.

There are potential downsides, though. What if this man does progress? He'll have to interrogate and torture some of our own spies. How many people can we allow to die to protect his identity?

For the time being, at least, these are hypothetical questions. Steak Knife is FRU's number one asset at the moment and I am his MI5 liaison contact.

As soon as he starts feeding us information, I am to authorise the MoD's Cranborne Bank in SW1 to pay him £80,000 per year to a bank in Gibraltar.

It rather puts my salary into perspective. But then I'm not taking anywhere near the same risks.

[4 July 1978]

Bill has been behaving a little oddly recently. The problem is that he's a bloody good officer and, despite his modest exterior, he knows it. He has become rather slack in his protocol.

I've put him on to a new assignment — Operation Leapfrog — which makes the most of his talent for acting out a role. The aim is to recruit publicans as informers. The logic is that they see and hear so much of what is going on. The casual exchanges witnessed across a bar floor can be as intimate and revealing

as a full-length meeting with minutes. The Irish are a garru-
lous, bibulous bunch. And they're especially talkative after a
few litres of Guinness in the local alehouse.

This kind of operation suits Bill to a tee. He hates being
stuck behind a desk and I don't know anyone with a greater cap-
acity for alcohol. In a couple of weeks, he has already amassed
a sizeable network of informers – most notably the landlord at
Rosie O'Grady's, a veritable vipers' nest of Republicans.

There is nothing that Bill enjoys more than disguising
himself as a drunk and checking up on these operations. He can
make himself look fifty years older, getting every little detail
right, from the smell of his clothes to the dirty hair.
Preparations take him up to three hours.

Occasionally, he warns the landlords that he is about to
appear. But more often than not, he slips in and out without
being noticed.

It might all sound rather childish, and I'm not sure I
approve entirely of these little jaunts. But Bill is so happy –
and so successful – doing things his own way that I think he
should be encouraged, in general.

That's where the army often goes wrong, in my opinion:
attempting to restrict individual creativity into a straitjacket
of standard operating procedures. What kind of security service
would we be if we did the same? We might be part of the government bureaucracy, but we don't have to think like bureaucrats.

[27 July 1978]

Disaster.

I have just witnessed Bill being kidnapped from Rosie O'Grady's. And the worst thing was that I did absolutely nothing about it.

I was there with a potential informer when I caught sight of Bill by the bar, dressed in one of his drunkard disguises.

Two men burst through the door, grabbed him by the hair and yelled, 'This man is a British spy.' They started to drag him towards the door. I tried to follow them as best I could. But they were professionals with decoy vehicles and getaway cars. It was impossible for one officer to tail them successfully.

The two men: Steak Knife and Patrick McCann.

[28 July 1978]

Looking back on the incident, it's clear that I could have done nothing about it. I am known to both Steak Knife and Patrick McCann. McCann has every reason to hate me after I killed two of his accomplices. Had I stuck my head above the parapet in Rosie O'Grady's, I would have compromised Bill as well as Steak Knife.

Right I might have been, but it is hard to accept that when you've watched one of your best friends being led away to an uncertain fate. And it's even harder to remove the niggling doubt that these tactical explanations are mere excuses for acting like a coward out of an overwhelming sense of fear.

For the time being, however, these rights and wrongs are

immaterial. All that matters for the moment is finding Bill. The climate has changed recently. I very much doubt he will be as well treated as me.

[29 July 1978]

I've spoken to Simon Cooper and was very disappointed with his response. He appears to be working along the old lines – wait and see; watch and wait. Informers will lead us to Bill soon enough. He doesn't seem to understand how much things have changed. And it is Bill and I who have changed them. McCann knows that.

I want the army involved but Simon has refused. 'You're getting too emotional about this,' he said. 'Let us do it in our own way, in our own time.'

Well, screw him. If he's not going to do it, I will. If they do it in their own way, in their own time, Bill will be dead. I have taken some annual leave and plan to spend it finding him.

[31 July 1978]

No luck so far. This is an agonising journey of twists and turns, false summits and dashed hopes. I have met every agent I run, every informer I use and shaken every cage I can think of. I know I said I wouldn't meet agents alone again since I was kidnapped. But this is different. This is about Bill.

There have been a few leads – a farmhouse in Galway, which

appeared to have been vacated just before I got there; a safe house in Belfast where I found a thread of Bill's shirt. But there has been nothing concrete. And we are running out of time.

[1 August 1978]

Simon Cooper finally appears to have understood the urgency of the situation. It is unprecedented for an MI5 officer to be held this long and he has now mobilised all our resources. 'No man left behind,' he keeps on saying, but there is a hollow ring to the phrase. Colonel Collins used to say that as well, but you always got the impression he meant it.

Cooper has started rattling a few cages of his own. This afternoon I watched him interrogate one of our prisoners in the hope of finding out more information. It was brutal and entirely counter-productive. The man clearly didn't know anything. What's worse, he knew that we knew he didn't know anything. You could see the hatred as well as the pity in his eyes. A thousand years of English misrule – or however many it's meant to be – and it hasn't got much better recently. It was like frying ants with a magnifying glass.

It might have taken out our frustrations, but it achieved nothing.

[8 August 1978]

Bill's body has been found – dumped outside his flat in the early hours of this morning. It was horribly mutilated – half burned away by a blowtorch. The poor man. I am going to have to tell his parents, of course. And his sister. But what do I tell myself? It seems that his captors worked out his link to me during their interrogation. A note was left on his body: 'One down; one to go. An eye for an eye, Harry.'

We believe the handwriting belongs to McCann.

Did I kill Bill? Hath man no greater love than this, that he lay down the life of his friend? And for what? His career? His country?

[10 August 1978]

I had a full, taped debrief with Simon Cooper yesterday. There have been murmured rumours in the service that I was in some way responsible for Bill's death. That my inaction had caused it.

It's one thing blaming yourself for these things; it's quite another hearing them from other people — unvoiced and cowardly, lurking in the shadows behind my back. It's that old metaphor, I suppose: stand on the inside of the tent and piss out; don't stand on the outside and piss in.

So, I defended my actions in yesterday's interview and saw a different, altogether more understanding side of Simon Cooper. He said I'd made the right judgement call. He put the murmurings down to jealousy at some of my successes in the past month.

Perhaps he's right. I've learned a lot about myself this week. But I've also learned a lot about MI5 and how it works. I've learned the validity of when to speak and when to stay silent. I've discovered its little hypocrisies, its bashful flirting, its ruthless betrayals.

What everyone knows — and no one voices — is that Bill Crombie was sacrificed to protect Steak Knife's identity. Bill was our rising star; now Steak Knife is more useful to us. We couldn't keep both, so someone decided. Means, ends, betrayals. As simple as that. And the worst thing about it all is that Steak Knife was my discovery, my tool, my pawn.

Is it an injustice? Or is it just realpolitik? I'm not sure I know. But this morning I knew I couldn't let it pass.

I walked into Simon Cooper's office (where he was mid-meeting with the DG) and called him a 'fucking hypocrite'. I just didn't care any more.

Perhaps I shouldn't have done it. Perhaps I should have taken some time, had a think, mulled things over, calmed down a little. But this was done on instincts. I told them that they would live to regret it, that humans were not pawns in their games, that Steak Knife would bring them more trouble than he was worth. 'How many more people will you let die to protect him?' I shouted.

All things considered, they took it rather well. Admittedly, the DG looked slightly shocked, but Simon Cooper appears to have reassured him. The outburst will not be mentioned on my record and I am to be seconded to MI6, somewhere in Europe.

As Simon put it, 'I think you are currently too emotional to continue working in Northern Irish affairs.'

Damn right, I am.

Oh dear God, Bill, forgive me.

1979

[14 February 1979]

Officially, I've been on secondment in Europe with MI6 since last August. But it didn't quite work out as I planned. I've just returned from an extraordinary month in Iran.

MI6 has a station chief in Paris called Juliet Shaw who is my immediate boss there. She can't be much more than a couple of years older than me but she's already risen very quickly through the ranks. She's a ruthless, right-wing crazy who will stop at nothing to get her own way, but I rather like her. She's feisty, intelligent and excellent company.

Juliet joined MI6 straight after Cambridge and looks set for the top.

MI6 has a different culture to MI5. They've retained that whiff of mysticism that the domestic security services are beginning to lose these days. The rules are looser; the person-alities more eccentric. They still labour under a strange, misguided sense that they're protecting the Empire in some way. The final frontier. No doubt half of them believe that India still belongs to us.

27

[spooks]

It has its downsides, of course. Many, in fact. But there is something rather appealing about the sense of freedom its officers enjoy, especially after the stuffiness of A Section. MI6 appears to be run along the lines of a progressive boarding school: creative anarchy rules. The house prefects decide everything. The more mischievous juniors get away with blue murder. And the masters turn a blind eye to almost everything.

Most of the time it works. But when it goes wrong, it goes spectacularly wrong.

Anyway, Juliet already appears to be a past master at the rules of the game. In January, she declared that she was bored with running the Paris office and there was nothing going on in any case that our allies, the French domestic SDECE, couldn't deal with for the time being. So she announced that Iran was where it was at, and she and her deputy (me) would be popping over there for a brief fact-finding mission because one day we'd be running the show and we better be well-informed about the state of the Middle East.

You have to admire her gall.

Well, our trip wasn't that brief – we were there over a month. But we certainly found a lot of facts. We arrived the day before the Shah fled the country and relocated his family in Egypt. The poor Shah: he'd had a fairly dreadful few months. Last August, Muslim extremists had set fire to a crowded theatre in Abadan. In September, army troops opened fire on riots in Tehran, killing 122 and wounding 4,000. In November, they sacked the British Embassy. And in December, two million people demonstrated against him.

We left – a month later – having seen Ayatollah Khomeini

return to Iran after almost fifteen years of exile, establish the Council of the Islamic Revolution and seize power for himself.

It was an interesting time, to say the least. Fortunately, we had diplomatic immunity – for what that's worth these days – and Juliet speaks fluent Persian and knows the area well. It was her first posting after completing training and her father used to be third secretary there twenty-five years ago.

Her father makes for an interesting historical comparison. In August 1953, MI6 and the CIA jointly engineered the overthrow of the democratically elected Prime Minister of Iran, Dr Mohammad Mossadegh. Crowds were paid handsomely in dollars to celebrate on the streets.

Here, two and a half decades later, that policy had finally come home to roost. No one really understands Iran. And I can't pretend to after a month there, even during one of its most turbulent periods of history. But it seems obvious to me that it will affect the course of the Middle East for the next half a century, whether or not anyone is aware of it.

[15 February 1979]

There is another matter – a personal one – which I feel I should record in my diary. Yesterday was Valentine's Day. I loathe the entire institution but I am not sufficiently stupid to make my feelings aware to Jane. I know that women set great store by these things.

I took her out for supper in the Latin Quarter where we proceeded to have a blazing row.

I had been distant, apparently, since Bill's death. I had always been fonder of him than of her, and I had become withdrawn. Why didn't I tell her anything any more? Why was I such a bad listener?

And then there was Juliet. Jane is suspicious of her, it would appear. Juliet is very beautiful. And very manipulative.

But Jane is also slightly suspicious of me at the moment. And perhaps I can't blame her. I am not being a good husband. I've dragged her away from her family, uprooted her to Ireland, uprooted her again to Paris just as she was settling into her new job and then I disappeared for a month with my attractive female boss to watch a revolution take place in the Middle East.

I can kind of see her point.

[16 February 1979]

There is also the problem that Jane is entirely accurate in her suspicions. Something did happen with Juliet while in Tehran. It wasn't meant to, and I regret it deeply. But at some point, we just became swept up in the whole adventure of the moment.

[20 February 1979]

Jane is finding it very difficult to get work in Paris — her French is almost as bad as mine — and we've discussed whether there might be somewhere else in Europe that I could work. Cologne is definitely an option, as I know there is a desk officer trying to find a quieter retirement sinecure. Jane and I both speak reasonable German.

I'll speak to Juliet ·about it as soon as I can.

[21 February 1979]

I spoke to Juliet this morning. She was angry, at first, and accused me of trying to run away. I told her it had nothing to do with her, that I was bored by Paris and that I couldn't work properly if Jane wasn't happy. France is very tame after Northern Ireland and Iran. West Germany does at least share a border with an enemy.

Juliet eventually relented and has signed my transfer papers to Cologne. But I fear this won't be the last I see of her.

[26 February 1979]

Arrived in Cologne today, which was their Rosenmontag festival. The Kölner Karneval has been going since 1823 and it was a boisterous and fun welcome to the city.

I've never quite understood why we've continually fought the Germans in the twentieth century. Ultimately, they're very similar to us: they enjoy beer, street processions, puerile humour and inebriated, tuneless singalongs. Why we ended up allied with the French against them is a mystery.

[28 April 1979]

Jane has found a job in a boarding school just outside Bad
Godesberg, Bonn, we've found a flat almost in the shadow of
Cologne's cathedral and my work has just got very exciting
again.

There is a far-left militant group here called the Rote
Armee Fraktion, or the Baader-Meinhof Gang — the Red Army
Faction. The RAF is essentially an urban guerrilla group with
origins in the student unrests of the late 1960s. Interestingly,
its foundations can be traced to the protests against the Shah's
visit to West Berlin in 1967.

In the subsequent twenty years, its activities have moved
dramatically from energetic street demonstrations to full-blown
terrorism. In February 1975, the conservative candidate for
mayor of Berlin was kidnapped to force the release of some of
their prisoners. Weakly, the German government relented — which
only served to encourage the RAF. In April, they occupied the
German Embassy in Stockholm and murdered two hostages.

Then, in July 1977, following the life imprisonment of
three of their members, the RAF shot dead the head of Dresdner
Bank outside his house. In September, the President of the
German Employers' Association, Hanns Martin Schleyer, was taken
hostage, sparking a month-long crisis that became known as
Deutscher Herbst (German Autumn). The following month, a
Lufthansa flight was hijacked and flown to Somalia via Rome,
Larnaca, Dubai and Aden. Demands for prisoners to be released
were issued.

This time, however, the German government didn't give in.

The pilot had already been shot. The elite police unit, the GSG9, stormed the plane and saved all the remaining hostages. The next day, the RAF inmates were found dead in their cells, supposedly having committed suicide (although the details are highly suspect). Schleyer was executed by his kidnappers the day afterwards.

So, what has all this got to do with MI6 and British interests?

The answer is twofold. First, it has come to our attention that the RAF has been heavily infiltrated by the East German Stasi. This effectively means that the Iron Curtain has shifted by several degrees longitude to the West, bringing the Cold War even closer to home. The Stasi is one of the most organised intelligence organisations in the world. This makes it very much our concern.

Our other, more pressing, fear is the lackadaisical manner in which the German authorities appear to be tackling this threat. MI6 has been warning them, almost from the outset, about its seriousness. Several times in the past, the government has been guilty of appeasing the group, notably when they caved in to the RAF's demands in return for the release of the Berlin mayoral candidate.

We would have hoped and expected that the Deutscher Herbst might have strengthened the authorities' resolve. In one respect, at least, it has. They made a pledge after the hijack-ing crisis that they would never again negotiate with terrorists.

But as far as the RAF and other left-wing organisations are concerned, they have become complacent. The groups have gone

33

underground again, leading the authorities to conclude that they won this particular battle. Our analysis shows that the opposite is true: the RAF and others are taking this opportunity to regroup and rearm. And when they come back, they'll be even stronger than before.

They might have been silent since last autumn, but that doesn't mean we can stop worrying about them. Silence is not necessarily evidence of inactivity. Just as a great deal of noise does not prove the opposite.

The question now, of course, is what do we do about it? A threat has been identified, so how do we act?

I'm currently the only MI6 representative in Cologne, so I've been briefing the overall section head in Berlin, Robert Campbell. He is a cautious man, approaching a cautious retirement, at the end of a cautious career, and unsurprisingly recommends caution.

We are to continue to monitor the group's activities while maintaining a low profile ourselves. At no point are we to endanger the lives of German nationals by provoking the RAF into a hasty reaction etc., etc.

My analysis, on the other hand, is that this requires a more dramatic approach. I have a meeting with C, the director of MI6, at the Century House headquarters in Lambeth next week to argue my case.

[4 May 1979]

Margaret Thatcher has just become Prime Minister, quoting the prayer of Francis of Assisi outside 10 Downing Street. I'm not sure what to make of her yet. I like her instincts but I'm not sure I'm going to like her methods.

Still, she can't be any worse than the last lot. Britain has an admirable history of strong women and we could certainly do with one now.

[9 May 1979]

The meeting with C went well, if a little bizarrely. I was searched twice — once at the main doors, and a second time before entering his office. He's relatively new to his job and looked more nervous than I might have imagined.

Perhaps his nerves were something to do with the subject matter we discussed. I gave him a full briefing on the situation with the RAF: my unease with its current silence, our inability to infiltrate it with trustworthy agents, Campbell's inertia on the subject, and so on.

C looked grave.

'Do you really think that, Pearce?' he said.

'Yes, sir,' I replied.

'And are you prepared to act on the strength of your convictions?'

I hesitated.

'It's not a trick question,' he continued.

'Yes.'

'Good. Then, do you know what a black op is?'

'Yes,' I said. 'Of course. We used them the whole time in the army in Northern Ireland . . . or rather, they were *allegedly* known to be used by the army in Northern Ireland at a time when I might or might not have been there myself.'

C laughed.

'Excellent. Well, that's the kind of linguistic evasion that we'll need with this one. A black operation is similar to a false-flag operation. In the old days, flags gave coherence and a degree of legitimacy to military engagements. One side wore one uniform, the other wore a different uniform. You shot at the people wearing a different colour to yourself. Everyone knew where they stood. Or lay. Dead. Espionage, of course, is a little more complicated. We sometimes have to work on the principle of deniability. Dress your man up in a different uniform, give your own uniform to someone who's not one of us. In other words, fly a false flag.'

C went on at some length – I don't recall all of it – but it boils down to this: I am to run an illegal black op in Cologne, code-named Omega. The only two people to know about it are C and myself. Neither Campbell nor Juliet Shaw are to be given any inkling of our intentions. The meeting with C himself will be stricken from the record. C's diary will be altered accordingly and an alibi accorded for the forty-five minutes he spent with me. I am flying back to Cologne on the same assumed name that I used to come to London. In essence, this means that the only person in the intelligence agencies to know about Omega is me and me alone.

The thrust of Omega is as follows: I am to do everything within my power to provoke the German authorities into clamping down on the RAF – C: 'And I mean *everything*, Pearce.' I will work with anyone, exploit anyone and perform any task, however unsavoury.

C: 'If I've read your psychological profile right, I think you'll enjoy this.'

Not for the first time, I'm glad I'm keeping a diary. If this ever blows up in my face, here is my evidence that I received a direct order to carry out the op.

Omega starts today.

[27 May 1979]

I've started the operation at a low level. My ultimate aim is to stage large-scale terrorist attempts (with minimum to zero loss of life) that will provide the excuse/justification for a government clampdown. The Italians have been doing this for much of the 1970s to keep their far left under control – often in conjunction with their far right.

However, I don't want to start at too high a level. The RAF are suspicious, well-trained and enjoy many friends in the media. C: 'Remember God's eleventh commandment. And my first: don't get caught.'

So, I've begun simply by stirring up a bit of tension between the extreme right and left in Cologne. Some of my budget went on quadrupling the circulation of the far right's newsletter, *Das Rote Kreuz*, which contained a scathing polemic accusing the left of cowardice and capitulation. This was then circulated to all known members of the RAF in the city.

I have also been allowed to use three British Army explosive experts currently stationed in West Germany. I like working with soldiers. They don't question your orders and they don't ask too many questions. They hate civilians, and they're not very keen on spooks, either. But a former officer who's become a spook is just about acceptable. 'Theirs not to reason why, Theirs but to do and die' was meant as a criticism by Tennyson, but it has its uses in modern warfare, conventional or otherwise.

The three explosives experts are called Howard, Roupell and Price.

We've started a low-level bombing campaign against soft governmental and corporate targets in Cologne, as well as the traditional focal points of the far left. On Monday, it was a burger bar. On Friday, it was Dresdner Bank. Today, it was the German Post Office.

All the attacks have been carefully camouflaged to pin authorship on the RAF. We achieved something of a coup today with the post office bomb – which caused an impressive amount of damage to infrastructure without harming any members of the public. The RAF felt moved to put out a statement saying that the bomb hadn't been detonated by them, leading the evening paper to conclude that the RAF were adopting a more sophisticated approach involving the concept of deniability used by many intelligence agencies.

The ironies are almost too delicious to comment upon.

Howard, Roupell and Price are excellent technicians and appear to be enjoying working outside the confines of regiment life. As Roupell said to me this afternoon: 'It's nineteen seventy-nine and I'm getting paid by the British government to blow up German infrastructure. My father would have been proud.'

[26 June 1979]

Our biggest coup to date. Yesterday, we successfully stage-managed a failed assassination attempt on Alexander Haig, Commander of NATO forces, as his car crossed a bridge in Mons, Belgium. Again, blame has been pinned on the RAF.

The attack was carried out with East German landmines, which were insufficiently strong to cause a lethal explosion. Moreover, our intelligence was good and we detonated the bomb after Haig's car had passed, injuring instead two of his staff in the following car.

Most importantly, the German government has finally sat up and taken notice, spurred into action by an extremely irate Belgian Defence Minister and the Mayor of Mons, embarrassed by the American general almost meeting his Maker on his bridge. The German parliament debated the RAF today and the story led most of the newspapers.

A telegram arrived for me from Tonbridge Wells: 'Congratulations Stop Second wedding anniversary is paper Stop Sorry late Stop Much love Stop C Stop'

The crafty old bugger. Anyone intercepting that would have thought it was a long-lost friend who'd been to my wedding two years ago. But it's still scary, sometimes, how much they know about you in this job. I can't imagine any other career where you get mysterious telegrams from your boss disguised as nuptial congratulations.

[28 June 1979]

The honeymoon was shortlived; the backlash has started.

The CIA is livid about the assassination attempt on Haig and suspects foul play. Our man in Brussels has had a thorough going-over — disgracefully thorough in my opinion. America is our ally; I don't see why it has to act like the fat kid in the playground so often. We know where we stand.

Fortunately, the deniability principle advocated by C has held up well. Brook — our man in Brussels — is a first-rate officer and wouldn't have given away anything. But it's rather easy if there is nothing for him to give away in the first place.

Brook, however, is no fool and suspects something is going on. He has flown back to Lambeth to request more information. It is well known that he has his own eyes on the job of C one day.

In the meantime, we are also experiencing problems here on the ground in Cologne. My attempts to build up a false impression of strength among the left has perversely ended up strengthening the far right. Initially, they enjoyed baiting the left's cowardliness and weakness in their newsletters. More recently, they have been outraged by the left's renaissance and rallied many to the right's cause.

Stupid of me not to realise earlier, but it shouldn't take a genius to see how the pendulum swings in these things. Every political action has an equal and opposite action. MI6's danger — or, more specifically, my danger — is that we get caught in an elaborate and prolonged pincer movement between the two.

We have to remember why we're doing this, after all.

Politicians are fond of saying that history will judge them. It's partly true: they're judged by the present as much as by posterity. But in the world of espionage, we really do take the long view. If we succeed in provoking the German authorities into destroying a dangerous, nihilist far-left group, I think the German public will forgive us, whenever and however the true facts eventually emerge. If we succeed in creating running street battles between extremists from opposite sides of the political spectrum, they will rightly feel rather less charitable towards intervention from a foreign power that has already destroyed their country twice in half a century.

[10 July 1979]

Again, I've made the mistake of mixing work and pleasure. My own stupid fault, but the pressure of Operation Omega was getting to me. This is why people work as teams. There are escape valves in either direction. You can take out your frustration on your juniors and confess your fears to your superiors. Working alone is not only very lonely, it can also be quite terrifying. Black ops are black because they're deniable. Does that mean I'm deniable as well? And what happens if I am hung out to dry?

Yesterday, I went to Paris to visit Juliet. I hadn't seen her since 21 February when I'd left for Germany under something of a cloud. We'd spoken a bit on the phone since then — mainly work matters — but I felt I really had to see her.

It was a foolish thing to do. Spontaneous but foolish. We spent an enjoyable day together, but it ended up, inevitably, where we'd both expected.

Even more foolishly, I told her all about Operation Omega. Maybe that's why I'd gone to visit her in the first place — as much as for the other reason. At any rate, somehow I found myself blurting it all out. She was a sympathetic listener, but I couldn't resist thinking that this was more to do with her training than any affections she might hold for me. I've just given her a golden bullet to use on me in the future, should the need ever arise. She can use the nugget of information to damn me in whichever way she chooses. Either I'm a blackmailable officer who oversaw an illegal operation, or I'm a naïve fool who's not capable of keeping a secret among his own. She can feed whichever line she likes to suit the audience.

I feel very stupid.

[28 July 1979]

My liaison with Juliet has escalated into a full-blown affair. At first, I thought this was out of fear. I'd dipped my toe into the water, why not dive right in? If she knew something, why not tell her everything? She could be a useful ally for me in the future.

But there's something else there as well. I have rather fallen for her. And love, careless love, makes one say things one shouldn't. She now knows as much about Omega as I do. The only advantage of all this cavorting is that the operation itself has suffered from a bit of neglect recently, which is probably no bad thing. The Americans have backed down in their investigations and Haig is more interested in securing a job in the private sector.

[2 August 1979]

Jane is pregnant and I have ended the relationship with Juliet. It is six months too late, but it was the only decent thing to do. I might not be a good husband, but I refuse to be a poor father as well.

[17 August 1979]

Recalled briefly to London for another meeting with C. Omega has again begun to produce results but Lambeth is frustrated with the speed. C: 'I envisaged this as an SAS-style mission, Pearce. In and out before they know you're there, not trench warfare.'

C wants one big event: a one-off episode of such cataclysmic proportions that it is impossible to ignore. Our conclusion: we have to target the people who are making the decisions. Politicians are cowards who will choose the path of least resistance. But put their own lives in danger and they will react quicker than you can say 'chauffer-driven car'.

Out next target: Minister for the Interior, Thomas Bergen.

[27 August 1979]

A disastrous day. Mountbatten, the last Viceroy of India and the uncle of the Duke of Edinburgh, was assassinated by the PIRA, who planted a bomb in his holiday boat in Donegal Bay. Three other people were also killed in the boat.

Elsewhere, eighteen members of the Parachute Regiment were ambushed and shot dead in County Down.

It makes me so angry. I still haven't managed to control my emotions entirely when it comes to Northern Irish matters. For me, they will always be the murderers of Bill.

It also makes me angry that I'm stuck out here in Germany playing silly buggers with a bunch of loonie lefties. I'm really not convinced any more by the merits of Omega. The real work to be done isn't here.

Still, life goes on. As does work. Plans to target Bergen are going well. I have obtained his schedule and he appears to be particularly vulnerable at the beginning of November when he is due to attend a series of business conferences in Cologne. That will be our time to strike.

Howard, Roupell and Price are back on board. It's going to be a particularly fine balancing act – scaring the hell out of Bergen but not doing any serious injury. It also has to be completely untraceable. Bergen is too big for our prints to be anywhere near the weapon.

[29 September 1979]

The plans are all in place. A paid informer inside Bergen's private office has told me he's attending a conference on the morning of 6 November. A decoy car will be in place at the front at 1 p.m. At the back of the hotel will be his real car, ready to whisk him away to a lunchtime meeting in Bonn. We will detonate a bomb in the decoy car – in front of the media – just before anyone gets into it. Bergen will be unharmed in the other car, but will have no choice but to react strongly if he doesn't want the media baying for his blood.

We have obtained explosive materials from the DDR via a Stasi defector. We have also prepared a fax from the RAF to be sent to all major newspapers within minutes of the bomb being detonated.

Everything is prepared.

[4 November 1979]

Thousands of Iranians invaded the US Embassy in Tehran today and took ninety hostages — the majority of them American. Again, it makes my work here feel like little more than a sideshow. I phoned Juliet to talk about it, but her secretary said she'd already left on a plane for the Middle East. I have a feeling this one might drag on and on. There are a few British missionaries in there as well.

[6 November 1979]

A disastrous end to Operation Omega: our bomb today killed the Minister for the Interior, Thomas Bergen.

As far as I can ascertain, Bergen had expressed private fears that he might become the victim of a staged bombing campaign by British Intelligence. God knows how that might have leaked out. Nothing is watertight, it would seem.

Accordingly, he altered his plans, left his conference five minutes early and double-bluffed by using the decoy car at the front of the hotel instead of his intended vehicle at the rear. The bombs were detonated by timers, not remote control, so it was too late to intervene. The Minister for the Interior was blown up by British Intelligence within twenty feet of the world's media. The only consolation is that the bomb injured a few of the journalists as well.

[7 November 1979]

A report appeared in a newspaper today quoting the suspicions of Bergen's widow and pointing the finger of blame at MI6. Fortunately, the deniability chain has kicked in and all responsibility has been strenuously refuted. The story was dead by the evening, when an unfortunate lackey from the RAF was arrested and charged.

I have no idea what kind of machinations are going on back in Lambeth. A black op is isolating enough when things are going well. When it goes wrong, you are left entirely out of the loop. We had a bit of freedom to manoeuvre when there were no suspicions. Now it is imperative that I carry on as normal, whatever normal might be.

[11 November 1979]

Juliet called, offering to cover for me should the need arise. Lambeth have asked me to write up a brief report in response to the allegations — the layers of untruth! — in which I have attempted to convey a tone of suitable shock and annoyance.

Rumour has it that this might be considered a suitable moment for my secondment to MI6 to expire and for me to return to Five.

[16 November 1979]

Anthony Blunt – the fourth member of the Cambridge spy ring – was revealed today in a parliamentary answer by Margaret Thatcher.

It makes me admire her much more. The intelligence services have known about his involvement since 1964, but it just doesn't seem right that he should carry on without the rest of the country knowing as well.

We have a tradition in the security services of not throwing our officers to the wolves. If they go bad in the field, we look after them in our own way. But treason is something altogether different in my book, however laudable the expressed motives of conscience.

[30 November 1979]

Recalled to London. My time in MI6 is over for the time being.

1980

[19 February 1980]

I'm back in London at MI5, in Section D, whose current remit covers anti-terrorism and serious crime.

I was never debriefed over Operation Omega. It is as if my meetings with C never took place (which, officially, of course, they didn't). There were no more telegrams disguised as friendly wishes; no more searches outside his office; no more skulduggery on foreign shores. Just a simple recall to London because my secondment to MI6 was over and I was an MI5 recruit.

It was a strange limbo to be put in. I'd expected a reprimand for Bergen's death. A black mark for a black op, at the very least. But now I wonder whether that was what they'd wanted all along. Maybe they'd put me in that impossible situation to see just how far it would push me. Where would I draw the line? What would I be willing to do? Just one more stage in my ongoing assessment.

As far as I know, the German authorities bought the story about the RAF's involvement. A few conspiracy theories continue to circulate, but that's the beauty with conspiracy theories:

49

they're always there, so even the credible ones can be dismissed as the output of nutcases. Look at the moon landings. Or JFK's assassination.

So, it's case closed — for the Germans, for MI6 and for me. And I don't even know if I'm thought to have done a good job. Probably no one knows.

It has, however, given me a lasting suspicion of MI6's methods. Initially, I was attracted to their sense of freedom — as I recounted here in my diary. But I have now seen the flipside of freedom without responsibility.

There is a moral dimension to the work ethic at MI5 that appeals to me. There are less grey areas over here in Gower Street. *Regnum Defende* — Defend the Kingdom. That's what we do. We also defend the *people* of this kingdom. When someone tries to blow them up, we stop them. When someone attempts to subvert and pervert the democratic process, we put obstacles in their way. We are like a slightly more intelligent — well, much more intelligent — version of the police.

MI6, on the other hand, has a more confused remit, I think. British interests at home are easy to define. But what exactly are British interests abroad? Where do you draw the lines in the sand?

Often, MI6 operates in hostile areas with wildly different laws to our own. How do you retain a sense of Britishness if you're in that kind of environment? How do you stop yourself from going native? What exactly are you defending?

So, no, I'd rather defend this *regnum* from within the kingdom itself. It is, after all, the organisation to which I applied. Joining MI5 and being seconded to Six was rather like getting a job as a maths teacher at a school and then finding out that you're required to teach Latin as well. To the scholarship class. And take the 3rd XI football team on Saturdays. It was an interesting insight, but it wasn't what I'd bargained on.

With a young wife and a baby due, it also makes sense from a practical perspective. We've found a small house to rent just off the Fulham Road. Jane seems happier now that she's back among friends. An old acquaintance from teacher-training college has offered her a part-time job as soon as she is ready.

[20 February 1980]

One of the best things about being back at Five is that I have a proper team around me again. As I've noted here before, I found aspects of my work on Operation Omega lonely and isolating. I had Howard, Roupell and Price, of course, but it wasn't a team of equals. Everything I told them was on a need-to-know basis and, for the most part, they were happy with that situation. Even C only wanted the big picture and none of the gritty details. This sense of isolation partly explains, even if it doesn't excuse, my behaviour with Juliet.

On Section D, I'm again surrounded by like-minded, interesting people. This is presumably part of the reason why anyone decides to go into a chosen career: I like journalism, but do I like journalists? I want to go into medicine, but do I want to spend all my waking hours around doctors? Espionage intrigues me, but will I be spooked out by spies?

These, after all, are the people we have to share our lives with, as much as our family and our friends.

[spooks]

I think I've been very fortunate with my team here at Section D. The current head is a man called Clive McTaggart and he is an excellent leader – very much in the Colonel Sam Collins bracket. He exudes that quiet authority of a man who doesn't need to raise his voice to be listened to. Yet he also has a knack of taking you into his confidence and making you feel special in his company. When he talks to you, it feels more like a cosy fireside chat than a direct order. The concerns of every team member, from his deputies to the cleaners, are always taken seriously. Debate is actively encouraged. And yet he is very rarely questioned by anyone.

An elaborate, charming confidence trick or the art of leadership at its very best? Perhaps it doesn't matter which. Working with Clive is a master class in man management. I'll learn a lot from him.

Clive has gathered a good team around him and, like all the best leaders, he has attempted to fashion it in his image. How successful he has been in doing this is perhaps more debatable.

Our senior field officer is a guy called Matthew Ellis. He's chummy, almost to the point of being annoying. 'Just call me Matt' was his opening salvo to me, delivered in a way that implied he was doing me a huge favour and most people called him Mr Ellis. He is only a year older than me.

Still, Matt appears to be very good at his job, although rumour has it that he has been delegating a lot of the more exciting field work since his wife gave birth to a son earlier this year. All the more fun for the rest of us, I say. But he certainly has the respect of Clive, which counts for much around here. He probably deserves that respect, although I have seldom encountered a more effective brown-noser.

Then, at my grade, there is a man called Archie Hollings-head, a former defence correspondent on a national newspaper who grew bored of writing about what we do and decided to opt for the real thing himself.

'Standing on the touchline or getting your knees dirty on the pitch?' he's fond of saying. 'It was a no-brainer in the end.'

Archie is delightful company — outgoing, witty, irreverent. He has the dubious distinction of being one of the few people here ever to have made Clive blow his top. It was on his first day here and he made one of his usual bad-taste quips to calm his nerves.

Clive raised a quizzical eyebrow.

'Chill out, mate,' murmured Archie under his breath.

'My name is Clive,' shouted Clive for the first time in living memory. 'And you are on probation.'

Clive apologised afterwards.

Archie's one of life's lucky winners, who gets away with things others would be sacked for because you can't help but like him. He always has the right thing to say in every situation, unlike the rest of us who think of the perfect turn of phrase ten minutes after the event. His journalist training, in particular, allows him to lie his way into most situations. Although a couple of years older than me, the rivalry between us is friendly. Matt, on the other hand, always gives the impression of watching his back.

Amanda Bennett makes up the final member of our immediate team. On my first day here, she provided that 'oh, no' moment that strikes you on entering an office for the first time and realising that there is someone unbearably attractive sitting on the same desk as you.

Clive treats her with a fond sense of paternalism. Matt patronises her (I think she scares him). Archie exhausts himself by keeping his charm zoned into her throughout the working day.

Fortunately, I've come round to seeing her for what she really is — a beautiful woman who will stop at nothing to get her own way. We get on well.

So that's us — a merry little bunch of the usual suspects. All of us went to Oxbridge. All of us are privately educated. There is little more than a single degree of separation between any of us. It didn't take long to find a godfather in common, a shared ex-flatmate, a favourite restaurant that we all know on the same slope of the same exclusive ski resort.

It's a world with which I'm familiar, a world in which I can navigate my way around without falling into its myriad traps. But it's not a world I'm particularly fond of, this thin veneer of misplaced elitism and its underlying snobbery.

I also wonder whether it's the kind of world MI5 should be embracing. Being 'clubbable' is all very well if you work in a leading investment bank. It might even make the day-to-day office life more manageable. But we have to look beyond our office walls. Can we truly protect a society that we don't reflect?

[25 April 1980]

Jane gave birth to a daughter today whom we have decided to call Catherine. I missed the birth as I was in a conference call with

Juliet Shaw (who has finally been moved full-time to Iran), my superiors in Section D and the CIA about the failed Operation Eagle Claw to rescue American hostages from the embassy siege in Tehran.

It was a pig's ear of an operation from start to finish. Sandstorms and mechanical failures put paid to almost half the rescue helicopters. The mission was aborted but there was a crash during its abortion, killing eight US service personnel. They also managed to leave behind the classified details of CIA operatives within Iran.

Juliet was on strident form during the conference call, throwing accusations and denunciations left, right and centre. But somehow she manages to get away with it. It's not just her charm. The Americans respect her as well. I think she provides a good example of how to act as the weaker partner in an alliance: she's deferential, but firm; polite but uncompromising. And she's not afraid to tell them when they've gone wrong. No doubt they'll ignore it all afterwards, but at least we can say we told them so.

[26 April 1980]

Finally made it into the hospital to see Catherine. Jane wasn't very impressed about my absence yesterday, but what choice did I have?

Catherine is beautiful and there is something strong-willed about her expression that reminds me of her mother.

[30 April 1980]

At 11.30 this morning, six armed Iranians overpowered a police constable standing guard outside the Iranian Embassy and took twenty-six hostages. MI5 and the police are in a complete panic about what to do. Of course, we have game-played these scenarios often before. But we're very unsure as to what this particular group wants. They call themselves the Democratic Revolutionary Front for Arabistan – their name for the oil-rich Iranian province of Khuzestan. Their protest is apparently against oppression by Ayatollah Khomeini.

For the time being, they are being friendly and co-operative, treating the hostages well. A line of communication has been opened with an MI5 negotiator. But long-term we have no idea how it's going to pan out.

Our most pressing concern is that we've got no one in there to give us any intelligence. Most of the hostages – apart from a police constable and a couple of BBC journalists – are Iranian. Only one of the gunmen speaks English.

I have asked Clive whether I might be allowed the opportunity to infiltrate the embassy in whatever way possible. His response was that this would be too risky today, but I should game-play a number of scenarios with Archie as a precaution should the siege continue. Clive has spent most of the day at a Cobra meeting chaired by the Home Secretary. Matt has spent it sulking because he's on another operation with Amanda and considers himself to be something of a Persian expert.

For the time being, it is difficult to see any way of getting myself into the building without arousing the suspicions of the gunmen. Their lookout is good — both at the front and to the rear. On Princes Gate we also have the obstacle of half the world's media to contend with.

[1 May 1980]

I'm seizing my chance later today. One of the hostages, a BBC journalist, complained yesterday of a severe stomach condition and his captors initially asked for medicine to be brought in. However, his condition appears to have worsened overnight and they are now releasing him this afternoon.

I am to use this opportunity to infiltrate the embassy and provide intelligence from the inside. Flights into Heathrow are going to be lowered in their approach paths to give extra noise cover. Archie's job will be to create distractions on the street outside the embassy. Contractors are going to be brought in to drill as many unnecessary holes as possible. Newspaper vendors will shout their headlines even louder than usual. School-children will be encouraged to whoop and holler in the street. Buskers will be pulling out all the stops.

The idea is to assail the gunmen with such a barrage of noise that they will be unable to distinguish its various components. Organising chaos: it's a job that Archie is uniquely equipped for.

My job, meanwhile, is made significantly easier by the embassy's new design, which was brought to Cobra's attention last night. Following Khomeini's return to Tehran at the beginning of last year, many Iranian officials left their diplomatic posts in London for quieter careers. Amid this confusion, MI5 succeeded

in making a few minor adjustments to the Iranian Embassy —
notably a tunnel running from the neighbouring building.

My task will be to use this tunnel to gain access to the
embassy while the gunmen are preoccupied with releasing the ill
journalist. Once inside, I will be wired up to Cobra, as well
as any SAS teams involved in rescue efforts. My goal is to provide as much intelligence as possible — on the exact number of
hostages and gunmen, their whereabouts and their intentions.

It's almost certainly the most dangerous thing I've ever
done. My only child is five days old. But I can't think like
that. The operation starts this afternoon.

[6 May 1980]

I couldn't move around the embassy too much for fear of getting
caught, but I managed to find a sufficiently good vantage point
between the walls to observe all the goings-on.

On the fourth day, the gunmen released two more hostages,
including a pregnant woman. On the fifth, they released another.
But by the sixth day, the situation had begun to turn ugly. A
demand to negotiate via an Arab diplomatic intermediary was
turned down by the outside — on my recommendation. I could
clearly overhear that they planned this as a stalling tactic,
potentially taking another ambassador hostage as well.

Then, an Iranian hostage was tied up, shot dead and pushed
out of the embassy window. There was no choice but to call in
the SAS. From my vantage point, I could direct them to where the
hostages were being held and warn them about the booby traps
that had been set on the way.

All the remaining hostages were released unharmed. All but one of the gunmen were shot dead.

Those hostages were heroes, none more so than the police constable among them, who kept both them and the gunmen as calm as humanly possible throughout the ordeal. He is rightly going to be recommended for the George Cross.

In the evening, there was a celebratory reception at the SAS barracks, which I was invited along to. This was my place, after all. No George Cross. No television reunions with smiling, pretty wives. Just strong, male camaraderie. Secrets taken to the grave. The satisfaction of a job well done. The private memories. And a visit from the Thatchers, which I missed as I'd gone to the loo.

Matt is even more jealous now. He's always wanted to meet the Thatchers, for some inexplicable reason.

[22 September 1980]

War has broken out between Iran and Iraq after the latter's command council ordered its army to 'deliver its fatal blow on Iranian military targets'. Our recent assessment of the Iranian siege back in May is that it was probably carried out by agents financed by the Iraqi government. Again, we have been played for pawns in the wider battle of the Middle East.

[4 November 1980]

Jimmy Carter became the latest (but not the last) victim of the Iranian hostage crisis today when he lost the US presidential election in a landslide to Ronald Reagan. Carter's handling of the whole affair is widely thought to have contributed to his defeat. It's not a result to raise my opinion of politicians in general, and American politicians in particular. Nor does it say much about the American populace that they could choose a man such as Reagan. I remember a time when actors used to act. I'm not a great fan, on first impressions.

1981

[20 January 1981]

Perhaps I was harsh on Ronald Reagan. Today, the day of his inauguration, Iran released its remaining fifty-two hostages, bringing an end to the 444-day crisis.

Then again, the entire charade has the whiff of conspiracy about it – to me, at least. The timing just seems a little too suspicious, and there are some quite serious allegations that a member of Reagan's staff was in contact with the Iranian authorities during the election campaign, asking them to delay the hostages' release until he'd entered the Oval Office. If true – and none of us knows yet if it is true – I cannot think of a more cynical example of political expediency.

That's the problem with politicians when it comes to this sort of major event. They know full well that they're blamed – often unfairly – by the public when something goes wrong. So they're even more eager to take the credit – again, unfairly – when something goes right. In the process, they politicise a neutral issue, wind up their opponents and antagonise the professionals in the intelligence industry.

Long term, I think the most interesting thing to emerge from this crisis are the effects of the so-called Algiers Accords, agreed earlier this month. In return for the release of its hostages, the US has pledged that it will never again intervene, directly or indirectly, politically or militarily, in Iran's internal affairs.

Experience suggests that Uncle Sam might well have made this pledge with two fingers firmly crossed behind his back.

[18 February 1981]

Back to domestic affairs — very domestic affairs, in fact. MI5 has found an excellent nanny for Catherine — a young Polish girl called Liliana — allowing Jane to return to teaching part-time. The security services certainly know how to look after their own. A lot of corporate firms are starting to compare themselves to families these days, but MI5 really is a family. A jolly dysfunctional one, perhaps, but a family nonetheless. And it takes a great deal of care to make sure that all its extended members are happy.

Archie and I sometimes joke about it in the office. Clive is the benevolent father figure. Matt is the haughty eldest sibling. Archie and I are the naughty twins and Amanda is the precious, spoiled girl.

Back in my real family, everything is going well with Jane again.

[1 April 1981]

Look at today's date: I thought it was a joke when they first told me about my current assignment.

Part of MI5's remit is to deal with organised crime and serious domestic disorder. That's not the problem. The problem is a little operation run by the Metropolitan Police called Operation Swamp 81. The name derives from a remark made by Margaret Thatcher back in 1978: 'People are really rather afraid that this country might be rather swamped by people with a different culture — the British character has done so much for democracy, for law, and done so much throughout the world, that if there is any fear that it might be swamped, people are going to react and be rather hostile to those coming in.'

A fair point, perhaps. Certainly a stringent one.

And the motives behind Operation Swamp are also correct, however abhorrent its code name. Brixton in South London has some serious problems with street crime. In the past, the police have been timid in tackling the issue, preferring to turn the suburb into something of a ghetto and leaving it to police itself. Doing nothing shouldn't be an option in a democracy, however tempting it might appear.

The problem, then, with Operation Swamp is its execution. Under the so-called Sus Law, the police have the right to arrest members of the public on suspicion ('sus') alone. Inevitably, in an area such as Brixton, this is perceived as a discriminatory way of targeting black youths.

It's the old banana-and-fruit argument: all bananas are fruit; not all fruit are bananas. In Brixton, nearly all street crime is committed by young men of colour. Not all young men of colour are criminals.

Conveying this through the medium of uniformed officers, however, is a different matter altogether. Brixton appears to have an ingrained suspicion of any kind of uniformed authority — and perhaps rightly so. The police are perceived as reactionary and racist. Their current activities are only serving to heighten tensions.

This morning, the Metropolitan Police requested an MI5 liaison officer to work alongside them. Amanda has a funny effect on police officers. Archie can't help winding them up and anyone in uniform reacts badly to Matt's smarm, so Clive sent me down to Scotland Yard. I had been briefed on the outline of the operation, but the specifics were even more cack-handed than I'd been led to believe. More worrying still was the role the police envisaged for me: they wanted full MI5 technical and operational back-up. We were expected to bug premises, run background checks, deploy surveillance teams on the street and so on.

All of which appears fine on the surface, but the police wanted this done in an overt, obvious way so that the community would be left in no doubt that they were being spied upon. 'We want to shit them up a bit,' said the commander. 'If they think MI5 is involved, they might start co-operating a bit more.'

I had to refuse, of course. That's not how we operate. And it's definitely not how we should run this kind of operation. We are not a big stick to be waved around at recalcitrant schoolboys. This is hearts and minds stuff as much as serious crime.

So we've agreed on some sort of compromise: MI5 will contribute back-up where we believe it helpful, but we're not going to bend the rules on this one. And we're certainly going to keep it covert.

More importantly — as far as I'm concerned, at least — I will be going undercover in Brixton. This hasn't been agreed with the Met, but I managed to persuade Clive of the merits of the idea. Brixton has a problem, and our current concern is that the police will be stoking that problem. We will be spying on the law enforcers as much as the lawbreakers. For obvious reason, it seems best to keep this to ourselves.

[8 April 1981]

Not the most glamorous assignment, this one. The boffins have found me a squalid bedsit just off Somerleyton Road. By day, I work in a burger bar. By evening, I morph into a tramp and sit outside the tube station.

But what the roles lack in charm they more than make up for in their intelligence-gathering opportunities. Tramps and fast-food workers are equally invisible and equally well placed to observe the comings and goings of a community.

Brixton's burger bars are a social nexus of gossip and intrigue. Customers shout and yell at you while dealing drugs to one another under their trays. I've seen an average of three knives pulled in the 'restaurant' every hour. The manager has called the police ten times in the last week and they've turned up once.

Meanwhile, outside, hapless youths are hassled and harried

by police officers. There is a feral atmosphere spreading among young people. I am seeing the young alienated and marginalised, the moderate radicalised. The root causes of the unrest — unemployment, poor housing — are not being tackled.

That's the liberal critique and the police are failing to answer it. Just as seriously, perhaps, they are also missing the bigger picture when it comes to acting tough. At the moment, they're acting like the proverbial fat bully in the playground. I've witnessed this in the evenings. They're quite content to stop the small kids and the shifty young men. But they're afraid to tackle the gangs and the gang leaders. The strong grow stronger and complacent; the weak get angry.

Operation Swamp is a mess and I fear for where it will end.

[12 April 1981]

Riots. That's where it ended.

I'd warned them. I'd warned Clive who even went as far to blow my cover with the Met. His, and my, fear of repercussions from the police was outweighed by the seriousness with which we viewed the current situation. It wasn't just a gut instinct I was acting on. I had specific intelligence. Three days ago, I'd overheard discussions about plans to initiate a riot on the next provocation by the police. I'd even been asked if I wanted to join. 'This isn't just about black men,' one of them said to me as I cleared up their meal. 'It's about the working class, the underclass, the oppressed.'

On the evening of the 10th, police officers arrested a young black man with a knife wound. As they took him back to their vehicle, they were ambushed by angry crowds. The violence escalated over the next two days into full-blown running riots with bricks, bottles and petrol bombs. It was the first time Molotov cocktails had been used in the UK outside Northern Ireland.

I was caught right in the middle of the violence, attempting both to mediate the police response and calm the crowds. It was an impossible task: at one point, I was almost lynched as an appeaser by an angry mob; at another, a policeman in the Special Patrol Group almost broke my legs with his baton, despite my giving the clear code word of an undercover officer. At least I have his badge number. I intend to ensure he's making tea for the next six months.

Crowd psychology is interesting, and there is always a tipping point in this kind of protest. Before a certain moment, the presence/threat of excess force is entirely counter-productive. After a certain moment, you can't have enough visible force on the street. This point was reached very early on in these riots – an indication of the groundswell of discontent.

I was able, at least, to provide some degree of live intelligence to the forces, but at the end of the day, I was the wrong man in the wrong place. If we're going to stop this sort of thing from happening again – and I think it will happen again – we'll need much better agents on the ground. The future threats to this country are going to come from minority, home-grown, marginalised groups as much as from high-level, state-sponsored terrorism.

[13 April 1981]

I made the mistake of returning home still muddied and sweaty from the riots. Catherine burst into tears when she saw me. She called Jane 'Mama' after only six months. She still hasn't called me Daddy. I do my best, but I still don't feel we've bonded. She'll be a year old soon.

[14 June 1981]

I have been seconded to the team responsible for the security of the wedding of the Prince of Wales and Lady Diana next month.

It is an unenviable job.

Three and a half thousand guests will be in St Paul's Cathedral – including most heads of state. Palace officials want our advice on seating plans: who could spark an international incident by sitting next to whom? Meanwhile, King Juan Carlos I of Spain has been advised not to attend because the honeymoon will involve a stopover in the disputed territory of Gibraltar. The President of Ireland is not attending in protest against our presence in Northern Ireland.

Despite these absences, St Paul's Cathedral will still represent the ideal target for anyone wishing to make a nuisance of themselves. We've shaken all the obvious cages: the PIRA have never been under closer observation. And we've locked ourselves into a few unexpected ones as well: Republican groups, disaffected anarchists etc.

Then there is the general public to worry about. Millions are expected to line the route. Almost a billion people will be watching on television. This is Britain on show. We have to give the impression of a confident country enjoying a moment of national unity — serenely organised, quietly and expertly policed.

Under the surface, of course, we'll be paddling like fury. I knew there were cranks around, but I'd never realised how many until I was assigned to this project. The royal family receives thousands of items of correspondence every day, much of it charming and benign. But there are also death threats, obscene insinuations and bogus claims. The green-ink brigade has truly come out in force this month.

While many of them can be easily dismissed, we're not taking any chances. We like to do this in a low-key manner. We're not a police state, after all. Nutters can be easily assessed by a police constable making 'routine' inquiries in the area. This is much more efficient than alarming a mentally unstable stalker, or giving egoists the MI5 glamour they desire. It is only the truly worrying ones that we bring in and scare a little.

We're all currently on a high state of alert after six blank shots were fired at the Queen yesterday during the Trooping the Colour. She managed to regain control of her horse, but it has put everyone on edge rather.

[30 July 1981]

There is a balanced level of monarchism at MI5, which I find satisfying. In the army, it was completely overblown. We were HM's forces who swore allegiance to the Queen. Every mess dinner had repeated toasts to Her Majesty.

[spooks]

At MI5, on the other hand, the Queen and the royal family are simply part of the status quo that we defend. *Regnum Defende*. But that kingdom also includes politicians, the public, democracy itself. It seems more nuanced, more acceptable somehow.

Charles and Diana's wedding yesterday passed without incident.

And as I moved through that crowd, listening, watching and monitoring, I felt — perhaps for the first time — an overwhelming pride in being British. Here was pomp and ceremony and circumstance. But here also were ordinary people, happy, laughing, united as a *demos*. It is my job to protect these people, this country, these traditions that I love. And it is a job that I am honoured to do.

1982

[12 January 1982]

Bloody Mark Thatcher has gone missing somewhere in the desert on the Dakar Rally and Juliet Shaw has been dispatched to find him. She has been something of a favourite of the Prime Minister's ever since her reports from Iran. Unsurprising, perhaps — the two women have a lot in common.

[15 January 1982]

The prodigal son has turned up, spotted 50km off course by an Algerian military plane with Juliet onboard. She rang to tell me the news. 'I was all for leaving him there,' she said.

A strange reaction, I thought at first. From what I know of Juliet, she's surely a rabid Thatcherite. But, like me, I don't think she's very keen on playing silly buggers in deserts with spoiled offspring when there are more important matters to attend to.

71

[5 April 1982]

We are at war with Argentina in the Falklands. It's strange to write those words. It doesn't have the same resonant impact as saying, 'We are at war with Germany.' For many here, it appears a spurious conflict about faraway islands about which we know nothing. Even patriots' patriotism is being stretched a little far with this one.

Still, I don't think Thatcher has much choice. She's gone very Palmerstonian on the public, promising to stick up for British interests, wherever they might be.

Meanwhile, it's a frustrating time to be at MI5. Our cousins at Six have all the fun when a major event like this pops up abroad, while we have to continue with the daily drudge of domestic security. The modern media is apt to focus on a major event like this and assume that everything else is put on hold. It isn't. There is probably no better time for the PIRA to attack, or for other renegade groups to catch us with our pants down. So we are all working around the clock on a state of high alert. Amanda has cancelled at least four dates with various members of the Square Mile in the last fortnight. Matt has taken to sleeping in the office and conference-calling his wife at hourly intervals during the evening. Even Archie has started showering at work.

Working late is never ideal in any job. Partners are missed, friends stood up, meals uneaten, children left without a kiss and a bedtime story. I don't think I'd be able to stay late in an office if our concern was the bottom line of a company's balance sheet. But when it's national security, the sacrifices are more bearable. There's a special camaraderie on these sorts of occasions, when we put aside our usual daily gripes and work much better together.

Our other problem, of course, is what to do with the Argentine community in the UK. At the beginning of the Second World War, all Germans (and perceived German sympathisers) were rounded up and incarcerated. But do we need to do that now with Argentinians as a precautionary measure? Can they really be a fifth column in our midst when our troops are thousands of miles away? It seems unlikely to me somehow.

[7 June 1982]

President Reagan is visiting London tomorrow when he'll be the first US President to address a joint session of the British parliament. The security preparations are similar to those for the royal wedding last year, only fifty times as bad. The Americans really do have the most annoying approach to security — 'POTUS this, POTUS that. He's our chief executive and commander-in-chief, blah blah.'

The President Of The United States' protection squad, in particular, really get up my nose. Burly thugs with curly headsets march around our public places as if they own them, babbling inconsequential nonsense into their microphones. It's all, 'I won't let this happen on my watch,' and, 'The life of the most powerful man in the world is in our hands,' and, 'I hope you understand that, Brits.' They've all been watching far too many B-rate films, in my opinion.

Reagan better have something interesting to say tomorrow.

[8 June 1982]

Reagan's speech *was* surprisingly interesting. He must have an excellent speechwriter lurking in the bowels of the White House somewhere.

There was a nice line that the Soviet Union 'runs against the tide of history by denying human freedom and human dignity to its citizens'. But more interesting was his analysis — the first by a world leader of standing — that Communism would soon collapse. We've been operating on the opposite model, that the Soviet Union is to be contained — occasionally bullied, cajoled and mildly provoked, but always contained. Reagan's approach, on the other hand, appears to be to go hell for leather at its very existence.

Either he ends up a hero or we all end up dead.

[14 June 1982]

The Falklands war is over. Thatcher's rhetoric has never been so Churchillian. It's all a far cry from her high-pitched recitation of the St Francis prayer when she took office: 'Where there is hatred, let me sow love. Where there is injury, pardon.'

Well, indeed.

[10 July 1982]

Yesterday an intruder, Michael Fagan, broke into the Queen's bedroom at Buckingham Palace and spent ten minutes chatting to her. It's the sixth breach of security there this year. Last year, three German tourists camped in the garden after mistaking it for Hyde Park.

I went to Buckingham Palace today for a debrief with the Queen's security teams. We are livid that they can allow this sort of thing to happen. It makes a laughing stock of the security industry and it persuades other misfits, losers and more serious groups that they, too, can have a crack. We have proposed a range of much tighter measures.

To my amusement, the Queen was very relaxed about the whole thing. And to her credit, she had kept Fagan chatting until help arrived.

'A lot of my job is very boring, Mr Pearce,' she told me. 'Nervous people at another nervous charity whose names I can't remember. This was the first proper conversation I've had in a long time.'

It reminds me of a conversation I had with an Arab during my time in Germany.

'So, your monarch is a woman?'

'Yes. Queen Elizabeth the Second.'

'And your Prime Minister is a woman?'

'Yes. Margaret Thatcher.'

Pause.

'Harry, what's wrong with all the men in your country?'

[12 December 1982]

More troublesome women.

Thirty thousand of them arrived at Greenham Common

yesterday to 'embrace the base'. Clive told me it's high time we started infiltrating agents into the group and I agree. I'm sure the women all mean very well, but a nuclear deterrent is a vital component of our defence strategy at the moment. Of course, it would be very nice if we could all disarm and live peacefully together but we should never, ever do it unilaterally.

Amanda has been put in charge of recruiting a suitable nexus of agents to infiltrate the Greenham protesters.

We were all there this morning when Clive briefed her.

'I'm sure you can think of the kind of person I have in mind,' he said. 'Maternal, a little unwashed, straggly hair, smelly cats at home, a fondness for peppermint tea, rainbow jumpers and CND badges.'

Clive paused to look Amanda up and down.

'Do you know many people like that, Amanda?' he asked.

'It's as if you've just given a pen portrait of your youngest female field officer,' replied Amanda with a smile, smoothing down her Prada trouser suit.

The funny thing about Amanda, though, is that it wouldn't surprise me at all if she ended up donning a rainbow jumper herself and heading down to Berkshire. This job attracts some interesting split personality types — equally at home in Harvey Nichols and muddy fields, gentlemen's clubs and urban riots.

In the end, we're all actors. Except that the script's unwritten, the audience is vicious and the pay's risible.

1983

[24 March 1983]

A fine month for President Reagan. On the 8th his speechwriter again excelled himself, labelling the Soviet Union an 'evil empire'. And then yesterday he announced the Strategic Defense Initiative, or 'Star Wars' as the media like to call it.

I suppose it's a slightly less depressing alternative to the current deterrent of mutually assured destruction (MAD).

[25 April 1983]

An extraordinary thing happened in the US today. Samantha Smith, a sixth-grade schoolgirl from Maine, wrote a letter last year to the Soviet Communist Party General Secretary, Yuri Andropov, expressing her concerns about the tense relations between the USA and the USSR. It was a charming letter. 'Congratulation on your new job,' it started.

Andropov wrote back and invited her to visit his country this summer to see for herself that the USSR wants peace.

[spooks]

Of course, the whole thing has the heady stink of propaganda about it, but there is something rather touching about this correspondence between a ten-year-old Western girl and a grizzled Communist leader.

It's a reminder to us all while we scheme in smoky corridors, turn agents, infiltrate institutions, eavesdrop via satellite and invent bigger, nastier and more expensive destructive weapons. It's a reminder as to what really counts: a young girl who enjoys roller skating who'd like to be alive next year and can't see what all the fuss is about.

[18 June 1983]

Jane gave birth to a son today whom we've decided to call Graham. Catherine has been worried for ages that we'd 'no longer love her' once we had a second child, but I took her along to the hospital this afternoon and she was delighted with her new brother.

'He looks just like you, Daddy,' she said.

'Yes, he is an ugly baby,' said Jane, smiling.

[29 June 1983]

Two events have just conspired to make my life very difficult indeed.

One: Boca Juniors, the Argentinian football champions of 1981, have decided that they are going to come on a pre-season tour to Europe. As a gesture of goodwill to the country that recently defeated them in the Falklands, they will be starting this with a friendly match against Chelsea in August.

A 'friendly' match against Chelsea? If a better oxymoron exists, I'd like to hear it.

We are currently in the midst of a horrible spate of football hooliganism. It's one of many reasons that I'm more of a rugby man. Chelsea, in particular, is a nightmare at the moment. A lot of ex-servicemen have season tickets there. It is difficult to imagine them taking kindly to a visiting team of Argentinians with their attendant fans. If ever a match has the potential to descend into a mass brawl, it's this one.

There is a particularly charming crime technique at the moment known as the Chelsea Smile. The victim's face is cut from the edges of their mouth to their ears. They are then punched until they scream, stretching the wound as far as possible.

As for the Boca Juniors, their nickname at home is *bosteros* – horse-shitters. That they now wear this insult as a badge of pride says, I think, all anyone needs to know.

Two: Margaret Thatcher has decided that she wants to attend the match.

[2 July 1983]

I had a meeting with Thatcher this morning about the football match.

God, is she an iron lady! The eyes of Caligula, the mouth of Marilyn Monroe.

She is surprisingly attractive, with particularly well-turned ankles, but you forget that in her presence. Her femininity isn't the vulnerable kind. It's an overwhelming, powerful, emasculating, ball-twisting, terrifying form of femininity. She reminds me of an old school friend's nanny, but with ten times the brain power.

I'm not very keen on Thatcher's economic politics – I studied enough economics at Oxford to realise that her monetarism is targeting a very narrow band of the money supply – but I always felt scorn for the Wets in her cabinet. What were Gilmour, Pym, Carrington etc., all thinking? Why couldn't they rally round their leader? But after spending twenty minutes in her presence today, I think they were braver men than I could ever imagine. Defying her is like attempting to defy a dreadnaught.

No, she would not reconsider her decision to attend the match. No, she would not put pressure on the clubs to play the match earlier in the day, thereby making drunken rioting less likely. Yes, she was fully aware that we had fought and won a war against Argentina last year, thank you very much, but no, she couldn't see what that had to do with anything.

I eventually left Downing Street feeling like I'd gone ten rounds in the ring with a heavyweight boxing champion. I'd been there less than half an hour but it was absolutely exhausting.

The only concession I'd managed to wangle was that Thatcher would keep her attendance at the match a secret. Otherwise, she might as well go back two thousand years, find a nearby lions' den, walk in and say, 'I'm a Christian; what would you like for starters?'

[5 July 1983]

God, I hate journalists.

The front page of today's *Sun*, or *Moon*, or whatever it is they call it: SHE'S GOT BALLS. THATCHER TO ATTEND ARGIE-BARGIE FOOTBALL MATCH.

They've printed her seat number, her attendance time and details of her security arrangements. It's about as close to an assassination manual as you can get. They've even given a few suggestions for chants she might like to join in with. 'Stand up if you bombed the *Belgrano*,' was a particularly sensitive favourite.

Stupidly, I then did what no intelligence officer should ever do. I rang up the editor and gave him a blasting.

'What's your name?' he kept on demanding.

'That's none of your fucking business,' I kept on shouting back at him.

[6 July 1983]

Front page of today's paper: JAMES BOND ON THE PHONE, along with a fairly accurate transcript of my conversation yesterday with the editor. It would seem that we're not the only organisation in this country that taps telephones.

Clive has been reassuringly lenient with me. I think he shares my dislike of the media. Archie has been calling all his old contacts to try to get this to go away as quickly as possible.

It's not that I loathe journalists per se. They can be good

company. They have some value. And occasionally we use them to leak useful stories. It's the way they've got so far up their own bloody arses recently that annoys me. I blame Watergate and *All the President's Men*. Half of them run around as if they're the only official opposition, bleating about the Fourth Estate and holding people to account and all that self-righteous nonsense. The other half has absolutely no sense of morality these days. It's all about sales and scoops and advertising promotions. Who can be there first with whichever story it is that no one else in the public cares about at all etc. It's all 'unattributed sources' and 'leading industry experts' and insiders and outsiders sounding off about this, that, the other and the next thing ad infinitum.

And they never think about the knock-on effect of their actions. Fly-by-night interests are picked up, chewed up, spat out and ignored. And then we have this week's little shenanigans, putting the security of the Prime Minister at serious risk.

I am not happy.

[7 July 1983]

I am even unhappier.

It transpires that the story was leaked by Downing Street itself. I might have been a little unfair in my rant in yesterday's entry against the media. They are only printing what they are being fed in the first place.

I spoke on the phone to Thatcher's press secretary. Why the hell had he authorised this leak? I asked.

'It puts her in a good light,' he said. 'In victory,

magnanimous; in defeat, gracious.' He gave a horrible nasal little laugh and added: 'Not that she's ever been defeated, of course.'

'No,' I said. 'It makes her look like a crowing, silly old biddy. Populist, but never popular. And it means you're not doing your job properly.'

'Just do yours, Harry,' he said. And then he hung up.

The problem is that he's right. At the end of the day, I have little say in the matter. Thatcher is elected; her advisers are appointed by her. I am a civil servant. If she wants to sit in the middle of a football stadium with thirty thousand people who would happily kill her, then that's her choice. My job is to make sure she comes to no harm.

[14 July 1983]

The match is taking place on 4 August and I've been recruiting agents in as many different locations as possible. The apprentices who clean the boots at Chelsea: in my pocket. The hotdog seller at Standford Bridge: reports to me. I have an informer among season-ticket holders in every section of the stand.

Amanda has managed to charm her way into a corporate box for the match itself. Matt's decided that he would like to join her there and leave me to direct events from the crowd. Archie is trying to get a job as a ball boy for the day.

The problem, as expected, is on the Argentinian side. Our agent networks there were stretched to the limits during the Falklands conflict. Half of them are dead, resting or exhausted. MI6's traditional snobbery doesn't help either. While we know exactly what is going on in all the polo *estancias* around the country, our intelligence on football teams is sketchy, to say the least.

Worse still, Thatcher has decided to take a tabloid editor, Mark Sharrocks, with her to the match as a thank you for his support during the difficult early years of her premiership. If anything happens, the most poisonous toad in Fleet Street will have a front-row scoop on proceedings. Our only hope is that any Argentinian assassination attempt will mistake his bouffant hairstyle for the Prime Minister's.

Archie has started keeping low-level tabs on Sharrocks as well, just in case the need arises.

[3 August 1983]

The match is tomorrow and we've identified fifteen specific threats on the Prime Minister's life. Ten — Argentinians living in this country — have been arrested. Five were identified by MI6 from among the travelling fans and picked up at Heathrow. We've never had so many sniffer dogs and policemen on the lookout there.

Still, I have an uneasy feeling about the whole thing.

[4 August 1983]

I was right.

It all started last night when I was looking at the squad list of Boca Juniors. We'd profiled every known troublemaker among the fans but it occurred to me that we'd been a little slacker when it came to the players. Footballers are like gods in Argentina — as they're slowly becoming over here as well. Getting close to them is impossible. Suspecting them is close to treason.

Boca has a striker, Miguel Mendoza, who is one of the best players of the decade. He has scored more than fifty goals for his country and has a strike rate of almost a goal per game for Boca. He has one passionate hobby besides football — rifle shooting.

The call came from Six's man in Buenos Aires. Mendoza had been left out of the starting line-up at his own request. He was going to be sitting on the substitutes' bench instead.

'So what?' I said.

'Thatcher is sitting five rows behind the bench,' he said.

It wasn't enough in itself. But it had a suspicious ring to it. I got someone in Five to get every detail they could on Mendoza. Two hours later, she came back to me. Mendoza has two half-brothers with a different surname. Shared mother. Both on the *Belgrano*. Both dead. Both sunk by Thatcher's decision.

I rang up Downing Street straight away and spoke to Thatcher's Special Branch liaison.

'For the last bloody time, you have to keep Thatcher away from that match,' I said.

The Special Branch man wasn't impressed: 'Do you have any specific intelligence? Perhaps Mendoza's tired. Perhaps he just wants a rest. Perhaps the manager doesn't want to exhaust him against a weakened Chelsea team before the rest of their European tour. Perhaps he's got the shits from our English food.

85

Perhaps, perhaps, perhaps. This is all just meaningless speculation.'

I took my concerns to Matt and Clive but it wasn't enough for them, either.

'It's not concrete, Harry,' said Clive. 'We can't interrupt the PM's schedule like this. She'd kill us.'

Thatcher was coming to the game and that was that.

The match kicked off at 4 p.m. Mendoza was in the starting line-up after all, which made us lower our guard. I could see the Special Branch guy glancing pityingly at me as Mendoza scored just before half-time.

But then, in the sixtieth minute, Mendoza was substituted. I've learned enough about football in the last month to know that he is almost never substituted. And when he is, he reacts appallingly, throwing down his captain's armband like a spoiled child and jogging off sullenly to the dressing room, refusing to watch the rest of the match.

This time, however, was different. The armband was handed gracefully to one of his teammates. He appeared to be savouring the moment, basking in the adoration of the crowd, walking slowly towards the dugout. He had the demeanour of a man bowing out of the game altogether and saluting his fans. Or he was acting like someone about to do something very stupid indeed and savouring his last moment of freedom.

Mendoza is twenty-four and a long way from retirement. This couldn't be his footballing swansong. As he finally approached the bench in the dugout, he kept on casting surreptitious glances up to the row where I was sitting — one behind Thatcher and Sharrocks. All my instincts screamed that I had to do something. But how? And when? In front of me sat the most powerful person in Britain and a tabloid newspaper editor. Fifty feet away, one of the world's best-known footballers was rummaging in his kitbag for something. All around me, fifty thousand people were watching a match while the television cameras whirred.

Do nothing and I might witness the first successful assassination of a British prime minister right under my nose. Overreact, and I would be the laughing stock of the world.

The only solution was to get Mendoza away from the scene while causing the least fuss. Neutralise the threat and all other repercussions could be taken from there. We needed a distraction.

I radioed two of my agents in the crowd. 'Two minutes,' I said. 'On my count. I need you to take your clothes off and run on to the pitch. All subsequent fallout will be taken care of.'

I wondered how I'd react should I ever receive such an order.

Then I radioed the ambulance team I had on standby in the stadium: 'In 110 seconds, two streakers will enter the field of play. That's your signal. Manhandle Miguel Mendoza on to a stretcher and get him into the tunnel. Give him a jab of something if you need to.'

In the sixty-seventh minute of the football game, two naked men ran on to the pitch. The crowd — including Thatcher and Sharrocks — dissolved into fits of laughter. Mendoza was ushered out of the stadium with barely anyone noticing. My ambulance men also managed to pick up his kitbag in the chaos. It contained pictures of his two dead half-brothers, a part-assembled rifle and the tabloid newspaper report of Thatcher's attendance at the game.

[7 August 1983]

It was decided not to press charges against Mendoza. The man — or the man's image, at least — is simply too big to touch in the current climate. And after the scare a group of interrogators led by Matt gave him in the cells last night, it is unlikely that he'll ever contemplate anything like this again.

Sometimes, you get a glimpse of your superiors in action and you realise what it is that got them to where they are today. I'd never really warmed to Matt. I thought his initial handling of this case was cavalier and it annoyed me that he constantly took Clive's side against me whenever I expressed my concerns about the match.

But watching him in action interrogating Mendoza, I saw just how good he can be at his job. It also made me realise how much I still have to learn.

Meanwhile, the story was spun to the press that Mendoza had fainted at the sight of two naked men running on to the pitch. The media has the nice little vignette it craved, and no one is any the wiser.

No one, that is, except for Thatcher herself. I was invited for a personal meeting with her this morning.

'You saved my life, Mr Pearce,' she said. 'And no one is ever going to know about it. I'm not sure how to thank you.'

I'm ashamed to admit that I blushed.

'Now what do you think of these pictures?' she asked,

showing me the front-page picture of my two agents streaking across Standford Bridge.

'I think it was a rather cold night, Prime Minister,' I replied.

There was a horrible, long silence. And then she laughed uproariously, fixing me with those piercing blue eyes of hers.

'Gotcha, Harry. Gotcha!'

In the evening, Jane asked me how my meeting had gone.

'Oh, it was OK,' I said. 'Very formal. Bit stuffy.'

Jane looked at me suspiciously. I haven't told her about Mendoza. I don't think she'd approve of someone saving Thatcher's life. She votes SDP and entertains some kind of inexplicable crush on Roy Jenkins.

1984

[12 March 1984]

Thatcher rang my home telephone this evening and got Jane on the line.

'How did she know our number?' hissed Jane as she handed me the receiver.

'Have I not told you what it is I do for a living?' I said as I took it.

Still, it was a rather disconcerting feeling to be rung at home by Margaret Thatcher. I know I regularly eavesdrop on other people – and I know that she's the Prime Minister – but I still think there are some things that should be sacrosanct, my home telephone number among them.

Anyway, it transpired that the PM was ringing for a very particular reason.

'I'm sorry to trouble you at home, Harry,' she said. (I don't know at what point she thought she should start addressing me by my first name. Maybe when I saved her life, I suppose.) 'But something big has come up and I really want to entrust it to you.'

I'd already guessed what it was she wanted to talk about. Last week, strike action began at a Yorkshire coalfield. Today, Arthur Scargill, President of the National Union of Mineworkers, declared a national strike.

'I have a feeling this is going to turn into an epic battle,' she told me. 'And I want you to do anything you can to make sure we win it. I mean *anything*, Harry.'

Well, it makes me very uneasy, I must admit. What exactly does she mean by 'we'? And if we are 'we', who are 'they'? Who is one of us? Who is one of them?

Regnum Defende, as I keep on reminding myself. But whose *regnum*? Ours or theirs? And does industrial action lie within our remit? Yes, if it seeks to overthrow democracy by violent means. No, if it's yet another political battle between a subjective view of us and them.

Traditionally, MI5 has protected the country from subversive elements from outside. Now we are beginning to focus within as well.

We are going to have to tread very carefully.

[7 April 1984]

It's not just Jane who's jealous about the PM taking a shine to me. Matt, Section D's most rabid Thatcherite, has been making continuous barbed comments about it. Even Clive, Amanda and Archie have failed to hide the venom behind their teasing. It's the problem, I suppose, with teamwork. You want the team to be successful, but you'd still rather it was you, the individual, who carried away the plaudits. No one wants to be the back-up player, especially if, like Matt and Clive, you know you made the wrong call and your junior officer got it right.

Still, the dust is settling and we have more important things to focus on. We're tackling the threat of militant miners in the old-fashioned way: a huge network of agents and informers.

It's not difficult to do when it comes to the unions. Some of these workers might have banded together but there is still more that divides them than unites them. We have the 'scabs' — the picket line breakers — that we can work on. Those who aren't working are desperate for any sort of additional money to feed their families. And then there are tensions within the leadership of the NUM itself. They might be attempting to lead their men to a bright new Jerusalem, but they're squabbling over who gets to do it.

It's the old concept: divide and rule. It's just not a division that I'm hugely happy with.

[2 June 1984]

We've made a huge breakthrough with our agent recruiting. Matt has found someone at the very highest level of the NUM — one of Scargill's right-hand men — who is now working for us. Silver Fox is his code name and it was a textbook recruitment. I've never seen MICE — Money, Ideology, Compromise and Ego — work so well in combination. Silver Fox is a greedy, Trotsky-hating egomaniac with one wife, two children, two mistresses and a penchant for rent boys. We've really got this guy where we want him. He's going to be the NUM's Steak Knife.

He's already proved useful for us. According to Silver Fox, a mass picket is planned at the British Steel coking plant in Orgreave on 18 June. The NUM is attempting to blockade the plant and force its closure. Thanks to Silver Fox's information, we have instructed the police to start organising counter-measures.

[19 June 1984]

If ever there was an example of good intelligence poorly implemented . . .

Matt and I were there at Orgreave yesterday to observe the picket, and the police got it completely wrong. They had almost one officer for every miner, creating a sense of tension from the outset. There were also around fifty mounted police and a similar number of police dogs. Much like the Brixton riots, the whole thing was only ever going to end in confrontation.

There was another thing I felt very unhappy about. Matt put pressure on me to persuade various television news organisations to show doctored footage of events. In particular, the sequence was altered to show the police in a better light. The way in which he told me to do it suggested that the order had come from fairly high up — higher even than Clive.

I don't mean to get too misty-eyed here. These miners aren't heroes. Many of them are militant, dangerous men. But many of them are also family men with hungry mouths to feed. I think we've escalated this into an unnecessarily large battle.

[19 July 1984]

Thatcher is not helping.

In a speech to parliament today she said, 'We had to fight the enemy without in the Falklands. We always have to be aware of the enemy within, which is much more difficult to fight and more dangerous to liberty.'

Sometimes, it's helpful to have a politician who thinks in black and white for a change. Most of them are too bloody clever for their own good. Not wise, not insightful, not intellectual. But clever. Clever dicks; smart alecs; interested in debate for the sake of debate; point-scoring; meaningless verbal joshing. They like to weigh up all sides of an argument, think everything through and end up pontificating into a paralysis of indecision. By the time they've actually made their mind up on anything, it's too late to act on it.

But there's black and white and then there's Thatcher's black and white. Lumping together miners with the Falklands? It's not only a crass and harmful analogy; it's a very inaccurate one.

Again, I'm reminded of the Brixton riots. We're ignoring the root cause of this anger.

[28 September 1984]

We're getting into murkier waters here. It's come to our attention that a far-left Labour MP has been giving support to the more militant elements of the NUM. His code name: Portcullis.

And I don't just mean moral support. Plenty of people – in the media and among politicians – have been speaking out against Thatcher and the police. They have arranged food and medicine for families out of work and other laudable and legal activities. Portcullis, on the other hand, has stepped over the line. We have good reason to believe that his parliamentary rooms are being used for militant meetings. His constituency office appears to be even more embroiled.

We've tackled the two offices separately. Archie has got a job as his constituency researcher in his West Midlands office. Ostensibly, he's there to act as a constituency help for Portcullis – a position that was widely advertised. In truth, however, he has become Portcullis's right-hand man and one of our best-placed informers.

It's surprisingly difficult shoehorning someone into a job like this. There are two major obstacles to consider: the first is the interviewer himself. You have to second-guess their motives and their tastes. What kind of employee would appeal to them? Are they a chauvinist? Or a letch? Once you've worked out exactly what they're looking for, you can tailor your chosen candidate to their taste.

Most MPs would warm to someone like Amanda. Our file on Portcullis – including some alarmingly detailed surveillance shots – suggested that Archie would be more his type.

The other major obstacle, of course, is the other candidates applying for the job. I've had great fun over the last week, starting rumours in various university campuses to stop people applying for the job. Adverts have mysteriously disappeared from careers offices. Applications have gone missing

in the post. Candidates have been made late for their appointments after a pernickety ticket inspector made them miss their
train. And so on. In any case, it worked. Archie is in place and
doing an excellent job.

Portcullis's office in the House of Commons was a slightly
trickier affair. Getting an agent in there isn't easy — he has
a battleaxe of a PA who's been with him for thirty years and
acts as a ruthless gatekeeper to his Westminster life. So we
decided to bug his rooms and his telephone instead.

Security around the Palace of Westminster is worryingly
lax. It's also a couple of hundred years out of date. Tight-
wearing, elderly ex-soldiers wander around aimlessly, looking
about as likely to stop an attack as they are to run someone
through with their cumbersome swords. Pretty much any member of
the public can walk in or out. There are rarely bag searches.

In some respects, it says a lot for our democracy. I like
the idea that we're governed by the people, that the physical
as well as the emotional gap between the governed and the
governors is bridgeable. Our Prime Minister has a house number
on a (fairly) normal street. Our representatives have offices
and you know where they are. But it is also something of a
security nightmare.

On the other hand, if you're a member of MI5 and you want
to get into the offices of those representatives and bug
them . . .

Well, it was laughably easy. Derek from the technical
department and I dressed up smartly as lobbyists (our briefcases
were stuffed full of bugging equipment). A policeman politely
asked us if he could help and we asked him where Committee Room

B was. He waved us on in the right direction.

We found Portcullis's offices easily enough, waited until he was called down from his postprandial nap (no true hero of the working classes he) to go and vote on something or other and bugged every nook and cranny of his office.

It's not the first time we've done this in the House of Commons. We've done it in the House of Lords as well — not the hereditaries, but some of those life peers have some very shady acquaintances, particularly the ones who've donated so much to the political parties that they're too grateful to ask any questions.

Still, it's a sobering moment to enter the office of an elected representative — even one you suspect of undermining a stable society — and cover it with MI5 wizardry. The people voted this person in. But then the people presumably didn't expect he was going to end up involved in illegal activities. The people are funding those illegal activities. But they're also funding me to snoop on his illegal activities. Should they know? And when should they know? Or is their ignorance bliss?

Sometimes, one can see the advantages in Thatcher's black-and-white approach to complex issues.

[5 October 1984]

Portcullis's bugs are reaping benefits. The long battle against strike action is beginning to swing our way. Maybe this is what this all boils down to: a means-and-ends debate.

[12 October 1984]

I was on holiday this evening when I got another call from Margaret Thatcher in our hotel room. Jane rolled her eyes as she passed the receiver over to me, wondering how the PM knew which room we were occupying, in which hotel, in which small district of Venice.

Of course I'd heard the news on the radio. In the early hours of yesterday morning, PIRA had detonated a bomb in the Brighton hotel where the PM and much of her cabinet were staying during the Conservative Party conference. Five people were killed; several others were seriously injured. I'd considered returning home, but PIRA wasn't my responsibility any more. I'd even checked in with Clive, but he told me to enjoy my holiday. 'Stop being a workaholic, Harry,' he'd berated down the phone. 'Give your family some of your time for once.'

Now here was Thatcher with some awkward words for me as well. 'I know it's not your responsibility, Harry. But I would really like it if you could help your colleagues catch those people.'

Next to me, Jane was giggling. 'She's got her own little pet spook now,' she whispered.

Of course, Thatcher has emerged triumphant from the whole affair. Events like these make statesmen out of leaders. And she's astute enough to know that. It's starting to put her above politics. Attack her at the moment and it looks like you're attacking the very fabric of British society. She gave a particularly stirring conference speech this morning.

But it's the words of the terrorists that will endure

longer. 'Today, we were unlucky,' read their statement. 'But remember, we only have to be lucky once. You will have to be lucky always.'

And that's the nature of the job we do. If we succeed 999 times and fail once, we are still a failure. What happens if a teacher makes a mistake in a lesson? Her pupils might lose one or two marks in an exam. If a businessman enters a wrong figure in a report? His company might lose some of its share price.

But if we fail, people die. If we cock up, catastrophes happen. And the worst thing is that there are thousands, perhaps millions, of people hoping that we do fail. There are also millions more relying on us to succeed.

We can do our job to the best of our abilities. We are professional, well-trained and dedicated. But, ultimately, we also have to hope that we are consistently luckier than our opponents.

1985

[12 April 1985]

It's been half a year since my last diary entry and, to be honest, it hasn't been a particularly interesting six months. This, I suppose, is the nature of work in the intelligence services. You are governed by events. Most of our activities are reactive, not proactive.

The miners' strike wound down officially on 3 March, a resounding victory for the government, but in essence it was won before that. In the long term, however, I think the Conservatives will find that they won the battle but lost the war. Vast swathes of the country will never consider voting for them again after their conduct during the last year.

Since then, most of my time has been taken up with writing reports on MI5's role in the strikes. These reports are inordinately difficult to pull off. The media speculates endlessly as to what we've been up to. They know, as well as we do, that the trend these days is towards increased freedom of information. But when do reports like these become declassified? After thirty years? Fifty years? Never? And what do we omit and what do we include?

Writing a report for your superiors is one thing. Writing a report that you fear will be read by journalists and members of the public in half a century's time is something different altogether.

On another note, Thatcher's request that I personally help hunt the Brighton bomber hasn't amounted to a great deal. Another department let him slip from under their noses and escape to Holland where Six are now tracking him.

[20 June 1985]

We have found the Brighton bomber — Patrick Magee — in Glasgow. He will stand trial next year and we fully expect him to receive multiple life sentences. Thatcher is delighted, although this had very little to do with me at all and everything to do with Matt. She would hear nothing of it, though, and Jane's constant teasing on the subject is wearing a little thin. I didn't tell Matt about her latest phone call.

[22 June 1985]

There are exciting plans afoot for a major defection from the USSR. As usual, Six are dealing with all the fun bits of the operation: the logistics of smuggling the defector out of the country and getting him on to friendly soil.

We, on the other hand, have the more laborious task of debriefing the defector once he's back in London. It's a task that can take a couple of hours if his information is low-grade material that we know already. If a high-grade defector, it can take years, even decades.

For once, however, we have absolutely no idea at all who this person might be. Six is being unusually discreet. Only Clive and I know about the case at Five. Matt and Archie are viewed as having too many Russian contacts, so alerting them might arouse suspicions in their numerous tails. It would only take one slip in their normal routine. Amanda is too junior.

Two officers from Section D — that's only one less than the total number of officers at Six in the loop. One of those, as I might have guessed, is Juliet Shaw, who is now stationed in Moscow.

[25 July 1985]

The defector is Oleg Gordievsky, a colonel in the KGB, and the highest-ranking KGB defector ever. He joined in 1963 and was the representative in London (the *rezident*) between 1982 and 1985. In May this year, he was recalled to Moscow, arrested and then released under surveillance. On the 19th of this month, he slipped his surveillance officers while on his usual jog, boarded a train to Finland and was then flown by MI6 to England via Norway.

Now he is ours to debrief in London and, I must say, he's a very charming man.

It's a curious concept, defection. To us, of course, he's a hero. He has gone from being the enemy to an ally overnight. We believe his recent actions will have significantly reduced the length of the Cold War. From our ideological standpoint, it is like a man who has finally seen the error of his ways and crossed from the dark side to the light.

To the Soviets, on the other hand, he's a traitor. He's betrayed his country, his friends and his family. And however much we respect him for swapping sides – and appreciate the vast volume of knowledge he brings with him, it is difficult for some of that scorn not to filter through.

You can end up respecting your enemy. A good soldier appreciates a worthy adversary. But when your enemy suddenly becomes your friend, emotions become confused.

There's also the problem of a defector adapting to his new environment. They might have loathed their previous regime, but often people grow to miss and admire what they knew. Routine and familiarity are reassuring, even when detested.

Take the Cambridge spy ring, for example, three of whom relocated to Moscow. They were never really happy there, partly, I think, because the Russians didn't give them the respect they thought they deserved. Kim Philby likes to boast that he was an 'officer in the KGB'. He wasn't – he was a simple foot soldier. When he was awarded a medal, he complained it wasn't as prestigious as a knighthood. Unused by the KGB once in Moscow, he now spends most of his time reading *The Times* and watching videos of Test matches. Guy Burgess was even unhappier in Russia, incongruously wearing his Old Etonian tie with a fur coat, before slipping into an early death.

It remains to be seen, then, whether Gordievsky will make a better fist of settling into the United Kingdom.

[5 August 1985]

My attitude to Gordievsky has softened considerably, not least because he has been feeding us some excellent information regarding hostile intelligence agencies operating in London.

When the Cold War finally ends — which I now believe it will, perhaps even before the end of the twentieth century – it will be remembered for the cloak-and-dagger nature of surveillance and counter-surveillance on the streets of the world's major capitals. Phrases such as dead-letter drop will enter mainstream vocabulary. Subsequent generations will marvel at grown men (and it is nearly always men) playing silly buggers, chasing rogue agents around dark alleyways and stabbing dissidents in the feet with poisoned umbrellas.

Talking to Gordievsky makes me wonder what we're fighting for any longer. On the one hand, we have the most destructive weapons humankind can imagine pointing at each other across vast oceans and divided land masses. With the wrong leaders in charge, we could wipe out the world several times over. On the other hand, we have people who are prepared to be smuggled into the boots of cars to go and live a few thousand miles away and talk to the people who've been aiming those weapons at their cities for the past forty years.

This is the future, I suppose. Incomprehensible technology alongside enduring human hopes and fears. Mass destruction and individual frailties. Never have the two seemed further apart.

In any case, Gordievsky's information has given us a unique insight into the current situation in London. We now know which cultural attachés are cultural attachés and which are 'cultural attachés'. We know who is working undercover without diplomatic protection. And we're aware of the weak spots — who could be turned and how we might go about turning them.

Just as usefully — but more alarmingly — we also know the potential weak links in our own side. Who is sympathetic to the USSR. Who our double agents are. There are many more than we thought.

Our response, of course, is to react as quickly as possible. Gordievsky is such a big coup that the news is already out. We have to act swiftly and swoop before people are tipped off. It's been very successful so far.

[20 November 1985]

Soviet Union leader Mikhail Gorbachev met President Reagan for the first time in Geneva yesterday and I went along as an observer, undercover as a Foreign Office representative.

I've never thought much of Switzerland — always there with their penknives and their cheese, capitulating here, prevaricating there, staying out of this, that and the other just as long as they can launder gold, make cuckoo clocks and live long, healthy lives in the mountains.

But it is a very beautiful place for all that.

I have a good feeling about Gorbachev, too. Thatcher has already described him as a 'man she can do business with' — a typical statement from the woman in many ways: patronising him as if he were a worthy, neighbouring greengrocer whom she could trust to give credit for his vegetable account.

Personally, I think it goes rather deeper than that. There

are many conflicting theories as to how and when the Cold War will end. Some think Star Wars will successfully negate the idea of mutually assured destruction. Others believe the West has to rearm until the Soviet Union goes broke with the effort of matching us and disintegrates in a mass of domestic chaos and poverty. The Campaign for Nuclear Disarmament (the poor misguided, idealistic mad souls that they are) would like us to shred all our weapons and hope that the nice, big bear in the East does the same afterwards.

But all these notions overlook the idea of leadership. I'm a great believer in the power of individuals to shape history. Cometh the hour, cometh Gorbachev.

1986

[20 January 1986]

The UK and France announced plans today to start the construc-
tion of a tunnel across the Channel.

Not the most exciting piece of news, and it has been made
even less exciting by my apparent role in the whole business.
The Secretary of State for Transport wants a full rundown on all
the possible security repercussions of such a tunnel.

'And I mean *all*, Harry. No point in writing a report if it's
under two-hundred pages long, is there?'

Well, what fun. Will the tunnel attract more illegal
immigrants? Will rabid dogs and cats scamper across to infect
us? Will terrorists use trains as huge, fast-speed weapons?
Could a bomb be detonated from above to flood it?

Who knows? But I suppose I will after drafting 201 pages of
this nonsense.

I'm in a rather terse mood because there's another structure — a personal one — that requires building more urgently: a
bridge between Jane and me. I'm not sure what's happened but
we've drifted again. I hardly ever see her these days. Either

I'm working late or she is. And if we are both around, we're tired and stressed.

My job also makes it difficult for us to go out and socialise together. Dinner-party conversation inevitably turns to, 'What do you do?' I'm fine at hiding it but Jane goes all awkward and tries to change the subject too rapidly. People start suspecting and she gets even more flustered. All we're meant to do is stick to the Civil Service line — which should be boring enough to deter any further questions. But she has a tendency to make my job sound so mysterious that people can't help inquiring further.

One group of near-strangers accused me last week of being an arms dealer (this is all the rage in London at the moment). Among some of our friends, it's become a running joke that I work for MI5. All I can do is play along in an elaborate game of double-bluff, playing dumb and saying silly things like, 'Of course I do. But if I told you more, I'd have to kill you.'

It's not Jane's fault, but it does make life rather awkward.

[22 January 1986]

There is something else, however, that is Jane's fault. I think she might be having an affair.

It started — or at least I think it started — with what my mother used to call mentionitis. Her headmaster's name started coming regularly into conversation. At first, it was always work-related. He was a great teacher and a great boss. Had I heard what he'd said in morning assembly? I should have seen the amazing goal he scored in the boys vs. teachers football match.

He was very good at soothing the parents' fears. He'll make a great teacher for Catherine and Graham one day etc., etc.

This didn't bother me too much. If I were allowed to talk more about my work colleagues, I would.

But then Jane's mentionitis slipped into social situations as well. Her headmaster had opinions on everything, it would seem. And she wasn't afraid to share them with me, or anyone else for that matter. His name would be dropped into dinner-party conversations on everything from the Cold War to Liverpool Football Club. 'Robin always says . . . Robin would disagree with that . . . Robin said a funny thing to me the other day . . .'

Until people would ask, 'Who is Robin? Your son? Your brother?'

And I would think, 'Yes, who the fuck is Robin?'

And she would blush and admit that he was her boss.

Well, it's got to stop. One way or another, it's really got to stop. I will not be made a fool of.

[24 January 1986]

Yesterday, after school was finished, I slipped into Jane's staffroom and bugged it. I've also placed a tracking-and-listening device in her handbag. Our home telephone number has a recording-and-call-tracing mechanism.

It is no way to go about tackling the issue. But I just can't help myself at the moment. I don't like what I'm being drawn into but I can't resist it all the same.

If you're planning on having an extramarital affair, make sure you're not married to a paranoid spook.

[3 March 1986]

The children have been drawn into this now as well. Catherine is almost six and a bright little child. This morning, she caught me opening an item of Jane's post. And I thought I was meant to be good at counter-surveillance.

'Daddy, that envelope's got Mummy's name on the front.'

'Oh yes, so it has. Silly me.'

'Silly Daddy,' she said, looking at me accusingly. 'Or maybe just *bad* Daddy.'

Almost ten years in the security services, and the first time I give myself away by blushing is under cross-examination from my five-year-old daughter.

[20 March 1986]

It all came to a head today. Horribly and inevitably, it has ended in tears. Jane's, the children's and the headmaster's, who is currently sitting in the Chelsea and Westminster hospital nursing a broken nose.

The worst thing about it: not only was I in the wrong in my methods; I was also completely wrong in my suspicions.

While the tracker in Jane's handbag showed that she was making regular visits to the headmaster's house after school, it appears that these were entirely innocent. I followed her there this afternoon, confronted her in a mad rage and a fight ensued with the headmaster. After I'd calmed down, it appeared that she had merely been giving some extra, private English tuition to his sixteen-year-old daughter. The headmaster's wife had been there all along.

The fallout, of course, is enormous. I was only able to stop the headmaster from pressing charges by getting the heavies round to scare him in his hospital bed. It is one of the lowest things I've ever done. Robin is now almost certainly aware of the nature of my job, which will make life very difficult for Jane and the children.

As for Jane, she is understandably livid. How did I know she was there? Why couldn't I trust her? Couldn't I see that she'd only taken the extra work because I earned such a pitiable salary as a civil servant? Why couldn't I get a decent job that paid properly like the rest of our university contemporaries?

This argument continued all the way home until I finally admitted that I'd put tabs on her.

'I've married a freak,' she yelled in front of both the children, who started crying.

And now she's taken them both off to live with her mother and I'm alone in a house meant for four. The only thing I have to look forward to at the moment is Archie coming round tomorrow night to help me drink my way into oblivion.

[18 April 1986]

Still no communication with Jane, but at least work has become interesting again.

Yesterday, Israeli security guards at Heathrow airport found Semtex explosives in a bag of a pregnant Irish woman who was attempting to board the plane. A detonator had been placed in a calculator. Apparently unaware of the contents, they had been planted there by her fiancé, a Jordanian called Hindawi.

Hindawi was arrested today after a tip-off and is due to stand trial soon.

Our problem is that this has the whiff of a Mossad sting operation all over it. Hindawi claims to have been working for Syrian intelligence, but we suspect that he was actually being manipulated by the Israelis. According to this version of events, the El Al security staff were tipped off by Mossad that the poor Irish girl (duped by a dupe) would be arriving with explosives in her luggage. A risky strategy, certainly, but an effective one if they wished to exact revenge against Syria.

The question now, of course, is how far will that revenge go. How will Thatcher react if Hindawi is found guilty? Play along with Mossad's games and cause a stink by breaking off diplomatic relations with Syria? Or cause even more of a stink by fingering an Israeli plot that was irresponsible from start to finish?

Here, I suspect, the enemy of our enemy is going to be our friend.

[30 September 1986]

More Israeli excitement.

An Israeli called Mordechai Vanunu flew to London at the beginning of this month, accompanied by a journalist from the *Sunday Times*. Vanunu used to work on the Dimona nuclear site in the Negev desert and was intent on spilling all his secrets to the Sunday newspaper.

Israel's nuclear armoury is something of an open secret. We know they have a nuclear bomb. The Israeli public think they know they have it. And, most importantly, their Arab neighbours think they know they have it.

But the Israelis have maintained an aura of mystique by adopting a policy of deliberate ambiguity. As a tool of foreign policy, it is remarkably effective. No one knows exactly how many they have, so they are able to spread rumours that it is more potent than it might be. Deliberate ambiguity, in theory at least, means that they could use the *idea* of a nuclear weapon as a deterrent, without ever actually possessing one.

Still, the actual revelation of nuclear secrets — especially by a former Dimona worker in a country renowned for its patriotism — would have devastating consequences. We have to stop Vanunu in whichever way we can.

Annoyingly, he vanished from our radar once he'd left Israel. It was only later that we discovered he'd gone to Sydney where he converted to Christianity and met the *Sunday Times* journalist. Back in England, he grew impatient with the *Sunday Times*'s painstaking research and subsequent delay in publishing his story and turned to its rival, the *Sunday Mirror*, prop. Robert Maxwell.

This was his first wrong move. Maxwell — who we suspect is a Mossad informer — rang and asked me to contact Israeli intelligence. I had little choice in this matter. Israel is our ally in the Middle East. Vanunu might be a decent man of conscience but he is still attempting to betray our ally. He is on our soil and we must return him to his own country to stand trial. It rather goes against my liberal principles, but there is the greater principle of political expediency.

There is the additional problem that we cannot be seen to manhandle an Israeli citizen out of central London. Mossad has decided, therefore, to use a honey-trap – Cheryl Bentov – who will pretend to be an American tourist and lure Vanunu to Rome, where the Italians have less sensibilities about this sort of thing.

The lift takes place today. Having met Cheryl, I must say that they've chosen their honey-trap very well indeed. It would take a will of steel not to do absolutely anything she wanted.

[28 October 1986]

Predictably, Hindawi has been found guilty of a 'callous and inhumane crime' and sentenced to a record forty-five years in prison. 'The bastard got what he deserved,' said one tabloid.

But did he? And did Syria? Thatcher has expelled the Syrian Ambassador (labelled the 'Ambassador of Death' by another tabloid) and it won't be long before reprisals start in Damascus as well. We'll be certain to lose some of our best men. And women. Juliet Shaw is also posted there at the moment after finishing her tour in Moscow.

Thatcher's rhetoric is typically belligerent but I think she knows we've been strung up like a kipper by the Israelis. The irony, of course, is that this suits our ends as well. It's just that we'd rather have chosen the option ourselves than be forced into it in this unseemly way. It's like breaking up with someone. They might want to do it as well, but you'd rather get in there first.

[30 October 1986]

Jane has filed for divorce, citing irreconcilable differences.

1988

[30 December 1988]

It has been a thoroughly awful two years on nearly all fronts. I have been too down to write anything properly in my diary.

The divorce went through at the beginning of last January. It was surprisingly clean, quick and easy, but that was even more depressing in its own way. A battle would have given me something to focus on. As it was, almost ten years of marriage was dissolved in a couple of hours. It made the whole thing appear entirely pointless and ephemeral.

There are still the children, of course. But there was never much doubt who was going to get custody of them. Shady spook father with alarming stalking habits? Or pretty young mother who's also a teacher?

I still find it ineffably sad to write about this, but I have almost no relationship to speak of with either Catherine or Graham. Catherine is now eight and coolly hostile towards me. I thought the father–daughter relationship was meant to be a special one, but I get on altogether better with my counterparts at the CIA than I do with her.

[spooks]

There is love. Of course there's love. But we just don't seem to understand each other. Perhaps we're too similar. She's argumentative, irrational, moody and hates to be told she's wrong. She has her mother's eyes. And her mother's sense of injustice. But otherwise, the poor girl has been landed with her father's genes.

So, we've turned into the family I always hoped we wouldn't. The kind of family I pitied during my own stable childhood. The children live with Jane and, when I can, I take them out for custody visits at the weekends. Snatched hours in stuffy cinemas. Sulky afternoons traipsing around zoos and museums. Always conscious of the time. Always aware of the guilt. Always eyeing up the other errant fathers doing their same Sunday-afternoon routines.

Then there is Graham who is only five but developing worryingly slowly. He's had child psychologists seeing him and concerned grandparents on both sides attempting to draw him out of his shell. But he's an unhappy child, born into an unhappy marriage. At least we can hope that he'll come through this now, living with his sister and Jane. But in the meantime, we can do nothing but blame ourselves for screwing him up.

Work-wise, too, it's been a miserable twenty-four months, cheered only slightly by Matt's departure (he couldn't avoid the temptation of the Square Mile's lucre any longer) and my promotion to senior field officer. In reality, though, it's made little difference to my day-to-day work. I've essentially been doing his job for over five years now.

Clive is still my immediate boss. Archie now works for me, rather than with me, but you wouldn't know it from his attitude.

Amanda is still Amanda — even more so since a new recruit called Esther joined six months ago and she has someone to compete directly against.

One person, in particular, they seem to be competing over is Archie. Esther appeared smitten from the moment she arrived, which seems to have galvanised Amanda into jealously protecting a territory of which she was previously unaware.

Archie, of course, is lapping it up, playing them off against each other. Yesterday, I saw him and Amanda attempting to get into the same pod at the same time and giggling uncontrollably about it. Today, he and Esther emerged from the vicinity of the stationery cupboard, casting coy looks around them while Amanda shot them both daggers.

And so we have an intriguing little love triangle under our noses.

Elsewhere, British hostages have been kidnapped in Beirut, including Terry Waite who is an old friend of Juliet Shaw's family. After her expulsion from Damascus last year, she is now in Lebanon working for his release. It has been utterly fruitless so far.

Margaret Thatcher has been elected for a third term and is showing increasing signs of going mad. The city is full of slick-haired spivs earning the kind of salaries that civil servants (with the exception of Matt) can only dream about. President Reagan has been embroiled in Iran-Contra affairs and then travelled to Berlin in June to urge Gorbachev to 'tear down the wall', to little effect.

Last October, my brother, Ben, died in a freak accident during a huge hurricane that swept across the south of England.

[spooks]

Last December was taken up with proving that the King's Cross fire, which killed thirty-one, had nothing to do with Irish terrorists or Israeli secret intelligence agencies. It was a cigarette.

This year, there was some light relief when the government — on the advice of A Section — decided to ban broadcast interviews with IRA members' voices. The BBC gets around this by using actors' voices, which continues to amuse me. I've met Gerry Adams and he has a silly little nasal voice. The actor who dubs him is far more convincing and menacing than Adams himself.

It's a strange form of propaganda — allowing someone to speak their mind but not their voice. We can hear his words but not his cadences. The public can see his beard but cannot hear his vowels. I'm sure Goebbels would have come up with something altogether more convincing.

Adams did, at least, unwittingly provide a moment between Catherine and me. We were watching the news together during one of our custody weekends. (The fact that I thought this a suitable leisure activity for an eight-year-old probably says more than I'd like to admit about my parenting skills.) Adams was being interviewed. Catherine turned to me and said, 'It's like in Punch and Judy when the lips move differently to the voice.'

I picked her up and hugged her uncommonly hard, and she smiled and looked happy and surprised at the same time. It broke what remains of my heart.

Tomorrow is New Year's Eve. Like last year, I will be spending it alone with a bottle of Scotch.

1989

[4 January 1989]

At last, something to get my teeth stuck into again. I have been assigned to the investigation of the Lockerbie disaster — the death, last month, of 270 people (including eleven on the ground) when Pan Am Flight 103 exploded over Scotland.

It was a particularly gruesome crash. Investigators have established that tornado-strength winds would have torn through the cabin. A few of the passengers are believed to have been alive on impact. Some were holding hands. A mother was still clinging on to her baby.

The intelligence work is going to be painstaking. The place is already crawling with CIA officers (189 victims were Americans), and there were a few intelligence personnel on board as well. The conspiracy theories are winging around. A number of well-known people had tickets for the flight and then cancelled them at the last minute.

It's not the kind of thing I enjoy doing — this in-depth, page-by-page analysis of witness statements. I'd much rather be out in the field. But it can be good for a man to give that a rest every now and again. You could go mad if you spent too long always pretending to be someone else. I've just counted: in the last two years, I've gone undercover on fifteen separate occasions with twelve different identities. It's good to be Harry Pearce for a while again.

[28 January 1989]

I've been put on to something much more interesting concerning the investigation: interrogation of leading suspects.

I'm slightly ashamed to admit that it is something I enjoy very much indeed. I'd like to think this is because I'm good at it. To be a skilled interrogator, you need to have a profound understanding of the human condition. You need empathy as well as intelligence, emotional as well as intellectual authority. What does this person want to tell you? What doesn't he want to tell you? What does he think that you think he doesn't want to tell you?

You have to be able to look further than the facts (or, at least, what you perceive as the facts). You're looking for motives. Not what, but why?

Not when, but how? You have to be able to put yourself in their shoes to understand.

Interrogation is something I was trained in during my time in the army and it's a skill I've continued to develop at MI5. Juliet Shaw is particularly good at it. There is something in that stare of hers. She taught me much of what I know.

My preferred role is to play the 'good cop' to someone else's 'nasty cop'. I seem to have a face that people trust, even as I slowly and subtly twist the metaphorical knife. Archie is my favourite nasty cop to work alongside. When he goes into that room, you're no longer working with Archie, the twinkly, charming bon viveur, but Archie the consummate actor cum *inquisidor general* of Gower House. Even I'm scared of him in that interrogation room.

But what I like most about Archie is that he knows there's a line. All interrogators have a line, of course. It's just that he and I draw ours in exactly the same place.

Interrogation is a curious gladiatorial battle. It's you against them. Your wits against theirs. Like a political interviewer or a prosecution barrister, except with no audience. Of course, the playing field is hardly a level one. You can send in the heavies to rough them up. You can threaten to send in the heavies to rough them up. They can do neither. Nonetheless, they know there's a limit to how far you'll go, at least in this country. One of our most effective weapons is to threaten to hand people over to the Americans if they don't cooperate. The Americans have a fearsomely brutal reputation. It normally has the suspects singing like a canary.

Despite what people think, we do retain a moral dimension to our interrogation work. More practically, we're aware of the uselessness of most evidence obtained under torture. I know people who would swear that their mother was a man if it took the pain away quicker.

That said, there is still a queasy unease when you first walk into an interrogation room. You can call it all the high moral names you like, but, in the final analysis, you still have a man entirely under your power. It's both guiltily exciting and

profoundly terrifying. In most cases, it would also take a heart
of stone to prevent your professional empathising turning into
genuine empathy. That could be you sitting there. And however
angry you are about what that person has tried to do to your
countrymen, you have to remember that.

We often spout nice-sounding platitudes when it comes to
terrorists. 'That would make us no better than them,' is a
favourite one. But often we *are* no better than them.

The police in this country deal with criminals. Bad people.
Robbers. Murderers. Rapists. We deal with terrorists, which is
a very different form of criminality. It's why MI5 has its roots
in military intelligence. We might be fighting ragamuffin
armies, but many of them are armies nonetheless. With coherent
political aims and belief systems. We have to treat them with
respect, however much we abhor their methods.

Not that anyone could ever admit this publicly, of course.
It would be political suicide. And entirely counter-productive
as well. We have to maintain the illusion — and, as often as
possible, the reality as well — of moral superiority. Otherwise,
all the foundations of Western society would fall.

A hundred years ago, politicians were honest when it came
to foreign policy. Palmerston, the British Foreign Secretary
and Prime Minister, spoke of Britain's immutable interests
abroad. Bismarck talked of Germany's in similar terms. Was the
British Empire really built on a desire to spread democracy?
Or on trading interests? I don't doubt that they didn't hope
to spread a little civilisation along the way — we can't
become *too* cynical — but it was never the primary motivating
factor.

Show me an altruistic country and I will show you a liar.

This is the problem today. Few people talk about national interests any more. They all think it, of course, but they rarely say it. So instead we have smokescreens such as the 'global interest' and 'morality' and other such misnomers.

The unpalatable truth is more simple. I care more about my people than I do about yours. If you threaten mine, I'll blow up yours. And if you attempt to blow up mine, I'm going to give you a very hard time in the interrogation room, even though if I were in your situation, I would probably have tried to blow up my people as well.

That's realpolitik for you. It's honest and it's very, very brutal. So much for good cop. We're all bad cops as well.

[14 February 1989]

Valentine's Day, and I've spent it, somewhat unromantically, with the author Salman Rushdie who's just had a *fatwa* pronounced on him by Ayatollah Khomeini.

I'm not much of a fan of Rushdie's works. I started *The Satanic Verses* but couldn't make head or tail of it. I prefer the classics myself. The occasional thriller. And anything by Tom Sharpe on P.G. Wodehouse.

Anyway, I was given a rest from the Lockerbie assignment as it was felt I was the best person to deal with Rushdie. He's taken the news that one-fifth of the world's population now wants to kill him surprisingly well. I suppose it's good for sales, after all. No such thing as bad publicity . . .

Archie had a slightly better Valentine's Day. Clive told me

that two huge cards were waiting for him on his desk this morning. One of them played a tune when he opened it.

[7 March 1989]

It's not easy guarding someone around the clock. You get bored of them. They get bored of you. It's a break to both your routines. We try to vary it slightly so that different officers take different shifts, but Rushdie has taken something of a shine to me and demands that I work with him as much as possible. This is beginning to get tiring.

Then, there is the security routine to worry about. He has to move house, of course. And be disguised. But how do we keep him in touch with his family? Which friends can he trust? Which gym can he attend?

His literary agent and his publishers have to be protected, his neighbours interrogated in case they have extremist links. The list goes on and on. It's escalated into quite a crisis. At the end of last month, the Ayatollah placed a US$3m bounty on his head. The West is up in arms that people can take offence at mere words. The Muslim world appears incredulous that our traditions of free speech and satire make no allowances for their concept of the divine.

Today, Iran broke off diplomatic relations with us over *The Satanic Verses*. Normally, it takes a plane crash to achieve this. Or a massive spying row. Or pregnant Irish women with boyfriends duped by Mossad. But a couple of errant sentences in a book?

We live in mad times.

[02 April 1989]

Rushdie keeps on asking me whether I like his book and it's becoming increasingly difficult to pretend that I've actually read it.

'Yes,' I said for the twentieth time today. 'I really do love it. Fully worth printing. Wish I could write like that.'

'What's your favourite bit?' he asked.

'Oh, I like the magic realism stuff,' I said.

'Which bit in particular?'

'Page 173 is very nice.'

[03 April 1989]

Thank God. Rushdie has asked for a different protection officer and I am released from my duties to return to Lockerbie. Time for Esther to play nanny. She studied English literature at Cambridge so might have more luck than me.

Poor man. Goodness knows how much longer this will go on for. I hope he's not planning a sequel.

[17 May 1989]

Amanda has cunningly taken advantage of Esther's literary leave of absence to snare Archie. They've tried to be subtle about it but it's easy when you know someone well to spot that something's changed in them. It's the studied casualness that betrays them – sitting a little further away from each other in the pub, the lowered glances, the affected politeness and indifference in meetings.

It first became obvious last month when I noticed Archie acting oddly around going-home time. He would make a great show of stretching, yawning and shuffling his papers ostentatiously.

'Well, I'm off,' he'd announce to no one in particular before shooting a surreptitious wink at Amanda. 'Just a quiet night at home for me.'

Then he'd walk out of the pods and hide in the corridor. Five minutes later, Amanda would perform exactly the same routine and then the rest of us would shuffle over to Derek's computer in the technical section and watch their security tags happily bleep out of the front door together, hand in hand.

[23 August 1989]

Exciting news in Europe. Two million people in Estonia, Latvia and Lithuania joined hands today — forming an uninterrupted human chain 600km long — to demand independence from the Soviet Union.

Six's intelligence suggests that this is more than just a one-off event. Had this happened fifteen years ago, Soviet tanks would have decimated a 600km human chain. Gorbachev's economic *perestroika* and democratising *glasnost* appear to be opening the door towards a new Russia.

What's going to happen, then? Will the Berlin Wall fall? Will someone draw back the Iron Curtain?

Who knows. But my job at Five now is to start assessing the

domestic effect of any thawing in the Cold War. What will happen to the British Communist Party? How will MI5 restructure its efforts if it spends less time shadowing KGB agents through the streets of London? What will the potential break-up of the Soviet Union mean for the rest of the world? Will we see the emergence of a Russian mafia as they embrace free-market capitalism? Will Eastern European countries be Atlantist or European in their outlook?

If we can steal a march on others here, we'll be well placed to take advantage of the next ten years.

[31 October 1989]

Archie and Amanda have finally come clean about their relationship, much to the relief of everyone else in the office. Even Clive had joined in winding them up about it – deliberately sending Amanda on honey-trap assignments, pairing Esther with Archie as an undercover couple, and so on.

Now that everything is out in the open, it's much easier for everyone to get on with the work at hand. It's surprisingly fun working alongside a couple. They complement each other in the office; in the field, they second-guess each other's next move.

Even Esther is fine with the new situation. She's now seeing someone from Six, who she claims has more style and sophistication than the rest of us put together. In fact, her constant praise of 'the friends' at the expense of Five is beginning to get on the nerves of the rest of us. I have told her that if she likes them that much, I could easily find her a transfer to one of the darker spots of Africa. She has been much quieter lately.

[10 November 1989]

Extraordinary. Yesterday, East Germany opened checkpoints in the Berlin Wall, allowing people to travel freely between the divided country. Today, they streamed across, tearing the wall down with their bare hands. I have never seen such a moving sight. East and West embraced. Literally. Water crossings that used to be riddled with sniper fire were filled with splashing revellers.

It feels like a time for someone of Churchill's stature to put it all into words. The person who invented the phrase 'Iron Curtain' would have found the mot juste, I'm sure. Is this the end? Or merely the beginning of the end?

[31 December 1989]

It was only the beginning of the end, but the end can't be far off. There have been revolutions in Czechoslovakia and Romania. At the beginning of this month, Bush and Gorbachev released statements suggesting that the Cold War was nearing its close.

Tonight was New Year's Eve and I'd resolved to make more of it than the last two. I took Catherine to Berlin. I wanted her to be able to say she'd been there, even if she didn't understand it until later.

Harry's Diary: TOP SECRET

We watched a pop singer standing on the wall and singing 'Looking for freedom'.

I tuned out and thought of all the good men and women who'd died, the silly espionage games we'd played, the deadly serious ones, the sleepless nights as innocent citizens worried about nuclear weapons overhead, the treaties, the bluffs, the high politics, the low manoeuvrings, the little American girl who'd visited the USSR, Vietnam, Cuba, mutually assured destruction, Gordievsky, Blunt, Philby and all the rest of it, and I shuddered and wept a little and held my daughter close.

It's the end of a decade, but it might just be the end of an era as well.

1990

[15 January 1990]

Thousands stormed the Stasi headquarters in East Berlin today in an attempt to view the files kept on them by the intelligence agency. It might just herald the end of one of the most feared organisations in the world. According to our estimations last year, the Stasi had 91,000 full-time employees and 300,000 informants. This approximates to one in fifty East Germans collaborating with the intelligence services – a penetration that far exceeds that of any other country.

Inevitably, it makes one wonder how a comparable situation might work in this country. Would Britain ever work as a totalitarian state? Would neighbours inform on each other? Children on their parents? Colleague on colleague?

I think it unlikely somehow. We might be a nation of gossips, but we're also a nation of libertarians and eccentric individualism. There is a world of difference between gossiping and sneaking. No one likes a grass in Britain, even though we make great use of them at MI5. Perhaps that's why few people like us either.

The general public still knows precious little about MI5 in Britain. Would they know which building to storm, even if they wanted to? (We're in Gower Street at the moment.) And if they did manage to get inside, I think they'd be pretty disappointed by what they found. There's a lovely new geek in our section called Malcolm Wynn-Jones, but he's not a patch on Q from James Bond. And while we have a few files on unexpected people – student union leaders, MPs etc. – it's nowhere near as bad as people might imagine. And it's certainly not of Stasi proportions.

I like it that way.

[31 January 1990]

If ever anyone had any doubts about the Cold War coming to an end, we now have the conclusive proof: the first McDonald's opened in Moscow today. It's a strange indication of victory, I feel. No tanks rolling into Red Square. No atomic bombs hastening the end of the Second World War. Just a forward division of fast-food burger outlets.

Welcome to capitalism.

Of course, the really interesting question is: what would have been the equivalent had the Cold War gone the other way? A neon display of a giant hammer and sickle in Times Square? New York renamed Gorbachevgrad?

Fortunately, we'll never know.

[14 February 1990]

Archie and Amanda have just announced their engagement. I am to
be best man.

[15 February 1990]

World events are still moving at a bewildering pace, many of
them entirely unrelated. Today, we finally restored diplomatic
relations with Argentina. Two days ago, Germany announced plans
to reunite. And four days ago, Nelson Mandela was released from
prison.

Many West Germans are worried about being swamped from the
East. But, personally, I think it is the rest of Europe that
should be worried. Nothing to do with militarism, but a resur-
gent Germany will completely dominate the EC — an association
that Thatcher is beginning to show an alarmingly hostile
attitude towards.

As Clive pointed out today, that's part of the problem with
this government: they're always fighting the last war. Colonial
nonsense in Argentina. Outdated isolationism in Europe. Indefen-
sible backing of apartheid. One day, it will count against them
more than they've ever realised.

[9 March 1990]

It's already beginning to do so on the domestic front. I was
back in Brixton today where poll-tax riots were taking place.

The crowd this time wasn't just the black underclass of 1981. There are grandmothers refusing to pay. Middle-class, middle-income, middle-England families. It risks turning into a serious problem, both electorally and for us as a security organisation.

There is softly-softly policing and there is softly-softly policing. How do you get the balance right when you're representing the state against the majority of the population, and you feel like you're on the wrong side?

[15 March 1990]

A British journalist was hanged today in Iraq on trumped-up allegations of espionage.

This is the extraordinary thing with spies. Abroad, we are very rarely caught. We're careful. We operate under diplomatic immunity, or we cover our tracks obsessively. Much of the time, we get local deniables to do our dirty work for us. How often do we see genuine spies paraded on foreign broadcasts and in newspapers? Answer: very rarely indeed. But we're forever seeing genuine journalists and aid workers and missionaries and so on arrested and treated in the most humiliating way.

It puts us in a very difficult situation. We have to carry on doing our job. But often, that job is putting people in much worthier professions at great risk. We do our best not to go undercover as aid workers and the like, but sometimes it's inevitable. It's then inevitable that others get caught in the crossfire.

But why do the Iraqis hang people they almost certainly know to be innocent? There are two schools of thought on this. One maintains that they think we are better at our job than we actually are. British intelligence still enjoys something of an invincible myth abroad — fuelled, it must be admitted, by some of the films our media churns out. The Americans are still widely viewed as bumbling idiots. We, on the other hand, have a reputation as conniving, cunning, successful schemers. Why would a journalist want to come to Iraq? Why would an aid worker go there? Why would anyone want to be an aid worker when they could be a spy? If you're British and you're abroad, then you're working in British Intelligence. That appears to be the logic of our foreign friends, at least.

Nothing is as it seems, they reason. If a foreigner is taking unsubtle photos of a military installation, then it's all part of an elaborate bluff. If they crack instantly under interrogation, then they're trying to confuse their questioners. If the entire British government protests the accused's innocence, they're merely trying to look after one of their own.

However, I think there's a simpler explanation. The Iraqis hanged this poor man because they could. Because they knew they could get away with it. They knew he was innocent. They knew he wasn't working for Six or Mossad, or whatever other nonsense they concocted at his 'trial'. But if they couldn't get their hands on a proper spy, they'd at least have a go at someone who could be framed as one.

It's horribly cowardly.

[1 April 1990]

More domestic problems for Thatcher yesterday with a huge

poll-tax riot in Trafalgar Square. As I've said before, it's difficult being the instrument of the state in a situation like this. Middle-class, middle-of-the-road Amanda spotted three family members and four of her close friends in the crowd. We've deleted that bit of tape.

[11 November 1990]

The Cold War might be at an end, but there is trouble brewing elsewhere in the world. In August, Iraq invaded Kuwait. Today, the UN Security Council passed a resolution giving it until 15 January to withdraw its troops. Otherwise, it's war.

More pressingly, on the home front, the IRA is again renewing its operations on the mainland. Since August 1988, we've had twenty-four terrorist incidents in Britain. Last December, Archie and I chanced upon evidence in a disused warehouse in Clapham that the IRA were intending to use DIY mortars.

Our intelligence from sources in Belfast suggest that they are planning another strike at the very heart of government – on a par with the Brighton hotel bombing in 1984. Our problem is that we have absolutely no idea when or where. Are we talking about Downing Street? Or the party-political conferences again? Or the Foreign Secretary while on tour abroad? We have to cover every possible angle and it would take a hundred times the manpower and the resources to be anything like certain of success.

[28 November 1990]

One thing now is for certain: if the IRA do attack the PM, it's not going to be Margaret Thatcher sitting in Downing Street. She resigned today, brought down by lily-livered mutineers behind her back. They'll regret it, I'm sure. Britons don't like grassers, and they don't like traitors either.

John Major appears to have won the contest to succeed her. God help us.

1991

[16 January 1991]

Operation Desert Storm started today with air strikes against Iraq.

[21 January 1991]

We've just returned from Archie's stag weekend — which I was in charge of organising.

Stag nights used to be such a simple affair. Alfred Doolittle only had to break into song for his loyal friends to get him to the church on time. Less bibulous grooms used to settle for a quiet half-pint with their best man the evening before the wedding. Now we are expected to go further, spend more and perform more and more exotic activities.

Archie being Archie, he was never going to be content with a weekend in a European capital or some manly bonding in a remote part of the UK. He wanted his stag to be 'unique, ridiculous, dangerous, memorable for all the wrong reasons and entirely unrepeatable at the wedding'.

[spooks]

At some point last March, we ended up deciding that it would be fun to stage an espionage game, complete with false identities, in northern France. Archie's closest ten friends (eight of whom work in the security agencies) would be divided into two teams of five, each with an opposite number whom he had to try to stop. Everyone would have different starting points around southern England. The end destination would be Paris.

I set up dead-letter drops, invisible ink notes and a series of clues all over Normandy. Tasks along the way included such things as stealing a road sign or persuading a French villager to accompany you to Paris. The ultimate aim of the mission was for all your team to arrive – intact, first and undetected – at a bar in the Latin Quarter. The weekend took almost as much planning and preparation as Desert Storm, but it was a fun diversion from proper work.

There was a twist, of course. No one was allowed to purchase a ticket, bring their passport or carry any money with them. A tab had been set up in the bar in Paris – owned by a friend of Archie's – and our passports and tickets home awaited us there.

It all seemed like a good idea at the time. The inevitable outcome was a farcical catalogue of errors.

Archie's school friend, David, got so drunk before leaving that he attempted to swim the Channel. He covered about 150 metres, swallowed a gallon of sea water, turned back and spent the rest of the weekend in hospital with pneumonia.

Two MI6 officers got caught by Customs and Excise attempting to smuggle themselves on to a small cargo boat in Dover and spent the next twenty-four hours extricating themselves from the local police station. They returned to London with their tail between their legs.

The remaining seven of us did, at least, make it as far as France. Archie, myself, another MI5 officer and a journalist friend talked our way onto flights out of Gatwick. Another MI5 officer simply walked into RAF Brize Norton, explained the nature of his strange weekend and blagged a lift over the Channel in a spare navigator's seat. Two guys from GCHQ – their social skills less developed than most – had to resort to getting a temporary shift as duty-free store assistants on a cross-Channel ferry.

Yet it wasn't until we all got to France that the real problems started. Only Archie and I – the captains of the respective teams – actually made it as far as Paris. One of the GCHQ guys was severely beaten up by a local farmer when he found him rummaging around his field for a clue I'd planted there. The other decided this wasn't his idea of fun, got cold feet and took the ferry straight back to Dover.

The RAF hitchhiker tracked down his opposite man in an attempt to stop him performing his next task and ended up in a fist fight in a bar in Lyon. The police were called, both men were arrested and spent the night being kicked around the cells by irate gendarmes demanding to know why they had no papers, no money and no obvious reason to be in France. They were eventually deported on Sunday evening.

Archie's journalist friend – one of the few people he's kept in touch with from his days as a hack – then decided this would all make a fantastic newspaper feature and dashed back to London to start filing a 3,000-word piece on" WHEN STAG WEEKENDS GO WRONG.

Archie and I had no idea what had happened to everyone else, so we decided to call the match a draw and set about celebrating in the bar in Paris, enjoying a tab that was meant for ten people.

It all might have ended more or less successfully had we not by this stage been in possession of ten UK passports and ten single tickets from Paris to London. Archie's friend, the bar owner, must have been used to his English friend's eccentric ways as he handed them over to us with barely a murmur of inquiry.

Unfortunately, an onlooker in the bar was more suspicious and called the police. The police then called the DST, France's nastier version of MI5, who spent the next twenty-four hours impolitely inquiring why we had ten passports (none of which matched our own names), ten tickets and a smorgasbord of friends who had been arrested, deported and beaten up in various parts of northern France.

Unable to provide them with a satisfactory answer, Archie drunkenly ended up telling them something approaching the truth. Clive was called, we were deported, and Amanda, who had spent her hen weekend in a spa hotel in Wiltshire, was far from amused.

Archie, on the other hand, believes the weekend could not have gone better.

[25 January 1991]

Back to work – and reality – with more worrying developments with the IRA. We've had reports – again from South London – of three men of Irish extraction looking for a very specific type of white van. They were adamant that the roof should be sufficiently thin that they could cut through it and adapt it.

This doesn't strike me as your average three white van men looking for a new toy.

The adverts appeared in a newsagents' window very close to where we discovered the DIY mortar kits in December 1989.

[28 January 1991]

Clive retired yesterday and we're going to miss him. It seems crazy that a man like that has to stop working at sixty. He had at least ten more years of useful service in him. It was Section D's gain but the service's loss overall that they never made him Director General. He was just the sort of person they need at the top of this organisation: a leader who has the respect of his troops instead of the usual desk fodder they churn out to fill the DG's spacious office.

All of us are a bit hungover today after his leaving party. You think you know your boss – I've probably spent more hours with Clive than I ever did with Jane – but until you've seen him dancing on a table with Esther at 4 a.m. he'll always be a stranger to you.

I just hope he doesn't find retirement too boring. Retiring from MI5 is rather like leaving senior political office. You miss the buzz, the excitement, the daily briefings, the knowledge that you're on the inside loop of events. You read the papers and try to work out what's really going on, but you can no longer read between the lines. You watch the news and realise that you're just another member of the public now, lied to and manipulated. When you go on holiday, you can no longer check the intelligence reports to see if there is any terrorist activity in the area. When you enter a crowded area of the capital, your life is in other people's hands and not your own.

To go from a somebody to a nobody overnight drives some people mad. To know that your life's work is finished, that there are dreadful things you've done that can no longer be undone: some people just can't cope with it. Retirement is handed down like a suspended death sentence, an unobtainable atonement that is both too short and too long.

Clive, I think, is made of saner cloth. He and Vanessa will move to a quiet spot in the country: Devon, perhaps. For a month or so, he'll probably do nothing at all. The occasional round of golf. The odd visit from his children. History books will be replaced with fiction, contemporary documentaries with films. He'll escape from his old world.

He'll relish not having to make decisions any more. A life of routine will be broken down, step by step. When he wakes up, he won't be reaching instinctively for his pager. No car will sit in his drive, its engine idling politely. The only thing to disturb him in the night will be nightmares of events past, not the pressing concerns of the present.

Then he'll travel. Look after grandchildren. Get involved with the local community — as a church warden, perhaps. And his new neighbours will talk about this kindly old man who used to be something quite senior in the Civil Service, but no, they're not sure what exactly it was that he did.

I'm getting elegiac; my own retirement is many years down the line. My point is that Clive is a man who understands balance in his life. He understood it while he was at Section D. He knew what mattered. He knew what he was fighting for. And he'll understand it once he's left as well.

I've promised to visit him – a promise he told me he doubts I'll keep. I hope to prove him wrong.

[1 February 1991]

I was walking along Whitehall today at 10.07 a.m. when I saw a white transit van drive up to the junction of Banqueting Hall and the Ministry of Defence, park at an angle to the corner, its rear end pointing towards the Cabinet Office and Downing Street, pause for around ninety seconds and then drive off.

Its number plate was blacked out.

It's only an instinct, but it looked incredibly suspicious to me. This was a trial run if ever I've seen one.

I spoke to the new head of Section D, James Helme, but he treated me like a madman.

'This is a ridiculous hunch, Harry,' he said. 'Do you know how many white vans there are around London?'

'Stopping at convenient angles outside the PM's residence?'

'Probably lost.'

'With a blacked-out number plate?'

'How many clean white vans have you seen in London?'

So I rang the head of Scotland Yard's Anti-Terrorist branch, who was slightly more understanding but similarly dismissive in the long run.

'What do you expect me to do about this, Harry? Close down Whitehall because you saw a white van stop? Where is your concrete evidence? Your smoking gun? Your witnesses?'

He's right, of course. We can't let the business of government come to a halt just because of a hunch. But I'm right about this. I really know I am. And I can't help thinking that Clive would have given my instincts the time of day.

Such is the nature of hunches. They appear from nowhere but then occupy your waking and sleeping thoughts so entirely that you *must* do something about it. The irony is that we're always being told by our superiors at MI5 to trust our instincts. This is why we were selected. This is what we were trained to do. And then the moment you announce a hunch that *is* based on instincts honed over years of experience, they dismiss you as a madman.

It will be heavily ironic if I turn out to be correct. But there are delicious ironies and bitter ones. This would be the latter.

So I've done the least I can do. I've registered my suspicions. I've written to the protection officers at Downing Street. But ultimately, I'm left on my own now. The IRA are sticklers for timings and timetables. My hunch is that their trial run is significant in some way. Maybe a week from now. Or a month from now. But at 10.07 a.m. on a particular day, I have no doubt that they'll be attempting some sort of atrocity in that exact spot.

There are two further options open to me now. Either I find who these people are before they do whatever it is they're planning. Or I have to catch them in the act. Find that smoking gun and block the bullet. Neither option appears very likely at the moment.

[6 February 1991]

I think I have a clear lead on who one of the white-van drivers might be. After talking to almost every second-hand dealership in South London, Archie and I have come up with a face match for a known member of the IRA whose brother was killed in custody under interrogation by the British Army five years ago.

Almost exactly five years ago, in fact. Five years ago tomorrow, 7 February. Which is also exactly a week after the trial run that I'm sure I witnessed. The cabinet is meeting in Downing Street tomorrow between 10 and 11.

Again, the evidence is flaky and my protests have fallen on deaf ears. Helme thinks I have some kind of strange bee in my bonnet about the whole thing.

'How many prime ministers do you want to save, Harry?' he asked 'You know they have their own protection staff, don't you? It's not your personal job to step into the breach every time.'

Stupid man. On his head be it.

[7 February 1991]

I was in a meeting this morning that was scheduled to last from 9 till 9.30. I knew that if it finished on time, I would still be able to get down to Whitehall to swat that bee in my bonnet.

But the meeting dragged on and on. An interminable affair about recruitment policies. I hate meetings. I'm no good at them. I like things to be short and sharp and to the point. I'm not good at the niceties, the small talk, the joshing, the petty politics. This was one of those meetings where everything had been said but not everyone had said it yet. It could have all been wound up in five minutes.

At 9.45, I excused myself on the pretence of being ill. Helme raised his eyebrows.

I ran towards Whitehall, reaching Trafalgar Square at 10.05. A white van overtook me on the corner, going significantly faster than my 8 m.p.h. I'm not in shape the way I used to be. The van had similar black-out markings to the vehicle I'd seen exactly a week before.

It pulled up in precisely the same location. Two men jumped out and on to a waiting motorcycle. I flung myself in front of it and it ran over my left foot before disappearing towards Parliament Square. Its number plate was blacked out as well.

The roof of the transit van was open. I dragged myself towards it and inside. As I wrenched open the door, I was flung back by the blast force of the first mortar launching. Two more followed in quick succession.

Two overshot their target by a hundred yards, landing safely in a patch of grass beyond Downing Street. The third detonated inside the garden of Number Ten. There was a huge explosion.

Forgetting the pain in my foot, I ran as fast as I could towards Downing Street. I must have made a curious sight for the policeman on duty at the door: sweat coursing down my face, a bloody left ankle, a ruined suit.

If he'd been doing his job properly, he wouldn't have let me in. But I must have said something pretty convincing because he opened the door to me, wide-eyed with astonishment as the events unfolded.

Inside, it was a mess. The smell of cordite everywhere. Four people had sustained minor injuries, including three Diplomatic Protection Group police officers. If they'd listened to me in the first place, they wouldn't have been hurt at all.

Outside, there was another explosion as the bomber's van burst into flames. Smoke rose into the air. And then I heard John Major's voice, calm, bland and reassuringly British: 'I think we had better start again somewhere else.'

I passed out from the pain in my ankle and the fumes.

[8 February 1991]

There are many people you might expect to see on coming round from an anaesthetic: the anaesthetist, for one, might be a fairly safe bet. Or the ward sister. Or your children.

I didn't expect to see Margaret Thatcher's face looming over me. I wondered what they'd put in the anaesthetic.

'I thought I'd pop in here before the others did,' she said.

'Finding it difficult to fill your time in your retirement, are you?' I mumbled through my oxygen mask, wondering what Clive might be up to now.

She smiled broadly and then leaned conspiratorially towards me.

'A shame the IRA have such a bad aim,' she whispered. 'Don't think much of my successor.'

Then she touched an elegant finger to her nose, tapped it twice, smiled and left.

I soon found out what Thatcher meant by 'the others'. My

151

next little delegation included Helme, Major and the head of Scotland Yard's Anti-Terrorist branch.

It was Helme who spoke, but I could tell they'd agreed on what he was going to say beforehand.

'Good job, Harry. And bad luck,' he said, gesticulating at my foot, which was trussed up in plaster by this stage.

He turned at the door, attempting to make it look casual and non-deliberate, but failing badly.

'And Harry. No need to go telling anyone how close you got, eh?'

It was Major's diplomacy that saved the moment. I think he could see I was fuming. He doesn't amount to much on television but he certainly has charisma in private.

'I'm sorry,' he said, approaching the bed. 'I'm sorry we didn't trust you. And I'm grateful for what you did. But remember, we can't let the public know about failures in our intelligence. This is a propaganda war as much as anything else.'

'There were no failures in *my* intelligence,' I said, perhaps a little too snappily.

Major smiled. 'I owe you one, Mr Pearce. I'll remember that.'

[16 February 1991]

I'm out of hospital, but still on crutches. The doctors said my foot should make a full recovery, although I might be a little slower at running than I used to be. I spent Archie and Amanda's wedding yesterday hobbling around the edges of the dance floor.

But at least there was plenty of material for the best-man speech.

Back in the office, James Helme is being suspiciously friendly towards me, dropping constant hints about his retirement in two years' time — he is a fairly short-term replacement for Clive — and how they'll need a man with instincts as good as his to fill his shoes.

I find it hard to listen to this kind of claptrap without snorting.

What is it with leadership within an office structure? Is it about time served? Or promotions gained? I have no more than three acquaintances who respect their bosses. The rest complain of arrogant, lazy, pig-headed leadership. But presumably, everyone who makes it into a position of authority has, at some point, had authority standing over them as well. They, too, must have complained about the wrong sort of man management. Why is it that no one ever learns from other people's mistakes, let alone their own?

Mentors, that's what we all need. Someone to look up to. Someone whose example we can copy. Someone we'd like to be ourselves in twenty years' time. Someone like Clive. If I turn out like Helme . . . well, it doesn't bear thinking about.

Anyway, the state of my foot means that I won't be fully operational for a little while. One alternative is for me to join the research team. But for a field officer like me, that wouldn't be far off purgatory. The research team is stuffed with unbearable boffins. So Helme has offered me a more interesting solution: join the recruiting teams for six months.

Recruitment might not sound very interesting. Recruitment

in the traditional sense almost certainly isn't. It conjures up images of women with clipboards and pencil skirts and glassy stares. For some reason, they're always called Sandra. And they work in 'Human Resources', whatever that might mean.

Recruitment at university involves ghastly concepts such as milk rounds and recruitment fairs. It suggests blue-chip companies and name badges and warm white wine and vol-au-vents that you spit over the important person next to you whom you're trying to impress. It recalls silly interviews and application forms and group exercises where you subtly screw over all the other candidates, and golden handshakes and assessment centres and all sorts of other nonsense.

That's recruitment in the traditional sense. But recruitment at MI5 is altogether more fun. Taps on the shoulder, mysterious invitations from mysterious tutors, notes in the post. That kind of stuff still goes on, but my remit is to head up a more sophisticated approach to recruitment. As the Cold War ends, our attention must turn elsewhere. We're currently stuffed full of Russian speakers but barely have enough Arabists to rub together to make a fire.

Then there's the Oxbridge overload in the service at the moment. We like Oxbridge. Most of them got in there for a reason. They're intelligent. But I believe we're missing a trick by not extending our catchment net further to include other universities. OK, maybe not as far down as Swansea and Portsmouth. But Edinburgh, Newcastle, Manchester etc. There is much that is being overlooked there.

It's a cliché overused in many corporate firms: 'Our best asset is our people.' When they say it, they don't mean it, of course. Their best asset is the billions of pounds of money they're sitting on top of. Or their shiny new building. Or their company's good name. The only asset their people provide is the ability to work very hard and not give insider secrets to other people.

At MI5, it's very different. Our assets really are our people. Backed up by millions of pounds of technology, of course. But still very important in a way that they can't be anywhere else. It costs a lot to recruit and train the right person. It costs a lot more to recruit and train the wrong person.

Distinguishing between the two is going to be my new job.

[9 March 1991]

We've started with the traditional Oxbridge recruitment round.

The problem with these two universities is that everyone knows that we're on the lookout there. Students start to guess which one of their tutors is acting as our eyes and ears in their college. And the more devious ones play pranks on their friends.

There have been some entertaining tricks over the years. When I was at Oxford, we sent one of our friends a faked MI6 embossed letter requesting his attendance at an interview at an obscure location in Invernesshire. The password for entry to this location was, 'I'm a pink elephant.' The address, of course, was that of a mental hospital. The poor guy made an 800-mile round trip for nothing – although rumour has it that MI6 heard about his dedication to a potential job and eventually recruited him anyway (having performed some extensive gullibility tests).

More recently, I've heard of students sending their friends to different college bars to meet their 'handlers', only to find a hundred fellow students waiting there and jeering. One put a newspaper article in a friend's pigeon-hole about tutors recruiting students in the old-fashioned way for MI5. The relevant passage was highlighted and 'Come and see me about this some time, SC' was squiggled in the margin. Neither he nor the tutor was very amused when he fell for it hook, line and sinker.

We hear about many of these pranks and most of the time they put us off the pranksters. We like to have fun people working at MI5. But there's a world of difference between taking yourself seriously and taking your job seriously. Like the poor man who was sent to Invernesshire, we're often more interested in the people they've duped. We don't want credible fools, of course. But there's no substitute for getting people who are actually interested in the job in the first place.

That's one of the problems with recruitment as opposed to applications. Approach anyone with more than a smattering of ego and tell them that they've been hand-selected to work for one of the most illustrious and secretive elite organisations in the world and it's very hard for them to say no, even if they're entirely unsuited for the job.

One day, I hope, we'll have an open application process like normal organisations. Anyone who wants to should be able to contact us. Introducing that now, however, would be too much of a shock to the system.

On the ground in Oxbridge colleges, we therefore have a

network of tutors who know the students well — or at least, as well as they can in three sets of eight-week terms before they're thrown out in the holidays to make way for graduates with proper research interests and high-paying conference guests.

These tutors pass their recommendations on to us. These include all the obvious types: the linguists; the well-travelled; the rugby captains; the scholars with an interest in politics; those of mixed race who could pass for different nationalities. But there are always some surprise propositions as well. We can't go for the obvious people all the time. And MI5 would be a very boring (and rather inefficient) place if staffed completely by squared-jawed, well-travelled public-school linguists who could mix a good gin and tonic.

Our intake might be diverse, but all our employees have a few, non-negotiable things in common. We have a fairly exact idea of what makes a good MI5 officer. They must be highly intelligent, confident and resourceful. They must be honest. They must be patriotic. They should have a sense of humour.

But we're not looking for intellectuals. We do not tolerate arrogance. Nor do we employ prigs or jingoists.

Our ideal officer should be a leader but also a team player, an individualist who can also cope with mundane routine.

Essentially, we're searching for people with a unique set of qualities. They have probably stood out in their peer group since a young age. But they should be able to keep their talents in check. Egoists, fantasists and naïve idealists we can do without.

Once someone has been recommended to us, we then set about

finding as much as we can about them. This is the really fun part. We intercept their essays in their tutors' pigeon-holes to analyse their ideological slant. We befriend their drunken contemporaries at the bar and get the low-down on everything from their girlfriends to their drug usage. If they go to a debating society, we go along too. If they start writing articles in the student newspaper, we read all of them. If they act in university productions, we get tickets for the front row.

By the time we're ready to meet them for interview, we know almost as much about our prospective employees as their friends do. It can scare them slightly when we confront them with all this information. In the past, it's occasionally gone over the top. Some students have said they don't want to work for an organisation that snoops so readily and easily on its prospective workforce. Others are so impressed by what we've managed to gather that they leap at the opportunity to join us.

[7 April 1991]

I'm currently embroiled in something of a row with the rest of my team over recruiting outside Oxbridge. We're not as bad as MI6, but there's still a lot of residual snobbery at Five. Some people talk as if only two universities exist in the country.

In the end, I've had to lay down a bet that I will find this year's best recruit and he or she will have attended a university that was founded within the last five hundred years.

Fighting talk. Now I have to embark on a tour of provincial towns in order to win my bet.

Slightly regretting it.

[2 May 1991]

We've started the interview process. A few years ago, these were haphazard, amateur affairs. They were often run by eccentrics whom the service had tried to pension off into a less sensitive department. There had been horror tales of young men having rugby balls thrown at them as they entered the room. If you caught it you got through to the second round. If you caught it and spun pass it back, you'd get considered for Section D.

There's even a story of an eccentric old fart of an interviewer sitting in his chair with a newspaper.

'Surprise me,' he said to the young man who walked in.

The young man set fire to his newspaper. He now heads up F Section.

So no, we're going to adopt a more professional, rigorous approach to our interviewing. We're looking for brain and intuition. Exam results count for a lot. As do references. And security clearances. But we're also looking for something beyond the normal. A spark. An intellectual curiosity. An interest in doing something worthwhile with a career. A sense of duty.

Our problem is that the selection process can really only assess potential. We don't want to start putting candidates through shadow training exercises as they cost a lot of money. There's also the security aspect to worry about. Around one in ten of our interviewees will never be employed by MI5. We make them sign the Official Secrets Act, but that means increasingly little these days. If they start blabbing to newspapers – or in their memoirs – about our selection procedures, there's little we can do to gag them. We're therefore limited by how much we can give away to people we might never see again.

So how do we separate the men from the boys with one hand tied behind our back? We have two in-depth interviews: one political, one personal. And there is a psychologist's assessment as well. There are also a couple of role-play situations, where we play the character on the other side. These are complex and fairly realistic. We might be a rogue arms dealer and the candidate has to persuade us to accept a deal. Or we might play a scared agent whom the candidate has to calm down and persuade to continue to act as an informant. Or we'll tell the candidate that we're a suspect in a terrorist case and he has to interrogate us effectively.

We also ask them some pretty searching ethical questions. Could they kill someone? And under what circumstances? When do the ends justify the means? What constitutes an illegal order? What would they do if placed in an awkward moral situation during the course of an operation? Is there anything they wouldn't do for their country? What have they done that they're most ashamed of?

There are no right and wrong answers for these kind of questions. The candidates who swear blind that they would happily sit in a foxhole for six years with no other human contact if MI5 asked them to tend not to get through to the next rounds. We don't need a lie-detector test to spot that kind of untruth.

But it's the final stage that really distinguishes between the candidates. We send them into a pub in Clapham. It's a pretty quiet spot, full of alcoholics drinking their pensions away. The candidates are given a number of tasks they have to perform in that pub. They include finding out the names and occupations of the landlord's children, the passport number of one of the punters and the birthday of the bar girl.

Simple enough in some ways, but it's amazing how many otherwise excellent candidates freeze when they're put in a public situation like this. We also like to throw a few extra unknowns into the mix: sometimes we'll get a brawl to start outside. Or one of the punters will challenge the candidate directly and ask if they're on MI5 training.

What the candidates don't realise is that the entire pub is a set. Everyone is played by actors. We're watching from the 'kitchen' next door on secret cameras.

Our interest is how they react to any given situation.

[9 November 1991]

Just finished the recruitment round for the year. Top of the year's intake was someone called Rupert Smyth from Christ Church, Oxford.

Bloody Rupert. Bloody Oxford. Together, they've lost me a £20 bet.

1992

[24 January 1992]

I've grown quite attached to the recruits I interviewed and
assessed last year so asked Helme if I could stay on and help a
little with their training this year.

Helme seemed delighted.

'All the better for you, Harry,' he said. 'Give you a full
overview of the system for when you're running it next year.'

There was something in his expression that I didn't like.

As I've mentioned in my diaries before, training for new
recruits used to be a fairly simple affair. After my short-term
commission in the army, it was like a walk in the park, apart
from a couple of token exercises with the SAS who would stand
on your cold fingers as you did early-morning press-ups, yell
in your face and generally make you feel like a vastly inferior
human being.

It didn't have much effect on the civilian recruits. Many
of them still couldn't tell their arse from their elbow, or one
end of a gun from another, by the end of the induction.

I've therefore kept the basic structure of the course, but

altered its core elements so that it will stretch our new recruits to their limits. I also intend to use the course as a further assessment tool. The best recruits will go to the most interesting departments at the end. The duds will be thrown out altogether. Others will be assigned as befits their particular strengths and weaknesses.

[1 March 1992]

One of the most important things about training is that it should be a lot of fun. Even the research boffins and technical whizz-kids who'll never use any of these skills again should get something out of it. It establishes a sense of belonging and corporate identity. People should remember who they joined with. Their peer group should become a clique within a clique.

So we mix up the practical and the technical. There are a lot of lectures – on counter-surveillance, surveillance, interrogation, counter-interrogation, honey-traps and so on. We also instil a sense of pride in the service and its history. Retired officers are brought back to talk about past triumphs.

But we also need to make it as practical and hands-on as possible. So a lecture on 'how to be an effective honey-trap' is followed up by an evening 'in the field' (or, in this case, a bar). A seminar on effective driving is followed by a couple of days on the track. And so on.

Today, we started with surveillance – a primary tool for any half-decent officer. There was a slightly embarrassing incident in the afternoon when we were practising in Oxford Street and one of our recruits got thrown out for loitering around the ladies' lingerie section for too long. Later, another one got too close to his member of the public and she ended up calling the police.

We have decided that they should practise on each other until they've become a little more proficient. There's a limit to how many times we can extricate people from Paddington Green police station. It doesn't do for MI5 to look stupid in front of the police. They have a low enough opinion of us as it is.

[8 March 1992]

Yesterday was the physical-endurance test and the subject of much gossip among the new recruits. Few of them realised that it was every bit as gruelling as the rumours we'd spread.

Sadly, fitness no longer appears to be a badge of honour among the young. When I was in my early twenties, it was almost taken for granted. We ate well; we exercised well. These days, they appear more interested in watching television. Laziness has become ingrained. It means that the standard of basic fitness among recruits has fallen dramatically in the last decade.

In the army, officers train alongside their men. They are also expected to be fitter than their men. I therefore wanted to take part in the physical-endurance test as well.

Sitting here this evening, aching in areas of my body I never even knew existed, I rather wish I hadn't.

The recruits were woken unexpectedly at 2 a.m. and ordered to do one hundred sit-ups to freshen themselves up. We then entered the Thames at Waterloo Bridge and swam down to Tower Bridge. There, they were told to get out and get themselves dry and change into new clothes. As soon as they had, they were told to undress and swim back to Waterloo Bridge again.

Then it was five laps around Hyde Park, another swim and another two laps around Hyde Park.

Twenty per cent of the recruits had dropped out by this stage. After the final lap of Hyde Park, they were told to line up.

'Right,' barked the PT instructor. 'You're almost finished now. Just one more swim down to Tower Hill. Step forward anyone who wants to bow out now. It won't count against you.'

Five people stepped forward.

'Interesting,' said the PT instructor, making notes. 'I was bluffing. There will be no more swims. You can all go home now.'

[16 March 1992]

Today was one of the most controversial parts of my new course: counter-interrogation training. The controversy wasn't in the course itself. It was in how far we were prepared to go.

MI5 officers have always had counter-interrogation training. They are taught how to play for time, how to answer questions while giving away minimal amounts of information, how to play their interrogators off against each other. We give them examples of escape tricks that have worked in the past and successful rescue attempts that have made the headlines.

My argument, however, is that this does not go far enough. Colonel Sam Collins used to have strong opinions on it in my regiment: 'Train hard; fight easy. Train easy; fight hard. And die.'

I believe the same should apply at MI5. It comes down to what you hope to achieve by training people. Are you drilling them for the mundane routine of everyday work? Or are you preparing them for the extraordinary one-offs that might or might not befall an officer during their career? If you push them too far, is that scaring them unnecessarily? Or is it wrong for them not be prepared for every and any eventuality, both mentally and physically?

Put simply in this case, the question was: should we inflict pain on our recruits when training them to withstand interrogation?

Mossad certainly does. Some of their best agents — Eli Cohen, for example — were put through the most torturous preparation procedures. Electrodes. Cold baths. Beatings. Waterboardings. The lot.

The problem, of course, is that it's impossible to recapture the proper sense of fear that an MI5 officer would feel under a genuine interrogation situation. You can hurt a new recruit as much as you like, but he knows that there is a limit to how far you're going to take it.

There's also a very obvious limit to how far you want to take it yourself. You don't want to cause lasting damage. You don't want to inflict gratuitous pain (psychological pressure is far more interesting — and useful, too, from a training point of view). And you don't want to lose their trust. Start acting like a madman and they won't want to work for MI5 at all. The point where the entire exercise becomes counter-productive is reached very early on.

My innovation, then, this year was to add a bit of a twist

to counter-interrogation training. Recruits were taken from their beds in the middle of the night by people of foreign appearance who accused them of working for MI5. They were interrogated in adjacent, unrecognisable cells in the basement of Gower Street while we watched on screens from next door.

In retrospect, today, I can see that it might have been a misguided thing to do. The recruits are still too early on in their training. This sort of exercise should have been deployed prior to a specific mission and not as a basic induction procedure.

Having said that, I was impressed to note that fifty per cent of the recruits lasted the designated twenty-four hours. The others capitulated at various points during the exercise, but they by no means shamed themselves. My hunch is that most of them were aware that it was a training exercise, felt they'd done enough to prove that they weren't cowards and decided to put an end to their discomfort.

The problem, however, lies with Rupert Smyth, our first-place entrant after last year's recruitment round.

His interrogators stepped over the line a little with him while I was paying attention to a neighbouring cell. The result was that he flipped, yelling at them that he knew this was a fucking training exercise, and it was a fucking disgrace, and they'd better fucking wait the fucking fuck until he'd got the fuck out of there and had a fucking word with their fucking boss about the whole fucking shambles.

Well, I'm the boss on this one and we still haven't been able to calm him down. The interrogators have apologised personally for going too far. I've also apologised for not supervising them better. I've even gone so far as to assure him that he'll get whichever department he wants at the end of the training.

Still, Mr Smyth isn't convinced. He quit the training this evening, warning us that it wasn't the last we'd hear from him.

[18 March 1992]

Smyth was right. He's a highly intelligent, gifted young man who feels he's been wronged.

Today, I got a call from the Home Office press department. They knew this kind of thing was against standard protocol, but could they connect me to the editor of a Sunday newspaper who was on the line? Smyth had apparently named me fully in his report, so it might be easier if I spoke to the journalist direct.

I took the call.

'Hello, Mr Pearce,' said a triumphant voice at the other end of the line. 'I've got a bucket of shit sitting on my desk and on Sunday I'm going to pour it all over you.'

We immediately swung into full damage-limitation response mode. A team of rubbish experts were sent round to the editor's house. Another team was sent to speak to Smyth, authorised to promise anything and everything to make him keep quiet.

This sort of thing leaking out would destroy us. It doesn't help that Smyth's father is a very rich and influential banker, beloved of the Major government.

[20 March 1992]

Crisis averted, but not without a considerable loss of face and capital.

The bag men discovered sufficient evidence of an extramarital affair to make the newspaper editor keep quiet about the story. He was also promised a scoop the next time we have a significant lead on an IRA suspect.

Smyth has been found a position in the fast stream of the civil service with an open job at MI5 whenever he wants it. We've also had to pay him the equivalent fee that he would have earned from the Sunday newspapers – easily into six figures.

Helme is not happy with me.

[7 July 1992]

After that little hiccough, the rest of the training went fairly smoothly and I'm confident that I'm turning out one of the best crop of recruits we've ever had.

In addition to their practical skills, they've undergone extensive psychological and intellectual tests, as well as being assessed for core competencies on an ongoing basis.

They have a formal ceremony tomorrow with the Director General and then they start on their respective desks and I'm back to Section D, where I belong, as a field officer. It's been an inter-esting interlude, but I'm looking forward to getting back to proper work. I miss the rest of my old team as well. Esther is still working alongside Archie and Amanda in Section D. Amanda gave birth to a daughter yesterday and they've asked me to be her godfather.

[8 July 1992]

Disaster.

Rupert Smyth managed to get into the ceremony with the Director General. It's a shame he left, as he would have made a bloody good spook. Before quitting training back in March, he had managed to swipe himself a duplicate pass for Gower Street. We've also discovered that he was dating one of the girls who remained on the course.

To our embarrassment, Smyth took to the platform in front of the DG, shoved him out of the way and started to launch into a tirade against MI5's training programme. He'd managed to mention my name in a ten-second burst of vitriol before I got to the stage and manhandled him away.

Still, the damage had been done. I was summoned to an interview with the DG afterwards, which soon turned into a full-blown argument.

'They haven't joined a graduate trainee scheme at ASDA,' I railed. 'If they can't stand the heat now, it's just as well they get out before it's too late.'

But while it transpired that the DG didn't disapprove entirely of my methods, he certainly didn't approve of being humiliated that way in public in front of his youngest employees.

I am to spend a couple of months in Section X as punishment.

As punishments go, it sounds pretty bad. I didn't even know the section existed.

[25 November 1992]

Section X is a strange little place — a subsection within a subsection, where spies spy on the spies.

Its official statement reads: 'Section X exists to keep tabs on members of the security services. We monitor personal communications, spending habits and extramural activities. Our remit is to reduce the risk of blackmail and act as an early-warning system for renegade officers. These notes are retained on file, which are "No Eyes" as far as the subject is concerned.'

All very laudable, if a little creepy. Sometimes, we come up trumps with our investigations. We've spotted officers with huge spending problems. We've identified a number of blackmail cases, especially among homosexuals. And it does indeed provide us with early warning should an officer start turning bad on us. As with most things, prevention is better than cure.

But do we really need a Section X? The answer is that, in a place as sensitive and as secretive as MI5, it is probably inevitable. It does, however, make it rather difficult to meet some of your colleagues' eyes in the office canteen when you know exactly what they've been up to the weekend before.

The other problem is the way in which the section is run. At the moment, it is headed up by someone called Oliver Mace — a lifetime desk spook if ever I've met one. I've never seen someone get such voyeuristic pleasure out of poking his nose into other people's lives. He is one of nature's manipulators — slippery, sadistic and certain to go very far indeed.

We've also got a dreadful man on secondment from MI6 — Jools Siviter. He was born with two silver spoons: one in his mouth, the other shoved so far up his own arse that he can barely walk. He's everything I hate about the other service: smug, arrogant, elitist and ineffectual. It's not a winning combination.

The Queen has just described this as her *annus horibilis*. If she had to spend every day in an office with Siviter and Mace, I think she'd think again.

1993

[2 September 1993]

Just back from a very happy nine months in the field – on an extended joint exercise with Customs and Excise tracking drug smugglers into this country.

The operation was a resounding success, taking me to Afghanistan, Thailand and Barbados. We've confiscated a total haul worth more than £200m – the largest ever in this country. Twenty drug barons are now awaiting trial.

I enjoyed working with G Section, which deals with drugs and organised crime. It doesn't quite have the same frisson as working on counter-terrorism, but the aims are laudable nonetheless. I've seen what drugs can do to a man. I've seen what they do to the middlemen as well. Nailing the shits at the top of the tree is one of the most satisfying things I've ever done.

There's a crossover, too, with many of the skills developed on the counter-terrorism side. Trailing a suspect. Bugging him. Digging up dirt on his background. It's all part of this great game of espionage.

[13 September 1993]

Yasser Arafat and Yitzhak Rabin shook hands on the Oslo Accords
in Washington today under the watchful eye of Bill Clinton. The
US President dwarfed his counterparts, both in stature and
presence. I've never met him, but Juliet once did, back when he
was Governor of Arkansas. I remember her saying that no one
exuded more charm and charisma in a room. I remember feeling
rather jealous at the time.

More vitally, the world is awash with speculation as to what
this handshake might mean for the Middle East. Is this the
beginning of the end of the Palestinian problem? Or merely the
shuttle diplomacy of three statesmen in a hurry?

It's a truism in Israel that the left talks peace, but only
the right can bring it. It's a discrepancy we find difficult to
understand in this country where the link between political will
and outcome is more direct.

[1 November 1993]

The Director General has just offered me the job of Head of the
Counter-Terrorism Department, Section D.

'You only had one serious opponent, Harry,' he told me in
his office this afternoon. 'Helme, the outgoing section head. He
hates your guts.'

'Thanks.'

'But you've got two Prime Ministers — one former, one
current — both rooting for you. You've saved both their lives.
You've recruited two of our best agents of the century — one in

176

Northern Ireland, the other in the miners' strikes. You've freed hostages, debriefed defectors, protected authors, bugged MPs and gone undercover numerous times. You're one of the best field agents we've ever had. You've sworn at me twice in meetings and got away with it. You've even revolutionised our recruitment and training procedures. And you've seen action across most of the departments.' He paused, looked at me and smiled. 'And you're not quite in the shape you used to be.'

I laughed.

'But if you're going to sit behind a desk, we can, at least, make it an interesting one. I think you'll do a bloody good job, Harry.'

I hope so. Today is my fortieth birthday, and it's time for a new stage in my life. I've accepted. There is a handover period — in which I have to work rather too closely alongside Helme for my liking — and then I start properly at the beginning of next year.

[28 November 1993]

A Sunday newspaper 'revealed' today that secret channels of communication have long existed between the IRA and the British government and it has caused something of a furore.

Quite what everyone is so furious about, I'm not sure. Is it that they never knew about the channel? Or that it existed in the first place? Which is worse, the fact or the cover-up of the fact?

As so often, our detractors are wrong on both counts. Part of the role of any decent security service is to maintain a dialogue with 'untouchables'. No elected official can be seen talking to those whom the government have labelled terrorists, least of all the Prime Minister. That's where we come in. We can operate behind closed doors, quietly wheeling and dealing behind the scenes without the glare of media analysis and public condemnation. If talks break down, no one knows about them. Failed summits simply don't exist. If we bargain, or give in, or capitulate, it is done in private. Only when we have a significant breakthrough do we recommend going public.

It suits the other side as well, whether they're the IRA or any other organisation. They have to play to their gallery, just as we play to ours. For their leaders to be seen openly cavorting with the enemy — and the security apparatus of that enemy in particular — would be the death of their future in that organisation. It would probably be their death, full stop.

I've personally set up quite a few of these private channels. The first encounter is always a tense affair. No one wants to lose face on either side, particularly the senior members of either side, so the initial contact is made by a junior. The politicians might not be there, but politics itself always is. But once a degree of trust has been established — you can trust someone even if you loathe them — these private channels can achieve a lot.

It's the old principle: keep your friends close and your enemies closer. You can despise your enemies, scorn them, betray them, torture them even, but you can never stop talking to them. At some level, there has to be a degree of communication. Otherwise, what do you do when everything goes wrong and situations spiral out of control?

Lose the communication and you lose everything.

1994

[31 January 1994]

I've just finished my first month as full-time Head of Section D and I'm utterly exhausted. A car is sent to pick me up at 6 a.m. every day and take me to Gower House. I'm rarely home before 10 in the evening.

In some ways, it's like having lots of jobs. I'm a manager to my team, a politician on the JIC and an active armchair general during operations.

The political side, in particular, is something I was unprepared for. Previous promotions have always been within parameters to which I'd grown accustomed. My responsibilities were extended, but my core tasks remained the same. When I took over from Matthew, for example, almost nothing changed at all.

Suddenly, as Head of Section D, I find myself constantly caught up in petty politicking. Previously, my decisions have all been operational — vital life-and-death operational decisions but operational all the same. Politics is a thousand times worse.

I used to deal with people on a level that I understood.

179

Fellow officers. Agents. Terrorist suspects. Foreign security services. There is an understanding between us, even if we're on different sides.

Politicians I find altogether more slippery. And it's not just the elected ones now that consider themselves political. My counterpart at Six is one of the most devious, conniving, back-stabbing, lobbying, wheeling, dealing, politicised non-politicians I've ever come across. Then there's the Home Secretary, his advisers, the JIC, the Director General, the police, the media, the Americans. . . The list is endless and they all have their agendas.

I seem to spend half my life in meetings where we argue for such a long time that we forget why the meeting was convened in the first place. Different factions oppose each other merely for the sake of it. I'd never fully understood the concept of horse-trading until the beginning of this year: if you scratch my back, I won't stab you in yours next time round.

It's the problem with all jobs, I suppose. If you're any good, you get promoted. If you get promoted, you end up managing other people. Managing other people means doing less of what you enjoyed doing in the first place. Start out teaching and you end up as a headmaster who spends more time listening to parents' complaints than working in a classroom. Succeed in the army and you're soon behind a desk, shuffling paper around and sending bright young things to their deaths.

Look at the leader of any organisation and they're virtually indistinguishable. A chief executive of a large firm could run any other large firm. It doesn't matter if they're making paperclips or cars, toothpaste or satellite dishes. If you can run a university you can run the Civil Service. We are all just managers these days.

Well, I have resolved to be as hands-on as possible in this new job. Otherwise, I might as well give up now. I like leadership, but it's still strange getting used to the buck stopping with you. There's less chance for frivolity these days, less opportunity to pass on difficult decisions to those above you.

As Head of Section D, I answer to the Director General, the Joint Intelligence Committee and, ultimately, the Home Secretary. But there are also a lot of people answering directly to me now.

It reminds me of something Jane said when she started teaching: 'You can't try to be friends with the class.' And I suppose the same is true of managing a team. You have to lead from a distance. But I still want to lead by example; I don't want to be force-fed newfangled management theories.

Fortunately, I have the backing of the DG in wanting to remain operationally involved.

'That's why we hired you,' he told me today when I expressed my concerns during an appraisal. 'The gap between the ranks has widened far too much. We don't want another Helme.'

The DG's support means that I've been able to hand-pick my own team. Archie and Amanda have been rescued from a joint secondment to MI6 (they were both moved there after falling out with Helme) and returned to join Esther in Section D where they belong. Malcolm Wynn-Jones is still with us on the technical side. And I have put in a bid for a young Cambridge graduate called Tom Quinn (my eye was caught by his application form) as soon as he finishes training in June.

[11 May 1994]

Perhaps unsurprisingly, I am finding myself with little time to update my diary at present. Despite the DG's promises, I am still inundated with paperwork and politicking.

It's a case of keeping busy for the sake of being busy, for we appear to be condemned to live in uninteresting times. The Cold War is over and we're drinking tea in St James's with our Russian counterparts. Even the IRA is less of a threat now. Much of our work is becoming more police-based as we help our intellectually challenged colleagues with the mundane details of organised crime.

The main excitement keeping us all going is that we're moving offices at the end of this year – from the Junior Common Room squalor of Gower Street to the more glamorous setting of Thames House, on Milbank. Rumours are rife as to what the building is going to be like. There is ridiculous speculation of five-inch thick carpets, gold-plated ceilings, jacuzzis in the basement, tunnels that lead under the Thames to all four compass points of London, helipads under a retractable roof, submarines, missile launchers, and so on.

For the time being, however, the most pressing concern is who's going to get which office. Views over the Thames come at a premium, even if it means staring at Vauxhall for ten hours a day. It will be just our luck, though, if Section D is squirrelled away somewhere in the bowels of the building, far from any source of natural light. Not for the first time, human resources has far more power in this organisation than any of the rest of us.

In other news, the Channel tunnel opened earlier this month and the country has yet to be swamped by rabid dogs and Frenchmen. I'm delighted to see that the 201-page security assessment I wrote eight years ago has turned out to be reasonably accurate.

[12 May 1994]

John Smith, the man we all thought was going to be the next Prime Minister, died today of a heart attack. I think he would have been an excellent man to work with, despite all the files we had on him. It's a shame, too, that the public will have to wait several decades to see them. There was more to that man than met the eye.

1996

[18 June 1996]

Today was Graham's thirteenth birthday and Jane invited me
around to their house for his party.

Looking back through my diary, I realise that I haven't
written about the children for years. In some respects, little
has changed. They both still live with Jane. Catherine is still
coolly hostile towards me — even more so now that she is sixteen
and has become a fully fledged Marxist. I think Jane must have
finally told her what I do for a living.

Our early concerns about Graham have been borne out by time.
He has grown from an unhappy child into an unhappy teenager —
even more unhappy than most teenagers, it would seem. There was
a brief period around the age of eleven when I felt I was getting
through to him. He began to take an interest in cricket and I
took him to a few Test matches, looking for all the world like
a happy father-and-son combination on a normal day out. But this
window of interest was short-lived and the melancholy closed in
on him again.

My custody visits at the weekends continued, but they

became less and less frequent. The children and I grew further apart. Jane has recently started dating the headmaster I falsely accused her of seeing behind my back. The irony is not lost on me. Once, that would have destroyed me. Now I am numb to it.

Jane and I are politely detached towards each other these days, like strangers. A part of me preferred the shouting and the tantrums. At least it showed that something once existed between us.

So partly I stopped writing about my family because there was nothing more to say. But mainly it is because I prefer the numbness. Writing means thinking about them. And thinking of the waste is almost unbearably hurtful.

For these, and a number of other, reasons I was nervous about going to Graham's birthday today. Teenagers are bad enough when you know them well. Estranged, moody, unhappy teenagers are something else altogether. I'd last seen Graham a year ago, when he was twelve. We'd had a fight because cricket was suddenly 'sad' and 'boring'. A lot can happen between the age of twelve and thirteen. Worse still, Jane had invited Robin along to the party as well. God knows what she was thinking. The last contact he'd had with me, MI5's heavies were scaring the shit out of him in a hospital bed after I'd broken his nose and falsely accused him (at least at that time) of sleeping with my wife.

The party started badly, then got worse. Graham has morphed into a spotty, sulky thirteen-year-old, his voice alternatively too high and too low, hair sprouting sporadically in all the wrong places, the faint odour of unwashed socks mixed with too much deodorant: awkward in his skin, his clothes and his mind.

He greeted me with, 'What the **** are you doing here?' and

then later with, 'Don't worry, I have a surprise for you in a bit.'

Catherine was only marginally politer before running out with an unsuitable looking boyfriend to a CND meeting, whispering something in his ear as she clambered on to the back of his moped and gesticulating in my direction.

Robin, in comparison, was almost Zen-like in his calm attitude towards me. Perhaps he is still scared. Or, more likely, he just thinks he's won this particular battle. If so, he's welcome to his victory. Good luck to him if he wants to become a stepfather to these two.

There were about twenty kids there, mainly boys. Graham appears to be at that age when youngsters have outgrown the platonic, mixed friendship groups of their childhood but are yet to be interested in more adult mixed relationships. Or at least, that's the stage Graham would be at if he were a normal young man.

After a couple of hours of making excruciating small talk with the handful of adults in the kitchen – and listening to the thumps upstairs of what passes for music in 1996 – everyone was called into the sitting room to sing 'Happy Birthday'. Graham blew out the candles and then, to everyone's surprise, took up the chorused offer to give a speech, launching into a tirade of stunning viciousness.

It started harmlessly enough – thanking his friends for coming and his mother for hosting the party. Then there was a pointed and barbed reference to 'Mr Robin Tindall' who had 'helped out behind the scenes' (it can't do much for Graham's popularity having his mother dating his headmaster), before he turned his attention to me.

I can't remember what he said verbatim, but the gist of it went as follows: 'I hate my dad. I don't know what he's doing here tonight. He is a bad father, a bad former husband and a bad man. My mother teaches children for a living. My father destroys lives. He works for the secret police in this country, who are called MI5. They are like the Gestapo, but British and worse.'

I tried to stop him but it was too late. All eyes were on me. I tried to laugh it all off: 'How strong was that punch mixture, Graham?' – but Robin was standing next to me and nodding his head pointedly, as if in agreement with my strange son.

'What the fuck do you think you've put him up to?' I shouted, grabbing Robin by the throat.

Jane ran out. The kids screamed. One of the other parents tried to step in. Graham just stood there, a faint, smug smile playing around the corner of his lips as if I'd just proved his point and we were all worse than Himmler. The party ended.

[23 June 1996]

I tried to speak to Archie about this episode at work yesterday, but he was in one of his flippant moods – 'I hope you're going to be a better godfather than you are father, Harry' – and I felt like grabbing him by the throat too.

There's no one else I can really talk to either. I have a lot of admiration for Tom Quinn, our new recruit, and he's mature well beyond his twenty-four years. But it would be weak for me to confide in someone so junior, despite the mutual trust that we've established in the last year.

My problem is that I simply don't know what to do about

Graham. And the complete breakdown of our father–son relationship is exacerbated by the fact that he has now turned it into
a work problem as well. Twenty teenagers and their parents have
heard that I work for MI5. My reaction to Graham's outburst
would only have confirmed their suspicions.

If I played by the rules, I should report this – as you are
supposed to report all breaches in personal security – to my
superior, the DG. But I am too embarrassed. To report this would
mean going into all sorts of personal details that I'd rather
keep quiet from my colleagues. It could also be extremely
damaging for my career. Compromise is taken very seriously here.
If your cover is blown, you're not much use as a spy.

In any case, I can console myself that there was no one
particularly suspicious at that party. I've run background
checks on our database and no one flagged up any alarming
relatives or anti-establishment backgrounds. There were no Irish
there, either. Nor Libyans. Nor Iranians.

Thirteen-year-olds are a fickle bunch and I am probably worrying about nothing. This will be old news for them by next week.

[5 July 1996]

Robin rang me at work this morning to ask if I could come down
and see him right away. Apparently, the news of Graham's
outburst had been spreading like wildfire around the school and
he had acquired a degree of celebrity status by boasting that
his dad worked for MI5 (curious how he had suddenly become proud
of the fact now that it was considered 'a good thing' by his
peer group).

Worse still, a group of Irish students had banded together and given him a horrible beating on his way into school that morning. 'This is for your dad from our dads,' they said, punching and kicking.

Jane was already in Robin's office when I arrived and refused to catch my eye. Robin looked grave. Graham sat between Jane and me, bruised and cowed, all the defiance of the previous week dissipated.

It would have been a good time for me to apologise. To Robin, for assaulting him twice. To Graham, for being a bad father. To Jane, for everything. That's what I should have done. But I was angry and in no mood for conciliation.

There are always two ways, both equally extreme, of interpreting any given situation. On the one hand, here was a frightened, bullied boy, a scared and loving mother and a concerned headmaster. They were the victims; I was the guilty party who had brought everything to this sorry state of affairs.

On the other hand, all I could see was a man sleeping with my former wife, a son who hated me so much he was on the verge of destroying my career and a woman I used to love who couldn't even look me in the eye for shame.

So I lost it. I shouted at Graham. I matched him blow for blow, insult for insult, for the speech he gave at his birthday. It was a pathetic and cowardly attack on a thirteen-year-old. I shouted at Jane and Robin, too, for putting stupid ideas in his head.

It was never meant to be like this. I'd wanted my children to be proud of me, to be proud of what I did for a living. In the early days, Jane and I had even discussed how to tell them when they were old enough to understand, as if we were breaking the news to them that they were adopted and not our real children. We'd turned my career into the elephant in the room and now here it was threatening to trample us.

I walked out of Robin's office, ashamed and shaking, to return to my meetings, leaving behind an even greater mess than I'd found.

[8 July 1996]

I didn't think it was possible, but the situation has deteriorated. Catherine rang me two days ago to say that Graham had run away from home. She said that her mother was too upset and too angry to speak to me herself.

I'm not sure you really know how you feel about someone until they are in danger. Last week, I would have happily throttled Graham. For the last two days, I have felt nothing but love – a fierce, protective, paternal affection – as I scoured the country for him.

Of course, we considered the worst-case scenario: that he'd been kidnapped or abducted. Tom gave the parents of the Irish boys who'd beaten him up a thorough going-over.

And then after all that, Graham turned up in the fields near Jane's sister's house where he'd built himself a treehouse. She caught him sneaking into her house to steal her food.

So the prodigal son was returned home to London, but not for long. Jane has decided she can no longer live and work near me and is moving them all to Oxford. I doubt I'll see them for a very long time. Jane's parting words – all pretence of estranged politeness now vanished – were that she hopes I rot in hell.

   She wasn't aware that I am already there. Archie and Amanda died in a car crash last night. It was the fourth birthday of their daughter – my goddaughter – Lucy, who also died instantly. They were late for a promised trip to a pantomime, speeding along a country road, because they'd been helping to look for Graham.

1997

[4 January 1997]

There have been times, I admit, in the last six months when I've considered ending it all. Two best friends killed, myself partly to blame for both of them. A ruined family. Another spiralling problem with alcohol.

The funerals were almost unbearable. The last time I'd spoken in public about Archie and Amanda, it was their wedding. As I stood there at the lectern, all I could hear were Archie's words echoing around the empty hangover in my brain: 'I hope you're going to be a better godfather than you are father, Harry.'

And so we are left with the clichés: so unfair; so young; so tragic. Such an unfair, tragic waste.

But the clichés are true in this case. I don't know if the gods loved Archie, but he certainly loved life. No one else was capable of grabbing it by its throat and embracing it quite as much as Archie. He should never have died like this. Amanda should never have died like this. There was so much nobility there, such passion. If they had to go young, could they not have gone in a blazing trail of glory? On a mission that meant something. Falling together, as they lived and worked together. But in their family car on a country road? With Lucy in the back seat?

I blame myself. Of course I blame myself. The 'what ifs', the 'if onlys'. And a horrid, small part of me can't help but blame Jane and Graham as well.

I think of Bill, too. All the time. Would he blame me? I wonder.

My work might have destroyed them, but it has also been work that's kept me going. The service has offered me counselling, but I find that simple, hard toil is the best form of therapy. Distraction and denial: that's what I need. I don't want to pick at the scab by talking about it incessantly.

Clive has also been supportive. He came to the funerals and has kept in close contact ever since. I'd hoped after his retirement that we might meet again under happier circumstances.

So, I'll carry on in their name – or however it was that Clive put it – in the expectation that this somehow makes things OK. Give it a label and that makes it feel better. But the truth is that I'm carrying on for me, so that maybe, one day far from now, I'll be able to catch sight of my reflection without wincing. It's an ideal worth hanging on for.

As I say, I came close to ending it, but never *that* close. A man can lose everything – his family, his friends, his dignity, even. But he can't lose his honour. That, too, is worth hanging on to.

[24 February 1997]

I've started serving on the Contingent Events Committee, a new body established at the beginning of this year. Our remit is to operate worst-case-scenario exercises: imagine the disasters in order to be able to prevent them. Modern management jargon would probably refer to it as 'proactive' planning as opposed to 'reactive' response. 'Action not reaction.' It is an attempt to control events, compared to our traditional habit of floundering along at their mercy.

Cynics would probably say it's because we've got nothing better to do with our time in the current climate. But we're far from the first security agency to think along these lines. The CIA has been known to employ Hollywood's finest scriptwriters on a freelance basis to see what kind of terrorist plot they would envisage. The fiction is not always stranger than the fact.

In any case, the Contingent Events Committee is an interesting intellectual workout to keep my mind from looping around the same old emotional scars.

In the first month of the committee's existence, we sat in a room and brainstormed all the worst things that could befall the country. This month, we have started talking through these scenarios, one by one. There are eight of us on the committee, two each from Five, Six and Special Branch, one from the Home Office and one from GCHQ. The discussion is recorded on to tape and also minuted by secretaries from each of the represented organisations. An executive summary is drawn up and presented for approval at each subsequent meeting.

Today, we discussed what would happen if either Prince

Harry or Prince William were kidnapped. It's an unlikely scenario – their security situation is assessed on a second-by-second basis – but it is a possible and worrying one nonetheless. Their value, both in political and financial terms, makes them a tempting target for the fanatical and the greedy, as well as the insane.

We started with the scenario that the kidnappers had no ideological motives and were simply after the largest possible ransom. We worked out the prices we'd be prepared to pay and the sums the kidnappers would expect (everything has a market, even ransoms). William as the future King would fetch significantly more than Harry.

We went on to discuss how we might dupe the kidnappers with false notes, traceable money transfers and exploding briefcases.

The media would also have to be managed meticulously. If the story got out too quickly, or in the wrong way, it could destroy all chances of making a deal. And being seen to make a deal openly would grossly weaken the image of this country. Just as we cannot be seen to negotiate with terrorists, we must not be perceived as an open ATM for anyone who decided to swipe a young royal off the street.

On the other hand, we concluded that there was almost no sum we would not pay if it meant securing the princes' release. Whether we told the taxpayer could be decided if and when the scenario ever arose. Monarchism is not what it used to be in this country.

The second part of the discussion focused on the aggressive response to any kidnap: how and when would we deploy the SAS? If the kidnap was politically motivated, what immediate sanctions would we take against the sponsoring country?

We also held an overall review of the princes' current security situation, which is done on a periodic basis in any case — their teachers at school, their friends, their friends' friends. And we debated how much they should be told about the risk to their person. It's a fine balancing act to perform. On the one hand, we want them to be conscious of their security. It should become second nature to them. They can help us do our job by not putting themselves in stupid situations. On the other hand, we want them to have as normal a life as possible. They should be wary, but not distrustful.

We give each of our contingent events three ratings: one for likelihood of occurrence, another for seriousness and a third for possibility of successful resolution. Out of ten, the kidnapping of Princes William and/or Harry was given 1, 7, 7 respectively.

[3 March 1997]

Today, we discussed a possible assassination attempt on the Prime Minister.

Likelihood: 2.

Seriousness: 8.

Successful resolution: N/A.

Four US Presidents have been assassinated while in office. To date, no British First Lord of the Treasury and Minister for the Civil Service has been killed.

There's one obvious explanation for this: more people would like to kill the American President than the British Prime

Minister. He has a higher profile, domestically, internationally and constitutionally. The British Prime Minister is first among equals. The American President is Commander-in-Chief.

While it's obviously a scenario for which we've prepared before, it is the belief of the Contingent Events Committee that the security around the Prime Minister — and other senior government figures — is not as tight as it could be. The accessibility of the Houses of Parliament to the general public is of particular concern. During Prime Minister's Questions, for example, the entire cabinet could be taken out from the public viewing gallery. Access to this is currently monitored in a very lackadaisical fashion.

We don't want to go down the American route necessarily with Air Force One and huge motor cavalcades and Neanderthals with earpieces jostling the PM whenever he walks anywhere. Obvious security does not mean good security. But we do need to tighten up our current protocols. As we often have to remind ourselves, we are protecting the office — the status of Prime Minister — not the man himself.

We also game-played what would happen in the wake of a successful assassination attempt: the measures we'd need to take to calm the country, the transfer of the chain of command.

This discussion then segued into the worst-case political scenario — the assassination of the entire cabinet — provoking a rather ugly debate between officers of Five and Six over who would take precedence in the case of emergency laws being passed. I shudder to think of any of them running the country.

[15 March 1997]

Military coup:
    Likelihood: 1.
    Seriousness: 9.
    Successful resolution: 5.
    A military coup is the staple of tinpot dictatorships and the worst nightmare of a democracy: take your strongest men, arm them, train them to be killers and then watch them turn against their own. The army hasn't borne arms against its own in this country since Cromwell, but it is still a terrifying and possible scenario.

    If it ever happened, the intelligence services would be the final line of defence. But the grim reality is that, if it did happen, elements of the intelligence services would probably be in on the coup as well.

[24 March 1997]

Another bumper week of disasters, including the Thames flooding, a nuclear power station leak, medical strikes, major food shortages, a complete electricity supply blackout, poisoned water supply and a banking collapse. Civil unrest, mass rioting, insurance companies collapsing, radioactive waste, looting, collective psychosis and a plunging stock market.

    I was rather relieved to return home for the weekend and remind myself that none of it had happened. Yet.

[2 April 1997]

Suicide bombings in Britain:

    Likelihood: 2.

    Seriousness: 9.

    Successful resolution: N/A.

This country has endured IRA bombs for years but the public and the security services have grown used to their pattern of deployment – generally aimed at structural, not human, damage and often preceded by a warning.

The concept of suicide bombers, as seen in countries such as Israel, is altogether more frightening. Our advantage when it comes to conventional forms of terrorism is that most people value their lives and their liberty. This is their weakness. But when someone has decided they have nothing to live for any more, they go under the radar of all our normal methods of detection. They don't need to prepare an escape route or an alibi or back-up. Detection is, in fact, the very goal of their entire operation. As are maximum civilian casualties.

A suicide attack in Britain would change everything. And not just our modus operandi. It would also affect our foreign policy and our domestic civil liberties. But our current intelligence is that a suicide attack would be very unlikely.

[10 April 1997]

Renegade, high-ranking spy:

    Likelihood: 4.

    Seriousness: 7.

Successful resolution: 8.

Junior spooks go bad the whole time. We catch them pocketing money meant for other people — like George Blair in Northern Ireland — or going native while abroad, or giving someone too hard a time in the interrogation room, or fabricating lazy intelligence, or talking about their job when they shouldn't, or any other number of minor and serious indiscretions.

But renegade junior spooks are fairly easy to deal with. We sack them. Or we shuffle them off sideways into a harmless administrative role. And if they complain, or go public with their concerns, we can make their lives very difficult indeed. Try to publish a book, and we'll pursue them to the other side of the world.

Everything in the intelligence services operates on a need-to-know basis. And junior officers need to know very little. They might have a couple of juicy titbits to entice the Sunday newspapers, but their actual high-grade intelligence is minimal. We can swing easily and seamlessly into damage-limitation mode.

But what would happen if a senior intelligence officer — at my grade or above — lost the plot? Most of them know enough scandals to shake the very fabric of society. They could bring down governments and destroy lives with a misplaced word in the wrong person's ear, or an unsanctioned memoir that went beyond saccharine details about the colour of the carpets in Thames House. Or they could go about releasing the details of all our undercover agents and officers, with similarly disastrous consequences.

Fortunately, it's an unlikely scenario for two reasons. First, the kind of person who succeeds at Five and Six is unlikely to be the type to suddenly go off-piste. Second, to be successful here you need to have done a large amount of unsavoury things on your way up. And so we have the ultimate security net: you start talking about us, we'll start talking about you. In an attrition battle of mutual destruction, the organisation is always going to win out against the individual.

Still, it's as well to be prepared.

[13 April 1997]

Princess Diana assassinated:

Likelihood: 2.

Seriousness: 8.

Successful resolution: N/A.

Of course we've game-played the assassinations of all the senior members of the royal family, but it's Princess Diana who causes us the most concern. While she still has her protection officers, she is no longer enveloped properly within the security considerations of the rest of the royals. She has become something of a loose cannon of late. Her liaison with the Egyptian has also raised her profile, making her powerful enemies both within the British establishment and abroad.

To protect the princess, we had to imagine how we ourselves would go about killing her. The most effective way we envisaged was in a car, in a tunnel, using a strobe light to distract the driver and passing the whole thing off as an accidental crash.

[1 May 1997]

The Labour Party won the general election today, ending eighteen years of Conservative rule.

There is a bit of concern in the security services at having to serve new political masters. Obviously, we'd grown rather used to the old lot and many of our officers (myself included) struggle to remember what it was like to serve under a left-wing administration. Will it mean budget cuts? Or a greater emphasis on civil liberties and the rights of the individual?

It's too early to tell, although our initial assessment of 'New' Labour is that they'll be good friends to us. The fight is over the centre-right these days. Thatcher might have thought she destroyed consensual politics, but all she did was create a new consensus — hers.

[7 September 1997]

Diana, Princess of Wales, died last week in a car accident in Paris. Her funeral took place yesterday.

The nation mourning her death is not one that I recognise. Flowers everywhere. Maudlin people lining the streets. Clapping during funeral orations.

I met her once — back in 1995. She was beautiful, of course. Charming, too. But she was just a woman for all that. It's a tragic death, but no more or less tragic than anyone else who has died in the last week. Or anyone who has died in a car accident in the past. Like Archie. And Amanda and Lucy.

Her death poses a problem for the Contingent Events

Committee, which was winding down its work in the last week anyway. By a horrible coincidence — and it really is a coincidence — she died in a way that is virtually indistinguishable from the scenario we'd game-played.

We could brazen it out, of course. Somewhere there are the full minutes of that meeting, which prove it was preventative and non-actionable. But the risk is just too great to take.

Our problem is that bureaucracy always leaves a slime trail. We can do our best to eradicate that trail — I've got one of Section D's new recruits, Zoe Reynolds, working flat out on it — but the stains always remain. All we can do is hide them as well as possible.

1999

[6 December 1999]

My life is back on something approaching a level keel. The most notable thing to report is the progress in Northern Ireland following the Good Friday Agreement last April. Earlier this month, political power was devolved to the Northern Ireland executive. It has meant a complete shake-up for A Section with many of their officers transferred to Six or generously pensioned off.

On the domestic front, it has also made things quieter. Our main concern at the moment is the millennium celebrations – in particular, the large gathering of VIPs at the Millennium Dome on New Year's Eve. Zoe took one look at the guest list and the building itself and muttered that it wouldn't be such a bad thing if we turned a blind eye for once.

There was also a general malaise of millennialism in the air until someone pointed out that the actual millennium isn't until next year, Jesus was born some time between AD 4 and 6, and anyway, how do we know that if God is going to end the world, he isn't working to the Mohammedan calendar?

The other main concern has been about something called the Millennium Bug. I can't pretend to understand exactly what it is — something about resetting all our computers to the year 1900 — but Colin has reassured me that it's all a fuss about nothing. He's our new technical guy working alongside Malcolm. Everything has become so computerised since Malcolm joined that we now need two of them working full-time in Section D.

They're a funny little pairing. Malcolm is the elder of the two and considerably more conservative. He's also an impossible snob. One of his least favourite tasks is checking out addresses in London postcodes he considers undesirable.

Colin, I think, fancies himself as something of a nonconformist, while deep down he's every bit as conservative as Malcolm. It will be interesting to see how he develops. In twenty years' time, I think he'll turn into a carbon copy of Malcolm.

Both men have their eccentricities — Malcolm is barely capable of making a cup of coffee for himself — but they are uniquely brilliant at their jobs. There are few codes they can't crack, few gadgets they can't whip up at a moment's notice, few systems they can't infiltrate. We're very lucky to have them.

2001

[11 September 2001]

Four planes, piloted by Muslim extremists, were hijacked in America this morning with the intention of causing maximum civilian casualties. Two were flown into the Twin Towers in New York. Another crashed into the Pentagon. The fourth came down in a field in rural Pennsylvania. Almost three thousand people died.

2002

[3 January 2002]

It's already become a cliché to say that the events of that day last autumn changed everything. In some respects, we're still too close to the action to say whether that's true or not. But my initial impression is that the world — or, more specifically, MI5's world — is not going to be the same again. Historians always liked to say the twentieth century didn't begin until 1914. Now, I think they'll say it ended on 11 September 2001.

What does this mean for MI5? The answer, I think, is that it means interesting and difficult challenges ahead. I'm not saying that the first nine years of my tenure in charge of Section D were lacking in drama. There was the ongoing fight with the IRA, the threat of organised crime, the emerging mafias of Eastern Europe and the former Soviet Union. It's been a good preparation for now. But now is going to be very different indeed.

The End of History — that's what many academics predicted at the end of the Cold War. They were wrong. Islamic extremism. Axes of evil. Ongoing wars on the nebulous concept of terror.

Not the end of history. This is the beginning of the future.

It's already started in some respects. Work has never been so intense as during the last three months. At first, it was the obvious fallout from 9/11 in the States. We had to rethink our entire aviation security strategy in the light of this new threat from the skies. There were intelligence leads to be chased up on this side of the Atlantic. Our so-called special relationship with America has never been more vital to either side. Juliet Shaw is currently Six's station head in Washington and she is performing an excellent liaison role.

But the Anglo-American relationship has already started to become a little one-sided. Danny Hunter, who joined us in June 2000, leads the communications with the CIA on behalf of Section D in this country. He is bombarded on an hourly basis with demands for intelligence sharing. And it is always demands, not polite requests. Their definition of 'sharing' is an intriguing one as well.

It puts a lot of stress on the rest of the team. Tom, Zoe, Malcolm and Colin are all still here. Tom, in particular, is an excellent senior field officer, now filling the role that Matthew and I used to perform. It took me a little while to work him out, but Tom is brilliant at his job. You always know where you stand with him. Enigmatic and highly intelligent, he is an excellent leader. Danny works particularly well with him.

There's also new recruit Helen, who's currently working in an administration position. Although rather green at the moment, she is learning fast. I think she'll go far.

And there's Tessa Philips who runs her own team and occasionally works alongside me. She reminds me of Juliet Shaw in some respects – ruthlessly feminine, ambitious and devious. The line between her being bloody good at her job and bloody bad at her job is a fine one. For the time being, she is just the right side of the line.

But it's not just liaising with the Americans that takes up so much of our time. Post 9/11, there is a sense that it is open season on the West, and the security services in the West in particular. Every crackpot, tinpot, nihilist freak has crawled out of the woodwork to give us a hard time. Events often threaten to overtake us. Things now happen on a weekly and monthly basis that used to stretch out over years. We are understaffed, under-budgeted and overstressed. But at least we're not bored.

[13 January 2002]

The most powerful man in the world almost choked to death on a pretzel today. This does not give the rest of us a great deal of confidence.

[9 April 2002]

I went to the funeral of the Queen Mother today in Westminster Abbey. She was always my favourite royal – tough, bloody-minded, irreverent and with a fondness for strong gin. An old era passed away with her.

[28 April 2002]

I've decided to change the way in which I write my diary in an attempt to move with the times. We work in an office that is almost completely paperless. Everything is computerised and wired up to the Internet. Sometimes, it is difficult for the Luddite in me to keep pace.

My temptation, therefore, was to transpose all my diaries into computerised form, but I was scared of these being accessed. MI5's firewalls are excellent. My home ones aren't. And I only ever write my diary at home.

Recently, however, Malcolm showed me a new device he had been working on. It is a normal hardback book – the complete works of Shakespeare – with memory chips secreted in the spine and a tiny receptive device. You would only know what it was if you ripped it apart. This is a prototype version that will only transpond within five feet when switched on. No one else can intercept the messages.

So I've bought a battered old laptop with no Internet connection. And when my bouts of insomnia come over me – or if I've come home early from the club – I transcribe my original diary on to the laptop, store the data in the book and then delete the original from the computer. Now that I've finished this process, the original paper manuscripts have been burned.

This is the safest method I can envisage of continuing to write my diary. It's an exercise that I've begun to find invigorating again. There is something addictive about recording one's thoughts on the events of the day. It's a mental workout that helps put everything in perspective. And if I focus on recent proceedings, I don't have to wander back into a past I'd often prefer to forget.

[2 May 2002]

In that oxymoronic direct yet roundabout way of his, Tom started asking me in the lobby today about MI5 and relationships. I told him my old story that I hadn't let my wife know about my career until after we'd signed the wedding register. As I thought at the time: good to get these things on paper first, isn't it?

He gave me a strange look.

More pressingly, one of Danny's agents — Osprey — has given us information that a car bomb has exploded in Liverpool. This isn't very run of the mill. We're used to cars being stolen in Merseyside. But bombed? This is worrying.

[3 May 2002]

The bomb killed a family-planning doctor and her daughter. The perpetrators call themselves Defenders of the Innocent. They're led by a pro-life extremist called Mary Kane, who's already been sentenced to death in her absence for a major bomb attack in Florida.

I find these kinds of people abhorrent. I signed up here because I knew who the enemy was and I wanted to fight them. These days, the enemy don't even have a flag. They're crazy, meddlesome extremists. If they care so much about unborn foetuses, surely they should care even more for young children?

Murder in the name of human life seems incredibly stupid to me.

Unfortunately, Kane's American citizenship makes the issue altogether more complicated. The CIA want her back in Florida. But should we deport someone to a place where they face certain death? Our government's policy, certainly, is not to do so. While the likes of Mary Kane repulse me, so does state-sanctioned execution. Lethal injections. Electric chairs. The cold-blooded termination of a life that could have continued. The scores of mentally ill who are also put to death. The complete absence of belief in redemption. It savages human existence.

It puzzles me that a country such as the USA, which otherwise marches in the vanguard of human history, should be so behind the times on this issue. It's Old Testament justice for a New World country. Look at the other countries that retain the death penalty: Saudi Arabia, Libya, Ghana, Sierra Leone etc. The last person executed in the UK was in 1964.

But of course there's a more pressing issue as well: there are up to twenty bombs at large around the country. If Kane is sent back to America now, we won't know where they are or what her accomplices are planning to do with them. We're going to have to play for a little more time.

There's the additional problem that we've got the Foreign Office breathing down our neck, bleating some nonsense about commercial interests in the States. They sent over one of their guys to talk to me. 'Bring out the garlic,' I could hear Danny muttering.

It's a fair assessment of the creatures of the night over on King Charles Street. I used to admire the FCO. It was a career

I'd considered when I was younger. Looking after British interests in far-flung hotspots. Witty chitchat with beautiful society hostesses over cocktails. Lawn tennis and Pimms before sundown. Important foreign-policy decisions.

But look at what they do now. They're completely emasculated. All British foreign policy is run by an unelected cabal of spin doctors in Downing Street. Or more accurately, it's run by America who tell those spin doctors what to do so that they can pretend they thought it up themselves. And then on the odd occasion when we do start doing something for ourselves, we find our European partners complaining that we're operating outside the Treaty of Nice or some other rubbish.

So our poor mandarins in far-flung hotspots are left with little to do any more. Modern communications have neutered the advantages of their presence on the ground. Modern geopolitics have taken away any power they once enjoyed. Instead, it's a lifetime of rescuing errant tourists, worrying that their children's school fees won't be paid for ever and hoping their wife isn't having an affair with the 'cultural attaché'.

Thank God I joined MI5.

[5 May 2002]

Zoe's done a first-rate job undercover, posing as Kane's intended victim. We successfully lured her to a marketplace where we jammed the bomb and arrested her. Tom offered Kane a deal whereby she'd be protected from deportation on condition that she give away the identities of the rest of her accomplices. He went back on his word, as, I think, he'd always intended to. The pressure from the CIA and the Foreign Office was just too great. And I think he also felt morally justified in doing what he did.

By Kane's moral compass, of course, this makes us no better than her. She is being killed in the name of life as well — protecting other people's lives and as a punishment for the lives she took. That is how she viewed the family-planning doctors she targeted.

But let's not be ashamed to say it here: her moral compass is wrong. Ours is right. It rather goes against what I've written earlier, but if the death penalty does exist — and we have to face facts — then I cannot think of a worthier recipient than Kane.

[12 May 2002]

I got an extraordinary phone call from the Americans today: they asked if I wanted to attend the execution of Mary Kane — presumably after she has languished on death row for the next twelve years as her lawyers file last-minute plea after last-minute plea.

Delivering justice — or at least their form of justice — is one thing, but revelling in it strikes me as something altogether less laudable. I have declined, for obvious reasons.

We are also having problems at home with Mary Kane. Her victims wanted to see justice done over here. And civil rights campaigners have got wind of the fact — God knows how — that we might have sent her back to her death in America. It's very difficult to keep these things entirely secret now in a 24-hour-media society. There's always someone with their ear to the ground, willing to line the pocket of someone with a loose tongue. Our organisation is fairly watertight, but we don't always have the luxury of working alone. The police, in particular, leak like the *Titanic*.

So the various civil rights campaign groups are kicking up a hell of a fuss, marching around with banners, comparing us to Hitler, Stalin, Chairman Mao etc. They're the bane of our lives, those people. We could help an old lady cross a road and they'd suspect us of planting a bug in her shopping bag.

[9 June 2002]

We've discovered an unpleasant connection between racist ringleaders, politicians and the mass killing of immigrants and I really need some officers to go undercover and find out what's going on.

We've seen a rise in extremist politics in mainland Europe recently. In May this year, Pim Fortuyn, the Dutch politician who was stridently outspoken about Islam, was assassinated by an animal rights protester. In the French elections last month, Jean Marie Le Pen finished in second place. We do not want to let this sort of thing take root over here.

The problem is that Tessa has insisted Zoe joins her on a separate operation that she's running. It can be very difficult to argue with Tessa. She's incredibly strong-minded. She's also got Zoe exactly where she wants her. She really admires Tessa.

So, Helen is going to go with Tom and pose as his wife. I'm a little nervous about this. There is a tradition of administration staff helping out on operations, but I fear this might be throwing her in at the deep end with weights around her ankles.

Still, the chemistry is there and that's one of the most important things about an undercover team. Tom and Helen are going to be posing as husband and wife to win sympathy with the racist ringleader Osborne and his wife, who we think he's beating. You can be an excellent actor and a first-rate liar, but if your undercover story appears unbelievable you'll be rumbled straight away. The best thing going for Tom and Helen is that they look like a newly married couple. And she almost certainly has feelings for him.

[12 June 2002]

Tom and Helen have done an excellent job so far – befriending Osborne's wife and getting themselves invited for dinner.

Osborne is a canny bastard though. Tom and Helen's backstops have been tickled. To date, everything is still in place and the stories have checked out OK.

[14 June 2002]

Today was my worst day at MI5 since Archie and Amanda died.

Tom and Helen were bundled into a van at gunpoint and taken to a restaurant kitchen. Osborne had found a fuse left behind from the bugging operation on his house and knew that someone was keeping tabs on him. When I find out who was in charge of the bugging, they will be drinking tea out of a straw through their nose for the next decade.

Helen's hand was plunged into a deep-fat fryer in a bid to force Tom to give details of MI5's investigations into far-right groups. When Tom prevaricated, they put her face first into the fryer. She was then shot.

This is the first person I've lost on an actual operation under my command at Section D. Helen was a sweet and intelligent and beautiful woman. She had an entire career ahead of her, an entire life ahead of her. And now we'll never know. Her file will be deleted, her desk emptied, her relatives informed and she will become just one more ex-officer who died in the course of duty.

Such is the price of leadership: the ghastly burdens we must bear; the guilt and the unanswered questions we must take to the grave. It demands two faces of us: the public, strong one where I reassure our team that I did everything I could and will continue to do everything I can in the future to protect them; and the private face, where nights turn into bitter, dark torments of sleepless personal recriminations and silent weeping.

Tom has demanded the use of the SAS to take out Osborne.

'We look after our own,' he argued.

We try. But not well enough, this time. Not bloody well enough.

[17 June 2002]

Sometimes we forget that grief, too, has its hierarchies. The deaths of Bill and Archie affected me greatly. It affected their parents, all four of whom were still alive, a great deal more. We were all upset on the Grid to lose Helen. Her family are beside themselves with anger, incomprehension and fear. Anger that she's gone, incomprehension because they don't understand how and why, and fear that she was caught up in something much bigger.

Helen's father squared up to me at the funeral today. He said he knew that I was not her boss in the fisheries directorate. He said there would be hell to pay over this. No one in her immediate family knew what she did for a living. Until now, at least. Now they all know and they plan to bring the rest of us down with them, 'to protect all the other Helens out there'.

The father's funeral speech didn't reference MI5 in so many words, but it might as well have done. It was a stirring oration, reminiscent of Earl Spencer's at Princess Diana's funeral in some ways. Tom, Zoe, Danny and I were sitting together and caught each other's eyes, grimly. This was going to be two families at war.

[19 June 2002]

The problem with this job is that to do it well, you often have to act against, and not with, your basic human instincts. Helen's father is a kindly, if angry, man who rightly did not expect to outlive his beautiful, healthy young daughter. In any other job, I would have been able to talk to him properly, offer him my genuine condolences, take his arm — instead of the weasel words of formal comfort I am restrained to give.

The result is that all his anger about Helen's death has been directed at MI5, and me in particular. We're not heartless. We look after the relatives of our own. We've offered every material and spiritual comfort to which we have access. Counsellors have been made available on a twenty-four-hour basis. The family has been offered holidays at any time they choose. They will be given help with every contact, from job promotions to rent negotiations, whose arm we can twist.

But none of this helps when all they want is Helen back and, failing that, the head on a plate of the officer who put her in that situation.

Helen's father wants justice and he is going about it in a maverick, uncontrolled fashion, ringing up newspaper editors, the Home Office, Downing Street's public-access line – any number, in fact, that he can lay his hands on – to shout his case. It means we have been put in the horrible situation of having to bug the house of the parents of our former officer.

Fortunately, he is currently too angry for anyone to take him seriously, but we could not let the situation escalate. He had become a loose cannon and someone was about to get hurt. So we brought him in today for a little chat. If bribery wouldn't work, then maybe blackmail would.

As I say, this job can reduce your sense of morality to the lowest common denominator. But what else were we meant to do? It was the right decision, operationally. Helen knew the risks she was taking. And awful though it is, we can't have the world knowing that an MI5 officer was killed in a deep-fat fryer. One, it makes us look inept. Two, it would give succour to our enemies. And three, how on earth are we meant to recruit new officers if this kind of thing is public knowledge? So you could say that we threatened a dead officer's father for 'the greater good'. It's just that the good doesn't feel very great at the moment.

[15 July 2002]

A man in the crowd fired at President Chirac during yesterday's Bastille Day parade in Paris. The shot went well wide of its mark, the man was arrested and no one was hurt.

When told of the attempt on his life, Chirac, apparently, replied calmly, 'Oh, really.'

It reminds me of John Major's insouciance after the mortar attack on Downing Street: 'I think we had better start again somewhere else.'

We like our leaders in these moments, simultaneously humanised and raised above us, both vulnerable and fearless. There is a more cynical interpretation, of course: they know that their reactions will be recorded for posterity and nothing is more likely to lose votes than the news that they whimpered like a little girl at the first whiff of any danger.

[2 August 2002]

Zoe found herself embroiled in a siege at the State Consulate of Turkey today when the building was stormed by Kurdish freedom fighters.

Obviously, it took me back to the Iranian Embassy siege of

1980. But this time it was different. We didn't need to get an officer in from the outside. By chance, we already had one in place. But how much could she do there? She wasn't expecting this. We had no intelligence at all that this was going to happen.

There is also a suspicious diversionary element to the whole thing — a hunch that was confirmed this afternoon when Tessa recognised Johnny Marks, a former British spy and secret lover of hers, on the CCTV footage taken before the siege.

Five doors down from the State Consulate of Turkey is Cranbourne Bank, an obscure private bank that is used as a cover to pay agents. Marks was intending to take the money and sell on agents' details. Both Five's and Six's. It's information that could bring British Intelligence to its knees.

These agents put a lot of trust in us as handlers. They risk a lot; they sacrifice a lot. In return, we promise to protect them. It's an unwritten contract signed in blood that I learned during my time in Northern Ireland.

We were lucky this time. Tessa — whose past gets more mysterious the more I hear about it — once had an affair with Marks. She was also pregnant with his child. After telling him this, he had a change of heart and left with only the money and without exposing our agents. And I thought we were meant to know everything about our own people.

I have ordered a full security review of Cranborne Bank. Only myself and the DG were supposed to know the bank's true function. If we can't protect our agents, then how can we expect to protect the country?

[25 September 2002]

There has been a recent rash of paedophile incidents in the UK with some horrible outcomes. However, the public reaction to it, stoked by a tabloid media, is out of all proportion to the number of occurrences. There is something of the mass Diana psychosis about all this.

I've just come out of a meeting in which someone seriously suggested co-opting Five's resources to deal with the threat, as if this were an elite and sophisticated group of terrorists. In particular, they wanted to borrow some of Colin's and Malcolm's expertise to trace paedophiles using banned Internet sites.

Paedophilia is a horrendous crime, but it is a police matter. If they don't have enough resources to cope with it, then I'm afraid that's their problem, not ours. I will not have Five turned into a better-dressed version of the boys in blue. We are not the FBI. We are not going to run into rooms screaming, 'Freeze, MI5!' and then release our best video footage to the media.

[13 October 2002]

Bombs exploded in nightclubs in Bali yesterday, killing over two hundred people. We suspect Jemaah Islamiyah.

All nightclubs in the UK have been put on full alert. They're an ideal target for terrorists — maximum casualties in a confined space and the perception that the victims are indulging in decadent, Western activities.

[8 November 2002]

Worrying developments in the Middle East, too, after the United Nations Security Council approved Resolution 1441, forcing Saddam Hussein to disarm or face 'serious consequences'.

Beneath the heady political rhetoric, few people are asking the real question. Which would the Americans prefer: disarmament or the opportunity to give them 'serious consequences'?

[11 December 2002]

I've just found out that Danny is in all sorts of financial difficulties and has been changing his credit rating on the CCR database.

I had to punish him, of course. I've put him on to staff training – and not the fun stuff that I used to oversee. Danny will be in lecture rooms with the least able recruits.

But a bit of me understands how this happened. MI5 pays its staff very poorly. It recruits some of the ablest graduates of a generation. Their friends and contemporaries might be earning ten times their salaries in jobs in the city. They themselves could easily be earning those salaries in the city. Earlier in my career, it became a source of tension between Jane and me.

Of course, we hope the job satisfaction that derives from an exciting and worthwhile career more than makes up for all the performance-related trinkets that make commercial life bearable. But we also put a lot of temptations in our officers' way. They're often required to live extravagant undercover lifestyles. And then there is the access they have to national databases such as the CCR. If I were in Danny's position, can I honestly say that I wouldn't have acted similarly?

He acted illegally. But did his behaviour actually interfere with him being a good officer?

His main sin is that he forgot the eleventh commandment: don't get caught. It's something C impressed on me during my time at MI6 and it has stood me in fairly good stead since.

[15 December 2002]

There appears to be a rash of officers going bad at the moment. In August, it was Marks. Now it's Peter Salter, one of our very best.

He was on a joint operation between us and Six in an effort to catch Istvan Vogel, the leader of an extreme anarchist group. Six suspected Vogel of attempting to disrupt the US President's visit to the UK. The operation was complicated enough without having to liaise with my old bumbling buffoon of an adversary, Jools Siviter, at Six. Then there's also the problem of Tessa, none of whose agents appear to be coming up with much at the moment. Given how huge her budgets are, this is rather alarming.

Anyway, Salter went native on his operation and fell in love with a pretty, posh girl called Andrea — one of Vogel's followers. He later explained that he was bored. 'Bum-clenchingly bored,' in fact. 'No one believed in anything any more.'

Well, I know what he means. This can happen to our best field officers. They feel that they have done everything, seen everything, saved everything. It's difficult not to turn cynical after a while when you see your operations continually botched by cack-handed politicians for their own ends. You start to feel invincible. You start to think that only your work matters. You suspect everyone else of cowardice at best, and corruption at worst.

It's why we don't let people stay in the field for too long. It's one of many reasons that I'm grateful I was made Head of Section D when I was.

You used to know where you were with the public-school traitor. Just look for the sixteen-year-old pipe-smoking sodomite with a copy of E.M. Forster under his arm. But treachery comes in all sorts of shapes and forms these days.

Salter said he liked Andrea, this 'posh girl turning herself inside out' for something she believed in.

Our problem, of course, is that Andrea — and by extension now Salter — believed in anarchy. That anarchy extended to attempting to disrupt air traffic control systems in order to crash the President's plane. Fortunately, Danny was quick and stopped it in time. He's a great officer. Now we just have to stop him spending money every time he feels a bit down in the dumps.

We had less luck with Salter. There is a tradition in the service that we don't burn our own. The strong can be proved weak. The service exacts a terrible price on its best. If at all possible, we like to find a compromise for our rogue officers: a quiet desk job somewhere, a generous pension etc.

What other profession can honestly say that they look after their own people in this way? Where else do you find such loyalty? Offend your political colleagues, for example, and you find them briefing to the media about your 'insanity' and denigrating you in their memoirs.

But Salter rejected the hand we offered him. Yesterday, he hanged himself on Tom's belt during interrogation.

There, but for the grace of God, go all of us.

2003

[2 January 2003]

Public opposition is growing to an Iraq war that looks increasingly likely. Predictably, the most vociferous opponents are currently the usual suspects among the loony fringe. We've just heard about a group of anti-war civilians from Western countries who plan to travel out overland on a bus and act as human shields in Iraq. They leave in a few weeks' time.

It's a noble thing they're attempting to do — I admire anyone who has sufficient courage of their convictions to translate opposition into action — but I don't think they realise how futile a gesture it is. You have to look at it from Saddam's point of view as well. He'll turn it into another propaganda coup.

[7 January 2003]

I had one of the more bizarre meetings of my career today: in the underground car park at Thames House with a former MP called Hampton Wilder.

Wilder was jailed a few years back for embezzlement. It was only one of the many things he could have been sent down for. We had files as thick as his stupid head on illegal things he'd done, including arms dealing. Embezzlement was just the easiest thing to get him on without revealing too many of our sources and our methods.

During his time in prison, Wilder had written his memoirs in which he fingered a current serving minister of the Ministry of Defence as his successor in the arms trade. However, he had subsequently gone on to 'discover God', changed his mind and now wanted to destroy these pages.

The minister in question is Richard Maynard, the best friend of the PM. Wilder wants us to track down his memoirs. The problem is that they've gone missing.

It's incredibly annoying, this operation. What exactly are we, on the great ship of state? The laundry room that washes the sheets of the officer class? Those men in the loos at expensive bars who wash your hands for you and give you a towel in return for a 50p tip?

Keeping a diary is one thing. I have my reasons. But memoirs that are intended for publication rarely fail to annoy me. I see them as a betrayal. How can anyone interact with you properly during your professional career if they fear that every false move will be turned into an innuendo for the public's delight thirty years later? It is no way to instil trust.

These kiss-and-tell memoirs are selling for huge amounts of money these days. What is wrong with the public? I wonder. Are our lives so shallow that we'll happily wallow in the triumphs and disasters of everyone else's? At what point did we all turn into such terrible voyeurs?

In this case, however, it would have been rather easier had Wilder simply gone ahead and published. Is it really our job to be salving political careers and fragile reputations? Is that defending the *regnum*? Or a particular political party and group of individuals?

I distrust these sudden prison conversions to religion as well. I have nothing against religion per se. I used to quite like smells and bells. But it worries me what it does to people. It turns people like Wilder into odious, hypocritical toads. At least in his pre-religious days, you knew where you stood with him. Now he's a slippery little number.

I've dispatched Tom and Danny to the prison to try to find the manuscript.

[9 January 2003]

Is there anyone Tessa hasn't had an affair with? We called in Maynard for a briefing today at the Grid and she took very good care of him.

[12 January 2003]

Jools Siviter might look like a bumbling buffoon, old Etonian, pinstriped, Wagner-loving MI6 officer that he is. But there's more to him than meets the eye.

He can certainly hold his drink as well. After a couple of

bottles of whisky at the Travellers last night (his tab), I've finally got to the bottom of all this. The memoirs were faked in order to disgrace Maynard who is a CIA asset. This was Six's way of getting him out of the country.

Maynard has taken up a teaching job at Harvard – sufficient punishment in itself, I would have thought.

A tidy end, then, to a messy affair, but I don't like being strung up in this way by Siviter. There's something intolerably insufferable about the bloody man: that priggish, elitist air that people like him carry as if they were born to run this country. It oozes out of every pore and screams privilege, from his ramrod straight back to the shine on his expensive shoes.

His job at Six is not to protect the country. It's to indulge his little whims for power games and playground tomfoolery at the highest level. He doesn't care about anyone but himself. The public are mere pawns in his game.

I hear he's due a posting in America soon. I hope the New World knocks a bit of humility into the Old Order. But I doubt it somehow.

[25 January 2003]

The human shields left for Iraq today, about fifty of them departing from London in double-decker buses and black cabs.

I sent a couple of surveillance officers down there to keep track of things and I've just studied the tapes. One of the people getting on the bus was Catherine.

So I rang Jane. We hadn't spoken since 1996. I told her what I'd seen, what I knew was about to happen in Iraq. I thought she might have been grateful for the knowledge. I offered to do everything I could to intercept Catherine en route, to bring her back safely. But Jane was having none of it.

'Let her go,' she said. 'She's not your responsibility any more.'

Maybe not. But she's still my daughter. I've sent Tom to join the bus as soon as he can in Europe. I don't want her to get east of Athens.

[15 February 2003]

Opposition to military intervention in Iraq has become global and mainstream. Today, more than ten million people protested in six hundred cities worldwide.

Here in London, there were almost a million people (although protesters predictably claimed a number nearer two million). The placards showed an eclectic turnout: Archaeologists Against War; the Eton George Orwell Society. A group of Social Worker Party activists marched alongside their mothers. Urban and rural, urbane and scruffy, the young, the old, the left, the right. It was almost certainly the biggest political demonstration in UK history. Five had problems monitoring the march as so many of our officers wanted to take time off to participate.

And what good will it do? Absolutely none. That's the problem with the British character. Everyone had a jolly nice walk around London today. They've all gone home feeling pretty satisfied with themselves. And nothing will have been changed.

We'll carry on with our 'policy' in the Middle East, if

that's the right word for it. What else can the government do? We're locked into an American timetable now. And what else can the people do? They can march all they like. They can write angry letters to their local newspapers. But it won't alter anything.

[17 February 2003]

Reassuring news, at least, from Tom who is doing a fine job of disrupting the human shields' progress to Iraq. Tyres have been regularly slashed, impromptu roadblocks set up, discord stirred among the group.

Catherine appears to have emerged as something of a leader. But if it carries on like this, she won't have anyone to lead.

[18 March 2003]

Parliament has just voted on a motion giving the government authority to join the invasion of Iraq. It was a meaningless motion — they would have carried on in any case — but this will be used as a post-hoc justification should the war turn out badly.

Democracy can throw up some curious anomalies. One million people march on the streets of the capital to protest against the war — dismissed. Party whips, political horse-trading and blackmail produce a narrow vote in favour of war — war legitimised.

Further afield, Tom's attempts to sabotage the human shields' efforts have been in vain. They've now entered Iraq and are negotiating with the authorities over who gets to defend which site. The situation has got completely out of hand. Nobility of purpose has crossed over into stupidity. I need both him and Catherine out of there.

He is lifting her tonight and taking her to our embassy in Amman. I'm not sure she'll thank me. But I'm not going to sit by and watch her bombed to death, live on BBC News 24.

[22 March 2003]

'Shock and awe' started today with massive air strikes on Baghdad. It is shocking and awful. This is the wrong war in the wrong place for the wrong reasons at the wrong time. I am not anti war, but I am most certainly anti this war.

The problem with Iraq is that the debate has already polarised into two extremes. If you oppose the war, you're pilloried as a head-in-the-clouds, leftie, pacifist, cheese-eating surrender-monkey appeaser. If you support it, you're a headstrong, neo-con, oil-loving colonialist.

Both caricatures are unfair. I'm opposed to the war for simple, practical reasons: it won't work. It won't work in Iraq. It won't work at home. Democracy won't be brought to the Middle East by force. It will descend into anarchy. And there will be a political backlash at home because the public is being spun the line that Iraq is a threat. It's not. One day soon, they will find this out and they will be angry. Distrust in the political process will grow to dangerous and unprecedented levels. Our standing abroad will be diminished; our self-respect at home will evaporate.

We can cope with an angry British public. But can we cope with an angry Muslim world? We're supposedly invading Iraq to make the world safer. The reality is that it will make Britain much more dangerous.

This is the unspeakable truth that we all know but are too afraid to share. The intelligence services won't be thanked for their role in this either.

[24 March 2003]

Tom has just returned home from Jordan, having left Catherine safely in Israel where she intends to start working with Palestinian refugees.

I asked Tom whether she'd guessed about my involvement in getting her out of Iraq.

'Yes,' he said. 'After she'd been drugged by me, driven over the border in a taxi and woken up in a secure part of the British Embassy in Amman, I think she realised that I wasn't actually a former hippy pacifist from Australia called Philip.'

'How did she take it?' I asked.

'Badly.'

There's a saying that the first half of our lives is ruined by our parents, and the second half by our children. It is one area where I think Catherine and I could find common ground, should we ever talk again.

[28 March 2003]

As if we didn't have enough problems around the world at the moment, I've just found out that I was right to suspect Tessa at the end of last year. Zoe has reported to me that she has been running phantom agents. Tessa had even tried to bribe Zoe to keep her quiet about it.

I could see Zoe felt awful about revealing this. She really respected Tessa. This kind of 'shopping-in' went against all her instincts. But I also know she did the right thing. Tessa has been running phantom agents for years and pocketing their sweeteners. It reminds me of George Blair in Northern Ireland back in 1978. He managed to get away with this kind of corruption. I was determined that Tessa wouldn't.

I think you can tell a lot about a person by observing how they react when the chips are down. Are they good in a crisis? Can they admit their mistakes? Can they face up to the consequences of their actions?

Tessa certainly can't. Her response to my discovery was to attempt to blackmail me. She went for the jugular — where she knew it would hurt most — accusing me of cowardice on the day that Bill was kidnapped in Belfast. How she thought she knew that kind of detail, I can't imagine. But it was a dreadful and dangerous thing for her to do.

The pain of Bill's death was something I thought I'd buried with him. But Tessa has unpicked a lot of old wounds.

I have decided that the code no longer applies to her. I am throwing her to the wolves.

[29 March 2003]

Tessa's not the only person to be dragging up my past in Northern Ireland. And now that she's gone, she's the least of my problems.

Patrick McCann — Bill's murderer and my torturer — walked into an MI5 safe house recently, promising information on a Middle Eastern terror plot in exchange for us turning a blind eye to his own splinter group's activities.

I couldn't sanction it. What couldn't they do if they went unwatched for thirty hours? What kind of mischief wouldn't they get up to? I know what these people are capable of.

But Tom went behind my back (with the rest of the team) and over my head (with the DG), running an MI5 within MI5. I'm aware I'm still emotional over Irish matters, but I do not like being made a fool of in this way.

The problem is that my hands are tied. How can I discipline Tom as his boss when he has my own boss on his side? Sometimes, I wish the new DG's prostate problem would just see him out, once and for all. He's a bloody liability when he acts like this. Has he got no idea of hierarchy? For a man who used to be in the army, he entertains a very nebulous sense of the chain of command.

Tom had better get some results with this one or there will be some serious hell to pay. McCann almost destroyed my life. I'm not letting him get away with this.

[30 March 2003]

The bastard almost blew up Tom Quinn. And his girlfriend, Ellie, and her young daughter, Maisie. A booby-trapped laptop exploded in his house this morning. The irony is that Tom's newly installed security system almost turned his house into a death trap. He was locked outside. Ellie and Maisie were locked inside. If the detonator had worked properly, I'd have to look for a new senior field officer. As it is, we merely have an expensive bill to foot for a new staircase for Tom.

Elsewhere, the government has to look for a new Secretary of State for Northern Ireland. The attack on Tom was a diversionary tactic for their real target. We have failed in our job to protect the cabinet minister.

My satisfaction at being right in my instincts – the DG has never grovelled so much – is negligible in comparison to my shame at failing in our duty.

If Tom hadn't almost been killed, I think he'd be in a lot more trouble than he is. But sometimes we have to cut our officers a bit of slack. Choosing between two evils is never an easy task. I don't want my people ever to be paralysed into indecision because they fear the repercussions of a wrong judgement call. If you stopped to think too much in this job, you'd go mad. Once we decide on a course of action, we have to follow it through. The least our officers deserve is some support in their decisions.

239

[7 April 2003]

Uplifting news in these dark times: Jools Siviter has just been expelled from Washington for 'committing an obscene public act' during a Wagner opera. Rumour has it that his next posting will be Baghdad. I hope he enjoys it.

[30 April 2003]

We've got a new recruit on the Grid called Sam Buxton. She's bubbly, blonde and Scottish — very much Danny's cup of tea. They've struck up an instant chemistry. If only he wasn't so hopelessly and unrequitedly in love with Zoe, he might be able to do something about it.

I like to see my officers romantically involved with someone — ideally one another. Partly, perhaps, because I am getting benevolently sentimental in my old age. But there's a more practical reason as well. Couples make great teams together in the field. Archie and Amanda made a great team. When they went undercover as husband and wife, it required less preparation time. And it does a man good to have someone to look out for, as well as someone to look out for him.

Inevitably, we keep a lot of things locked up inside — a fruitless battle when we know they have to escape at some point. Me, I have my diary. Others, they hit the bottle. But we all know that these are substitutes for something else, more tender and more lasting.

[1 May 2003]

The American President landed on an aircraft carrier today and gave a speech declaring the end of major combat in the Iraq war.

Mission accomplished, declared a huge banner behind him. As to what exactly they've accomplished, no one is entirely sure. This mission, such as it is, is far from over.

[9 May 2003]

Tom and Zoe successfully foiled an attack by a Serbian terrorist, Miroslav Gradic, on Cobra today. I was at the meeting. According to my calculations, it's the twenty-seventh time that someone has tried to end my life prematurely (not including the time my brother taught me to hold my breath under water in the bath as a child and got a little carried away with his instruction).

Twenty-seven attempts on my life. It's quite a sobering thought. Of course, Bush and the like get many more, but they rarely see it up close and they're only told about the more extreme cases. Otherwise, I think they'd find it impossible to do their job if they were continually living in fear of death.

Most of us think we'll have time to prepare to meet our maker. We imagine it happening in our old age, perhaps after a long and terminal illness. We'll have put our affairs in order, made peace with our loved ones and looked death in the face and smiled.

But at MI5, we have to deal with the possibility every single day. It works one of two ways. Either it sharpens your senses and makes every moment worth savouring. Or it paralyses you with fear until you can't cope any more.

After years here, it's something you rarely think about any more. But it only takes another near miss to open up all those old fears that you've spent so long teaching yourself to suppress.

[10 May 2003]

Back from these morbid, abstract thoughts to ruthlessly practical ones: what to do with Gradic?

I don't like hyperbole, but this man is an animal. He was due to be sent to The Hague for a war-crimes trial, but is that justice? He'll end up in a cell singing 'My Way' to himself for a decade while teams of lawyers run around arguing each other into stalemate until he dies a natural, comfortable death in his old age.

I'm not sure there's any justice any more, at least the way the world plays it. Look at Lockerbie: still ongoing after all these years. When was the last successful prosecution in international law?

I've altered Gradic's papers to smear him as a paedophile and sent him to Egypt. They're even less keen on them there than our tabloid editors.

A harsh sentence for a very harsh man. I have no moral qualms about this one.

[16 May 2003]

Thirty-three civilians died today in a terrorist attack in Morocco.

[22 July 2003]

The net is closing in on Saddam Hussein after his sons were killed by the US military in Iraq today. Money, it would appear, really can buy everything: $30m is going to be paid to a single source for the intelligence that led to their deaths.

Back in the UK, a British scientist at the Ministry of Defence, Dr David Kelly, was found dead last week, apparently from suicide. An inquiry has been established to look into the causes of his death — no doubt the first of many that will deal with, and around, the intelligence upon which the Iraq war was based.

Our colleagues at Six are in for a torrid few years. We, on the other hand, merely have to deal with the consequences of their blunders. They're scrabbling around in the past to work out what went wrong. We're dealing with their fallout in the present.

[3 September 2003]

One of our agents, a young Muslim called Johnny, has been horribly beaten in a mosque in Birmingham. They whipped him on the soles of the feet, a form of sharia punishment that is extremely painful, if not lastingly damaging.

Before Johnny's cover was blown, he did, however, manage to find out that the mosque was training a 'nest of angels', a group of young men who'd be willing to blow themselves up as suicide bombers. Israel has had to deal with this threat for years now. Are we finally going to see this strange and vicious cult of death take root over here as well?

The problem with mosques is that we have to tread very carefully indeed. Post 9/11, Muslims already feel persecuted around the world. The UK's multiculturalism is precariously balanced. We can't go storming into a place of God and start throwing accusations around left, right and centre.

As ever in these situations, we have to put ourselves in someone else's shoes and see it from the other side. How would Christians react if churches were raided? It's a fine line between tackling extremists of a faith and appearing to attack that same faith's central tenets.

Unfortunately, it's a fine line that Islamic extremists in this country well understand. They have much of the left-wing media wrapped around their little fingers. If we or the police so much as pass wind within sight of a mosque, we have a ton of human rights lawyers and hand-wringing columnists bearing down on us.

I also know that these people think MI5 is laughably impotent. I remember an interview transcript with an Islamic extremist in the past.

'Secret police in other countries can arrest, shock, beat and even kill,' he said with scorn. 'What can you do? A smear in the press?'

'Would he like me to beat and kill him?' I wondered. The irony that these people praise the strict regimes they were born into and then criticise our more liberal society while enjoying its tolerances is almost unbearable.

Mosques should be a place of refuge, just as churches are. But they are a place of refuge from the hustle and the sin and the sordidness of the modern world. Not from the law itself. The American President made a crass distinction post 9/11 when he said he would not differentiate between terrorists and those who harboured them. But there was a solid point behind his grandstanding as well.

We have to get an agent inside that mosque. For the time being, we've run out of likely candidates.

[4 September 2003]

Another new recruit on the Grid: Ruth Evershed from GCHQ. I'm not sure she's to the others' taste. There's something distinctly bumbling and unglamorous about her. But I'm already rather fond of her. She's got a quick little wit and she clearly loves her job. I hope we can persuade her to stay on here.

[5 September 2003]

In a team meeting this morning, we were discussing the possibility of closing down the mosque when someone pointed out that the Home Office might not take too kindly to this.

'Bugger the Home Office,' said Ruth.

Well, quite. Not the transitive verb I had in mind, but she voiced the thoughts of many of us.

She's also scored a hit by discovering a walk-in agent at Scotland Yard — an Algerian called Ibn Khaldun. Tom and I met him in Kensington Gardens this afternoon. He's an impressive man. Fearless and upright.

'Bring on your lions,' he challenged.

So we have. He's going to be our undercover man in the mosque.

[12 September 2003]

A pointless end to a good man's life. Khaldun's methods inside the mosque were unconventional — at one point, he told them he was an MI5 agent as part of an elaborate bluff — and this alarmed Tom. But they were almost very effective.

In the end, it came down to a showdown in a school playground. Tom had wanted to rush in with armed police. Khaldun wanted time to persuade the boy suicide bomber that he was making a mistake.

It was a mark of Khaldun's humanity, but it was also a fatal mistake, for him and the boy, but for no one else, thank God. Next time, we might not be so lucky.

Khaldun would have been one of our best agents had he lived. It's an oversight bordering on criminal that we have so few trustworthy people capable of moving undetected among the Muslim population. It's something that I intend to resolve as soon as possible.

[13 September 2003]

Another upsetting element to this operation was that we almost had to rely on Tessa for help. I thought I'd thrown her to the wolves; it transpired that she'd been thrown to a flock of very gentle and understanding sheep. She got away with little more than a slap on the wrist. Like most people here with any degree of seniority, she knew too much to be silenced. Blackmail is the darkest of the arts, and the most effective.

Tessa is now running her own private security firm entitled, imaginatively enough, Phillips Security. There was no sense of duty in her, no patriotism. She wanted my job. She suspected (rightly, I hope) that it would be a little while until it became available. She felt hugely undervalued.

But this is part of the problem with the job market these days. When Tessa says undervalued, what she really means is under-remunerated. We valued her highly here. Many people in the outside world also owed their lives to her. But she was paid on the same low sliding scale as the rest of us.

It was an issue that Danny wrestled with as well: how do you live a successful secretive life without the funds to oil the cogs? Danny, we rescued in time. Tessa was too far gone.

'What will happen to Phillips Security though?' I wonder. No doubt she'll make a huge success of it and will turn out filthy rich. The demand is certainly there these days for security firms such as hers. This is the century of the mercenary, where force is available for hire like DVDs and principles can be exchanged as quickly as an online transfer of enough money. Industrial espionage, high-income individuals, rogue states. Private security firms get involved with the kind of projects that we could never touch with a barge pole.

I just don't happen to think it's an honourable way to make a living.

[27 September 2003]

I've taken up my pledge to start resolving our lack of decent intelligence among the British Muslim community. This is MI5's *perestroika*, I suppose. For Six, it was the end of the Cold War and the sudden realisation that they had thousands of redundant Russian experts. For us, it has been the change in our home-grown threat. Exit the Irish, stage left. Enter fundamentalist Muslims, stage right.

But it's not an imbalance that we can correct overnight. Muslim communities in this country are close-knit. They're also suspicious of any sort of authority. Infiltration has to be carried out incredibly carefully. They are not afraid to cry wolf, or run to the *Guardian* at the first sign of any untoward activity.

So we have to tread carefully as we spy on our own to protect our own. It's the second and third generations we're particularly interested in. They're both integrated and apart, radicalised and conservative, susceptible to brainwashing by either side. We just have to make sure we get to them first.

I've got people scouring the universities and the schools. But we have to be careful we don't get carried away in our enthusiasm. Five obviously represents the ideal infiltration target for an Al Qaeda operative.

[29 September 2003]

More problems with former MI5 officers. Although, to be more accurate, this time the officer is long dead and it's his son that's caused all the trouble.

Victor Gleeson was an excellent MI5 officer working under-cover in Athens. His cover was blown and he was taken hostage along with his son, Noah. Victor was killed in the crossfire during a rescue attempt. Noah suffered huge mental trauma from the experience.

He never really recovered fully and continued to believe that his father was alive and telling him to exact revenge on MI5. Noah, who later took the name of Peter, is a computer genius and managed to hack into the MI5 server. He believed that if he could expose all our secrets, we'd have to bring our agents home, safe from danger. If we couldn't save his father, we could, at least, save his colleagues.

Noah led us a merry dance, which made us wrongly suspect a teacher at his school — a decent man called Gordon Blakeney — after we'd inserted Zoe undercover as a teacher. It was a job she was very good at. With someone of Zoe's abilities, it is difficult to imagine her doing a job that she wouldn't be very good at.

Blakeney was combative during interrogation. 'What's real for you?' he asked. 'Do any of you people know what reality is?'

The simple answer is that we know all too well what reality is. Better than most members of the public, in fact. Our reality is the stuff of nightmares, but it's no less real for that.

Weapons of mass destruction in the wrong hands. Huge civilian casualties. Armageddon. That kind of thing.

But Blakeney's also right in some respects. What is real for us? Interrogation rooms. Faked identities. Undercover legends. False accusations. It's a strange world we inhabit.

Where is the anchorage in our lives? Where can we escape, except inside ourselves?

[30 September 2003]

We've put Noah into a secure psychiatric hospital with strict instructions that he is to have the best treatment available.

It reminded me of Graham, with a horrible pang of double guilt — once for having forgotten; a second that it took this kind of event to remind me. He is twenty now and the only news I have about him is from occasional police reports I manage to steal from their files. He's not turning out too well.

Graham was always the one with the brains, but brains with no direction is worse than having no brains in the first place. He went to university for a bit and then dropped out. At the moment, I think he's living in some kind of squat in Brixton, up to no good at all, no doubt.

I have no relationship to speak of with him. Robin and Jane made it very clear that he no longer considered me his father after the events of 1996. I tried to ring once — on his eighteenth birthday — but he wouldn't come to the phone. I sent a card. It was returned in the post.

It's the opposite of Noah's devotion to his father's memory. And maybe it's a comfort that Graham won't end up in a psychiatric hospital playing chess against his father's ghost and willing destruction on Danny, Zoe, Tom and the rest. But it's not much of a comfort.

Neither Catherine nor Jane have spoken to me since the Iraq incident.

[24 October 2003]

Concorde made its final flight today and there has been a lot of whingeing about the march of human progress going backwards and so on.

Personally, I'm a little relieved. I've never let on to anyone, but I really don't like flying much. Travelling at 550 mph in a steel tube is bad enough. Going faster than the speed of sound is another thing altogether. I was due to fly out to the States later this year for talks with my FBI counterpart – my first flight on Concorde. I'll be relieved to be travelling a little slower.

[23 November 2003]

England won the rugby World Cup yesterday – the most excited I've been since 1966. I sent a rather crowing, encrypted message to my counterpart in Australia, which I fear I might regret next time they walk all over us at cricket.

In the office, only Tom has really shared my enthusiasm. Danny is more of a football and cricket man. Zoe only likes hockey. Ruth loathes all sport (although she did admit in our morning briefing today that she might make an exception if the England fly half wanted to make her Mrs Ruth Wilkinson).

I must admit to feeling a slight pang of jealousy. What does he have that I lack?

[25 November 2003]

We're having trouble with suspected money laundering at an old family bank, run by a friend of mine, Dickie Bowman. We go back a long way, Dickie and I. His sister was at university with me and my father used to work with his father. He's a fine man, the very embodiment of gentlemanly capitalism that has died a slow and protracted death over the last fifteen years.

There's the stink of government involvement here as well, so I've tasked Danny to go undercover as a trader in the bank. He has a history of swindling credit cards. I'm sure he'll be perfectly suited as a trader.

Ruth used to be in love with a 'big swinging dick' (her words, not mine) so she'll be teaching him how to get by as a trader. It doesn't say much for those barrow boys that their job can be taught to an amateur in a couple of hours. I'd like to see someone condense MI5 training into an afternoon of bite-sized chunks.

[27 November 2003]

Zoe's also at the bank, working in the rather less glamorous role of a cleaner. While Danny wears sharp suits, trades millions of pounds and goes out drinking in trendy wine bars, Zoe has donned an apron and is sweeping up the mess from under his desk.

There's nothing sexist about this. I do try to share out the fun tasks among my officers. They can be a jealous, whingeing bunch at times. If one of them has taken out the fast pool car, the other wants it the next time round. And so on.

Zoe will get her chance one day. But the job of undercover trader was always going to be Danny's, especially as one of our suspects is on the trading floor itself and is an attractive young woman called Maxi Baxter. Danny has already made something of an impression on her.

Also, Zoe has come up trumps by delivering buckets full of shreddings for Malcolm to piece back together again. I like to call Malcolm the 'Leonardo of the Dustbins'. It's a moniker he appears to accept with pride.

[7 December 2003]

The Bowman operation ended both well and badly. The money passing through the bank belonged to the Russian mafia. Danny managed to steal it and pass it on to the government. The NHS has just found itself $19 billion better off.

Unfortunately, Dickie was a casualty of the operation. Last week, he suffered a massive heart attack from the stress and died.

He was an immensely brave man to risk his life and his bank in this way to capture the mafia. I could see he was scared witless by his undertaking. Some people are born to sit behind a desk and Dickie was one of them. But bravery isn't the absence of fear. It's facing something of which you're terrified and doing it all the same. Despite the fear.

We chose this career, this shadowy world. That world knocked on Dickie's door one day and he was brave enough to allow himself to get caught up in it. Tragically, he wasn't strong enough to live through it.

[14 December 2003]

The team took part in an Extreme Emergency Response Initiative Exercise (EERIE) yesterday — on the same day as Saddam Hussein was finally captured in Iraq. None of us knew about it until today. It's a relief of sorts that Hussein is finally under coalition control. Whether this will actually change the situation in Iraq is another matter.

This particular EERIE was the nightmare scenario that every government plays out in minute detail: what happens if you find your capital city under attack, your lines of communication down and your command structure rendered useless?

At MI5, we have a very particular set of procedures for dealing with such an eventuality. An alternative seat of government is established at Turnstile in the Cotswolds, between Bath and Horsham. The compound can house two hundred and fifty leading politicians, officials and scientists. The royal family has a nuclear bunker in Windsor. Regional Disaster Committees are also implemented around the country.

In this exercise, however, we wanted to go one step further. Tom, the EmEx officer, was led to believe that a genuine emergency had taken place. Faked CCTV footage was shown of an empty and chemical-ridden London. We made it look as if the *Today* programme had gone off the air, signalling to the fleet of nuclear submarines at sea that the country was under attack. Tom was told that the government helicopters had crashed, leading him to declare a state of emergency.

It was remarkably realistic. Our boffins spend months devising training exercises such as this one. They have to get every detail absolutely right: the acting, the outside lines, the video link-ups. There is a world-weary cynicism in most MI5 officers, which means we hate training exercises. We spend enough of our time doing it for real. So you have to make the exercise as realistic as possible before people start paying attention.

We try to do approximately one EERIE per year. This was one of our better ones. Five years ago, it was so ridiculously far-fetched that we gave up halfway through.

Afterwards, I congratulated Tom on a superb display of leadership. This kind of 'crisis' shows people's true colours. Who is prepared to court unpopularity for what they think is right? Who is defeatist in the face of disaster? And who retains their cool while remaining convinced that there must be a solution to the situation?

For me, it was a rather easier day. I spent it quarantined in my office after faking the effects of VX poisoning. I must admit that I rather enjoyed the acting. When Tom came in, I was mumbling the words of St Paul to myself: 'Whatsoever things are true, whatsoever things are honest, whatsoever things are just . . .'

A rather lofty passage, perhaps, for a spook, but I've always been fond of those words.

'Whatsoever things are of good report; if there be any virtue, and if there be any praise, think on these things.'

If only we had more time to do so.

[26 December 2003]

Last week, Danny invited me to spend Christmas with his family. The only problem was that he did it in front of Tom and Zoe who then both felt guilty for not asking me first. Then Ruth started stuttering some nonsense about her cats.

So I decided I would make life easier for all of them — and myself — by pretending I already had plans. I didn't. I spent Christmas Day watching the British *Beagle 2* attempting to land on Mars, hoping for once that we might get one over on the Americans. *Beagle 2* crashed.

2004

[28 January 2004]

The findings of Lord Hutton's Inquiry were published today. It would be a lie to say that anyone here felt he had been unduly censorious of the intelligence services.

[12 March 2004]

Simultaneous bombs on rush-hour trains killed 190 people in Madrid yesterday. It feels as if Al Qaeda is circling this country like a shark, waiting for its moment to attack. New York, Bali, Istanbul, Casablanca, Madrid. Obviously, we're next. It's just a question of when.

Millions of Spaniards took to the streets today in solidarity against terrorism. It was a moving sight.

[22 March 2004]

The American President is visiting London next month and we've got the CIA breathing down our necks again hoping that nothing is going to happen to POTUS on their watch etc.

Their view of the world is like a medieval map. Anywhere east of Hudson Bay is marked with a large warning sign: HERE BE MONSTERS.

The pain of déjà vu is mitigated slightly by the fact that it's Tom liaising directly with the CIA this time. This is one of the joys of responsibility: delegation. You can take the tasks that appeal to you – however inexplicably lowly they might appear to others – and pass on the rest elsewhere.

Luckily for Tom, he gets to deal with Christine Dale at the CIA. She's very easy on the eye. But we ourselves have to keep an eye on Tom with women. He's going through another horribly messy break-up with his medical ex-girlfriend, Vicki. She has been a huge pest during this operation, putting call cards with his name on them around Soho and generally making a nuisance of herself.

No doubt, Christine will deal with the threat in her own inimitable way.

[4 April 2004]

Bush's visit passed without incident in the end, although not without a few hiccoughs along the way.

We came within a couple of seconds of shooting down a microlight that had strayed off course and was heading towards the President.

And then there were the Libyans, with whom we suspected the Americans of attempting to make secret contact. There's nothing like accidentally intercepting a box of diplomatic papers to give you an insight into what's really going on in the world (and spilling coffee over them so you spend half the night cleaning them up again).

Diplomacy is one thing, but it's based on lies and obfuscation. So much better to get hold of the real thing yourself and find out the truth. That's the joy of espionage.

UN resolution 3501: all diplomatic material remains the property of the member state.

Oscar Wilde: 'More than half of modern culture depends on what one shouldn't read.'

I know which bon mot I prefer. We played the Americans at their own game and nipped in there first to strike a deal with the Libyans.

It's not often we get one over on our cousins. I drank a lot of whisky in the Travellers to celebrate this evening.

[5 April 2004]

I was dismayed to discover today that a psychologist called Miranda Sawyer had been carrying out amateurish psychological assessments of my team during the American President's visit.

I'm delighted that Tom sacked her. She has gone off to work for a major American investment bank instead — no less than she deserves.

It was worrying, however, to read some of her comments. Most of the people here appear overworked and paranoid. While there is a degree of affection and loyalty among the team, there is an even higher level of bitchiness. I suppose this is inevitable in some ways: a steam-valve exercise is designed for people to do precisely that. But I wish it had been carried out in a more professional way.

It's difficult to see how the whole thing was anything but counter-productive.

I was interested, though, to read Danny's criticisms of the Public Access Line, a new project that is open to members of the public to report information. We spent a lot of money setting that up, but it's consistently failed to deliver so far.

The main problem is that we didn't really think through how it would work in practice. If we put a well-trained officer on the end of the line it's an expensive waste of a precious resource. Whereas if we ask a poorly trained, lower-grade employee to answer the phone, the chances are that they'll miss any important intelligence that comes their way. Either that, or they'll waste our time by passing on spurious titbits and irrelevant leads.

Then there is the question of what kind of person rings an MI5 open line. Madmen? Plenty of them. Lonely housewives? More than I ever believed existed.

These time-wasters are, at least, benign. More dangerous are the people attempting to use us as score-settlers. We've had innocent old men accused of terrorist inclinations by jealous family members and less innocent gang members attempting to get one over on their rivals.

I'm not sure the public needs direct access to MI5. It worked fine in the old days when they spoke to the police and the police contacted us on a need-to-know basis.

But having personally initiated this project, it's very difficult to stand up and admit it was a load of codswallop all along. The hubris of leadership, I suppose. And the hypocrisy. No one likes to admit they're wrong, and the further down that path you go, the harder it is to turn back.

It's the same at all levels. Just look at Iraq. If the American and British governments admitted they'd made a mistake, they might be able to salvage some credibility, both with their own electorates and in the eyes of the world. Instead, we soldier blindly on, incapacitated by our own stubbornness, in the hope that, if we carry on doing wrong long enough, we might one day prove to be right.

Yet admissions of fallibility and regret are akin to political suicide. For a nation of citizens so ready to apologise every time someone else stands on their toes on a bus, it seems curious that 'I'm sorry' remains the one last taboo of statesmanship.

[9 April 2004]

I was burgled this morning. My first thought was for this diary, but it turned out they'd taken my briefcase, which contains the codes to Firestorm (the weapon designed by a French arms expert, which we're all trying to get our hands on at the moment).

It's the first rule of intelligence work: never take your work home with you. I know I've been breaking it for almost twenty-six years by writing this diary, but still . . . I am livid to have been caught out like this.

[11 April 2004]

Our burglar is a fourteen-year-old called JJ. Even better, JJ's an orphan with a photographic memory and an IQ higher than Einstein's. And he'd just accidentally shot his friend. Terrorists manipulate youth; now we're going to as well.

[16 April 2004]

Incredibly, JJ succeeded in breaking into an office block for us and stealing the laptop we needed for Firestorm.

Even more incredibly – for me, at least – he turned down Tom's offer of a job with us. I'd always thought this would be every teenager's dream: your criminal record wiped clean, a successful operation under your belt and a career for life with MI5.

But then we don't all dream in the same way.

The problem, though, for someone of JJ's genius is that his intellect makes no allowances for mediocrity. He'll never lead a normal life. Either he'll soar to new heights or plummet to unimaginable depths. It's just a shame he refused our offer of a helping hand.

[18 April 2004]

I've decided to renew Ruth's contract with us here at MI5. She's very good at her job and we're lucky to have her.

I also didn't have it in my heart to send her back to GCHQ. I once spent a week on secondment there; it felt like a month.

So many bloody mathematicians everywhere. And Cheltenham. What exactly is a person expected to do in Cheltenham? The younger graduates at GCHQ are the only factor keeping the average age of the town below seventy.

Ruth came to us under slightly false pretences, but her report for Tom on her inter-agency espionage for GCHQ was more than satisfactory. It is a delight to have turned her.

Ruth has always expressed her desire to be a proper spy. I hope we can offer her the opportunity from time to time in Section D.

[21 April 2004]

My old friend Mordechai Vanunu has just been released in Israel after eighteen years in captivity. Somehow I don't think that will be the end of it as far as they're concerned. In Israel's eyes, a traitor who's served his time is still a traitor. Their constitution might be secular but the prevailing culture is still not so far away from the Old Testament's 'eye for an eye'. I doubt he'll be travelling the world and talking at will to journalists any time soon.

[25 April 2004]

Tom's the last person I would have expected to go native, but his current operation – the undercover investigation of Major Curtis – appears to have indoctrinated him into believing the army can do no wrong.

We'd heard otherwise. There have been rumblings among the trade unions of mass upheaval and co-ordinated strikes. I remember the 'winter of discontent'. We don't want that happening again.

One can't help but wonder what would happen if MI5 went on strike. Probably nothing. No one would notice unless GCHQ and Six leaked it to the press to make us look cowardly and stupid.

Anyway, our intelligence suggests that Curtis is intending to lead his men in a mutiny. It's a far-fetched notion, but one we have to take very seriously indeed. Tom, however, appears to think it's groundless. And, as I've written before, you have to trust the instincts of your men in the field.

[27 April 2004]

Tom was wrong on this occasion, and I was wrong to trust him.

Danny arrived at the barracks with the transfer papers, whereupon he and Tom were bundled into a military vehicle and taken to an oil storage facility near London. Curtis had intercepted nuclear waste and intended to explode a huge dirty bomb if his demands for better treatment weren't met.

Tom appeared to believe he could talk Curtis round. I disagreed. I ordered the sniper to shoot Curtis dead.

When Tom returned to the office this evening, he was still bitter about my call on Curtis and singing the praises of the military. But what exactly is it about the army that commands so much blinkered respect? Is it the uniform? Or the bravery? Or the natural sense of authority? Maybe it's simply the fear.

I admire the army. Of course I admire the army. I used to

be a soldier. But somehow the public has managed to glamorise and sanitise their role at the same time. Recruitment advertisements these days rarely show soldiers at war. They're always cooking together or jumping out of planes smiling or crawling through bushes smeared with ridiculous amounts of face paint. The public seems to have forgotten that they are trained to kill. And sometimes they die as well.

The media can't cope with them either. It's 'our brave boys' this and our 'men in uniform' that.

Well, I've served with them and a uniform doesn't purify a man. Some soldiers are the finest people you can ever expect to meet. Others are third-rate scumbags. And far from brave.

Curtis had some valid concerns about equipment and funding, but he pursued them through the wrong channels. He was an egomaniac. And Tom was naïve to fall for him.

It's not the only time Tom's been foolish recently. I've also ordered him to end his thoroughly unprofessional relationship with Christine Dale at the CIA. Many more mistakes and I'll start questioning his judgement. He's one of the finest officers I've ever worked with. But I'm worried by what I'm seeing at the moment.

[1 May 2004]

The largest ever enlargement of the EU takes place today, incorporating ten new countries, some of them former Soviet satellite states.

Opinion is divided in this country as to the merits of this. On the one hand, it has always been the policy of the British

Foreign Office to expand the EU to its logical conclusions. Dilute the Franco-German axis. Bring in more Atlantist countries. Welcome those who lived under the yoke of Communism. And so on.

On the other hand, it means a lot more work for us: the free circulation of people and goods; the union expanded to the shores of Islamic countries; the criminal gangs of Eastern Europe who have no qualms about entering into business agreements with the likes of Al Qaeda.

Not that the media seems to have understood the issues properly yet. The main concern for the time being appears to be how much you can get a Polish plumber for.

[19 May 2004]

A purple flour bomb hit the PM during Prime Minister's Questions in the House of Commons today, thrown by protesters from a group called Fathers 4 Justice. It's not a group whose aims or methods I have a great deal of sympathy with. It is, at least, some consolation that Jane has been saved from me embarrassing everyone in public in this way.

[28 May 2004]

It's bad enough having your number two losing his touch without your former number two conspiring against you in some form of elaborate revenge plot concocted alongside the most junior member of your team.

We've been investigating the Chala Cartel, Colombia's biggest drug traffickers, whom we've also suspected of bringing missiles into the country. They have contacts in distinctly high places, including a major drug company. So far, so expected. What we hadn't banked on was their involvement with Tessa bloody Phillips.

Such is revenge, I suppose. It gnaws away at some people — a festering, nurtured sense of injustice, always waiting, always lurking until it has its moment to get even.

Somehow, Tessa got to Sam Buxton during training and convinced her that one of her ongoing assessments was to report directly to her. How Sam could have been so credulous as to believe this, I'll never know.

Tessa told her contacts in Chala that she was on to us. Lives were lost, including an innocent girl that Tom had taken a bit of a shine to. He was livid with me, but I've had enough of my team sounding off whenever things don't go their way. They can be livid on someone else's time.

Sam is lucky to have kept her job. She is even luckier that I didn't have to interrogate her properly. It wouldn't have taken much to break a silly little girl like her.

I am reimposing a sense of order in the office. The whole team is on probation. The next person who messes up is out. No questions. No buts. No second chances. They are all on their third strike. I've had enough of this.

The only upside of all this is that I've finally defeated Tessa. I hope never to see her again. That woman has the morality of a puff adder.

[5 June 2004]

Ronald Reagan died today. I caught a glimpse of Juliet at his funeral.

[6 July 2004]

I don't think there is much doubt who's just had his third strike: Tom Quinn has gone AWOL.

At the moment, we have no idea what's driving him. Is it blackmail? Love? Money?

What we do know, for almost certain, is that he's gone bad. Clearly, Christine Dale has something to do with it. I've instructed him on several occasions to stop seeing that woman. I have nothing against her per se. I've met less attractive CIA officers, certainly. But she is a CIA officer nonetheless.

We stand shoulder to shoulder with them. We do not go to bed with them.

This is one of many reasons we try to persuade our officers to date fellow intelligence officers – from their own services and their own countries. Otherwise, it always comes down to a question to loyalties. A conflict of loyalties.

I can think of thousands of pieces of vital, sensitive information that Tom could never tell Christine. She probably has a similar number she couldn't pass on to him without destroying the relationship between our countries.

Good intelligence work relies on secrecy. Good relationships rely on openness. There's no two ways about it. So one of them has to crack: either your professionalism or your relationship. With Tom, it appears to have been the former. Sweet nothings on pillows become sweet somethings. Intimacy leads to trust and trust leads to betrayal.

Guy Burgess, the Cambridge traitor, used to quote E.M. Forster: 'If I had to choose between betraying my country and betraying my friend, I hope I should have the guts to betray my country.'

Well, Tom certainly has guts. But it's not the kind of guts I like.

The problem at the moment is that all our information is sketchy. Tom initially took Zoe and Danny into his confidence. Christine had told him that an American assassin had been sent to Britain by the Iraqis. The CIA was determined we should not know, but she thought it was the kind of information we could do with.

This is where the whole thing stops adding up. Why on earth would the CIA not want to let us know about an Iraqi-funded assassin turning up on our shores? They've played some pretty mean, lowly tricks in their time, but I don't think they would go this far. They owe us a lot of political capital for invading Iraq alongside them. An assassination on British soil would be every bit as disastrous for them as it would be for us. There's no way they would let it happen. None of it makes any sense.

So Danny and Zoe became suspicious. They trailed Tom and found he was setting up a legend with an Irish passport and Slovakian residency. When he persuaded them to investigate a Suffolk farmhouse, they were ambushed and interrogated. Tom has now disappeared and they rushed back to tell me everything.

I hoped it would never come to this. I have had to put out a warrant for Tom's arrest and issue a full national alert and a ring of steel around all cabinet ministers.

I've also interrogated Christine Dale but to no avail. She's either hugely in love or very foolish or very, very good at her job. Or all three.

[9 July 2004]

I didn't expect the twenty-eighth attempt on my life to be carried out by one of my own officers.

Two days ago, the Chief of the Defence Staff, Sir John Stone, was shot dead in Ipswich. Tom's prints were on the gun. Later that day, Tom shot me as well before swimming out to sea. I was hospitalised with a perforated shoulder, making typing with one hand rather slow. He is missing, presumed dead.

We still have the problem that none of it adds up. Why the hell would Tom want to shoot the Chief of the Defence Staff? Did his investigation of Major Curtis flip something in him? I don't think he took it to heart that much. Money? Tom lives a fairly frugal lifestyle. I've rarely met someone with such an ingrained sense of duty, an innate concept of right and wrong.

But it's impossible to conclude that he's right on this occasion. Tom rang to warn us that Stone had been shot and that his fingerprints would be on the weapon. It was the 'mother of all set-ups' he claimed. And if he's innocent, it is the father of all set-ups as well. I just can't see how he might be innocent. When Danny, Zoe and I went to meet him, he babbled all sorts of nonsense about Herman Joyce.

Herman Joyce is a former CIA officer. Very former, in fact. He died in a car crash five years ago.

A large part of me hopes that Tom has indeed drowned. Whatever happened in the end, he was an excellent officer for most of his career. A quick death would be preferable to him spending the rest of his life contemplating what might have been. I could never throw Tom to the wolves. But when you assassinate the Chief of the Defence Staff and the entire country knows about it, they tend to want answers. And retribution, of course. There's always retribution.

[17 July 2004]

Retribution has started but it's against us and not in the form we might have expected.

My old nemesis Oliver Mace is now chairman of the JIC. He's a former desk spook – the worst kind. A quizmaster general in Belfast. And political, too. So very bloody political.

He's got the PM's backing to launch an investigation into MI5. Apparently, we are 'rotten to the core'. They're 'cleaning the stables' and it's going to be 'something of a bloodbath'.

An investigation I could accept – after all, one of our officers has just murdered a very senior government figure. I could even accept an external investigation: it's difficult to maintain impartiality when it concerns your own. My objection, though, is that this is not an investigation, it's a witch hunt. It has little to do with Tom Quinn and everything to do with conspiracies in the darker corners of government. They want to see MI5 politicised and turned into a ministry of state security

271

with powers of arrest. They want to reduce Five to a firm of decorators, to be wheeled out only when they want a whitewash.

About two per cent of me understands where Mace is coming from. He's frustrated that he can't always get the results he wants from his intelligence. He'd like to do away with the niceties. But I like the niceties. They protect us from tyranny.

This is the way it has to work in a democracy. Five has its faults. Of course it does. But show me a government department that doesn't. We work pretty well as we are. It's not broke, and Mace is trying to fix it. Fix it good and proper, in fact. If he has his way, we'll become little more than the secret arm of a secret government.

I've lost a few battles over the years. I've occasionally conceded political ground to make my life and that of my officers easier. But this is one thing I will not back down over.

With age comes cynicism. With experience, scepticism. You cease to believe in things like you did in the follies of your youth. Most of all, you stop believing in the ability of individuals to effect change.

Cynicism, perhaps. Or maybe just realism.

But one thing I still believe in is MI5's role in this country. It is a decent and honourable job we do. I have devoted my life to it, at the expense of my former wife, my children, my friends and my bank balance. I will not stand by and watch Mace win.

If he wants a fight: goodie. Let him bring on his legions. This has nothing to do with Tom any more. He was merely a pawn in Mace's game. It's time for the kings to step forward.

[19 July 2004]

I was wrong: it's still got everything to do with Tom. He rang me this afternoon. It was a somewhat unsettling feeling to be on the phone to someone who 1) you thought was dead; 2) shot you in the shoulder two weeks ago.

Tom's promised to provide definite proof of his innocence. Does he have any idea what he's unleashed? I wonder.

Meanwhile, we've got Adam Carter over from Six helping us out. It was he who first alerted me and the team to the threat posed by Mace.

I like Adam a lot. He manages to distinguish between taking his job very seriously and not taking himself seriously at all. 'Just let it all crinkle out.' That seems to be his motto. It's not one that would ever work for me. And it's the antithesis of Tom in every respect. But it works for Adam. It also makes him a very likeable person to work with. He has made an excellent first impression.

I admire his faith in Tom as well. We're working on the principle that he *is* innocent. If Mace thought he'd intimidate us with these threats and investigations, he completely misjudged us. His aggression has had the opposite effect. We've never been more united.

All we need now is the proof.

[20 July 2004]

Proof enough for me, but not enough for Mace.

Late last night, Herman Joyce's dead body was delivered to

the steps of Thames House. For a man who'd supposedly died five years ago in a car crash, his body was still remarkably warm. And with a fresh gunshot wound through his head.

Tom had tracked Joyce to a church where he'd admitted that he'd set him up. Years ago, Tom recruited Joyce's daughter, Lisa, to infiltrate a European hardcore anarchist cell. She was horribly tortured and never recovered. Joyce never forgave Tom and recruited Iraqi Ba'athists to frame him for the murder of Stone. Joyce's death in a car accident was faked to give him more time to plan his elaborate revenge. It makes Tessa's attempts to get back at me look rather pathetic in comparison.

Tom's problem, though, was that he had no recording device on him when he confronted Joyce. He knew he'd never get a confession out of him in the long-term. Joyce spent a year as a guest of the KGB in the Lubyanka. So Tom hoped that his dead body would provide sufficient proof.

As I say, it's enough for me. But is it enough to save MI5? Mace doesn't think so. But then, why would he? His idea of a happy ending is very different to ours.

[22 July 2004]

We've lured Joyce's widow to London but Mace had clearly been working on Christine Dale. His goons were all over the hotel.

I feel quite sorry for that girl now. The betrayed became the traitor. Just as the bullied becomes the bully. The kiss of Judas. And all of it has been due to matters out of her hands.

[23 July 2004]

A thoroughly satisfying end to this little interlude.

Adam cleverly extracted a taped confession out of Carmen Joyce before talking her into shooting herself. It was a masterful performance, the best I've seen in any such situation. Tom listened alongside me in the van. Afterwards, he told Adam that he doubted whether he could have achieved the same result under the circumstances.

So, MI5 is saved, Downing Street is humbled, Mace is neutralised as a threat (for the time being), Tom is alive and back on the team, the Joyces are dead and we have an excellent new loan from Six.

Business as usual.

To show there were no hard feelings, I had a drink with Mace in the Travellers this evening. He's not such a bad man after all. Ruthless, ambitious and amoral, yes. But not necessarily bad. We spooks have to stick together, especially when no one else will drink with us.

He's said he'll never try a stunt like this again. I trust him about as far as I can throw him. And he's a heavy man.

[16 September 2004]

Security in Westminster was compromised again yesterday when pro-fox-hunting protesters stormed into the chamber. Back during the miners' strike, I wrote in my diaries about the benefits of minimal security in the Palace of Westminster. But this makes us look like a laughing stock: a bunch of guys in jeans running around the chambers where laws are made, sidestepping old men in tights.

What is it about fox-hunting that gets this country so excited? No one invaded parliament when we invaded Iraq. Or started deporting British citizens to Guantanamo Bay. But try to stop people on horseback from chasing small animals . . .

The government really isn't happy about this breach, especially in the wake of the purple-flour attack earlier in the year. The PM asked to see me personally today to ask for my assurances that parliament's security will be beefed up. I agreed, through gritted teeth. There's something about this PM that makes me want to see him hit with as many purple flour missiles as possible.

[5 October 2004]

Tom has just returned from Maine, where I sent him to check up on Lisa Joyce. Having destroyed her life on a mission back in 1994 and now orphaned her by shooting her father and allowing a colleague to talk her mother into suicide, I thought he probably owed her one.

In retrospect, I think it was a mistake to send him. My decision was prompted by a field report he delivered recently, which questioned Five's responsibilities towards Lisa. I thought it might be the honourable thing to send him out there to face up to the consequences of what it is that we do, to see what could be done to make her suffering a little more bearable.

He has returned something of a changed man. Lisa remains in a catatonic state of withdrawal. Five's financial assistance was angrily refused by an aunt who is now looking after Lisa. Tom suddenly appears to have acquired a conscience about the whole episode.

Consciences have their place in our line of work, but so does learning to ignore them. An officer who suddenly discovers one is a loose cannon.

[6 October 2004]

I've just had to reawaken a 'sleeper' — a Nobel Prize-winning chemist called Professor Fred Roberts.

Sleepers sign a contract with MI5 whereby we help them with their careers whenever we can. A nudge here, a word in the right ear there. We can open doors and close unwelcome ones that they didn't even know existed. In return, they agree to help us out whenever we require. That's how they repay their debt.

It's something of a Faustian pact. How do the sleepers know that we've helped them with their careers? How do they know that they couldn't have done it without us? Many of them agree to sign when they are young, unsuccessful and unworldly. It can be decades before their decision comes back to haunt them. Most of them aren't called upon at all.

It's something I could never do myself. At least I know when I wake up that I'm going into Thames House. But how could you deal with the suspense of never knowing when, if ever, the time might come? It takes the decision-making process entirely out of their hands.

Why do they do it, then? Ambition, maybe. Or excitement. To belong. A sense of duty, perhaps.

Our network is bigger than anyone would imagine. We try to hand-pick the success stories at a young age so that they can be useful to us once they've made something of themselves. A significant percentage of senior figures in the media, politics, law and business are all MI5 sleepers. We've had a handful of cabinet ministers, one Prime Minister even, two Archbishops of Canterbury, a dozen law lords and numerous university professors. Our network is like the Freemasons, but bigger, better and more secretive.

Most of the time, they're used for simple tasks: passing on low-grade intelligence; the occasional leak; rumour-mongering. It's only occasionally that we require something more of them.

Professor Roberts is one of these rare cases. We require him for Operation Flytrap. We want to spread the rumour that he has managed to obtain Red Mercury in order to see if terrorist groups attempt to purchase it from him. Which flies will swarm around the trap?

I approached Roberts today – at his daughter's graduation ceremony. He was reluctant. Highly reluctant, in fact. And I could see why: a vastly successful career, a happy marriage, bright children. Why would he want to risk any of that?

So I had to apply a bit of pressure: co-operate with us or we'll systematically ruin your life. He chose the first option.

[9 October 2004]

We've had to portray Roberts as a gambling addict who's lost all his money so that he appears sufficiently desperate to sell Red Mercury to a terrorist organisation. Otherwise, they simply wouldn't believe him. There's nothing in his past to suggest any kind of terrorist sympathies.

It's already worked well. A terrorist suspect has offered him $5 million for 5 grams of Red Mercury.

My concern, however, is directed at Tom whom I've assigned to babysit Roberts. He's displaying a raw, sadistic side that I've never seen before. Roberts and his wife fought; Tom laughed. He's meant to be there to ensure that Roberts sticks to his promises, but he appears to be enjoying the act of destroying a man. It's entirely counter-productive for all parties. A paranoid and resentful sleeper is no use to us at all. Neither is an officer who thinks he's playing god. Danny has also voiced his own concerns: Tom's behaviour has worried him recently.

This just isn't Tom's style. And that raises another question: if this isn't Tom, when is the professional old Tom going to return? If I had more manpower, I'd assign someone else to this case.

[15 October 2004]

I've just decommissioned Tom by the roadside as he was en route to reunite Professor Roberts with his family. This was against specific orders. He'd pleaded with me before to put Roberts's family in a safe house and I'd said no. It was far too risky a strategy. The Red Mercury contacts would have suspected something was up. Tom thought Roberts was being used. But show me someone who isn't being used by someone else. You just have to be on the right side yourself.

[spooks]

So Tom took things into his own hands. He had a crisis of confidence.

However you want to put it, the upshot is that I had no choice but to dismiss him from the service. This wasn't the first time he'd disobeyed specific orders but I had to make sure it was the last. For his sake. For his colleagues' sake. For MI5's sake.

I'm sad to lose one of my best officers (and it's not often I say that about someone who shoots me in the shoulder). He was loyal, enigmatic and utterly dedicated.

I hope he does well on the outside. In a sense, I envy him becoming a member of the public again. I've forgotten what it's like for no one to know where I am. To walk out of my front door and not have a driver waiting for me. To disappear on holiday at the last minute without checking in with the relevant desk officer in case of emergency. To return to Heathrow and not have a Customs official give you a little nod of recognition as he sees your passport.

When was the last time I watched the news without knowing what was really happening behind the scenes? Or read a newspaper without spotting all the stories we'd planted? Or listened to a politician without remembering what our bugs in his office had shown him doing with his parliamentary assistant during their lunch hour?

Eleven years now I've been Head of Section D. I could count the number of days' holiday I've taken on the fingers of two hands; the number of proper friends I have outside the security and government apparatus on one hand. The job and I are virtually indistinguishable.

'So what would I do on the outside?' I wonder. Have I become institutionalised? Could I adapt? Maybe start my own private security company? Or take a well-paid non-executive seat on a company that flogs death-sticks to children?

Former intelligence officers are a valuable commodity, but few succeed in cashing in on their worth. They should be able to pick up well-paid advisory jobs in business, but many find the sense of anti-climax hard to deal with. One day, you're protecting the country. The next, you're protecting someone's balance sheet.

For others, the memories continue to stalk them. Some of the happier retired officers end up as university lecturers. The more miserable end up alone, broken and verging on insanity. A number wind up in jail, having thought they could adapt their skills to more lucrative ends in the criminal world.

I hope I never have to think about it. I don't want to be like the sad old-timers in *Shawshank Redemption* who can't adapt to life outside prison.

Tom, I think, is still young enough to adapt. But it's a strange thought that I'll never see him again. We've shared this office for ten years, sat in meeting rooms together, walked through pods together, saved lives together. And now he's walking out into the real world.

[2 November 2004]

George W. Bush was re-elected today for a second term. God help us.

[5 November 2004]

Ruth called Adam Tom by mistake today. I think the team might be missing him more than they're letting on.

[9 November 2004]

I got a call from Professor Roberts today. Apparently, being a sleeper is no longer enough for him. Now that he's been woken up once, he doesn't want to go back to sleep again. Normal life appears rather mundane in comparison.

This has happened before with other sleepers. If they work with us for a couple of weeks, they start to think that it's always like this, that all missions revolve around them, and them alone. They forget the tedium that we also have to put up with. The paperwork. The politics.

Still, if Roberts wants a more active role, that suits our purposes. He was good during Operation Firetrap. Excellent, in fact. We've started him on something small. He can assess his students for subversive elements and potential officers. We'll see how we get on.

[10 November 2004]

We suspect Mace is up to his usual tricks again

Danny is on Close Quarter Protection of another author who's managed to offend the Muslim world. He's not nearly as charming as Rushdie and I pity Danny his task. He was almost killed in the line of duty a few days ago when a gunman burst into a bookshop and shot at the author, Zuli, and his bookseller friend, Harakat. Both escaped, shaken but unharmed.

Zuli now wants the CIA to protect him instead — a misguided sense of trust if ever I've seen one. He'll be dead within the month.

More alarmingly, a post-hoc analysis of the crime scene suggests that the gunman was actually aiming for Harakat. Our suspicions aroused, Ruth uncovered his application for UK citizenship. It reads like a bad MI6 legend, written up by one of those spotty mutants they keep in the dungeons at Vauxhall Bridge Road next to where C grows his magic mushrooms. They have brains the size of undiscovered planets and social skills to go with them.

I confronted Mace about this yesterday in the club. He denied everything.

But today we received a photograph from an anonymous source showing Mace talking to the head of a Pakistani terror group. We were worried. This is starting to escalate into something bigger. Adam is going to meet the source, an MI6 mole.

[12 November 2004]

Harakat was shot dead yesterday just outside Lord's cricket ground. He was a double agent who had been turned by MI6. The terror group chief Mace had met wanted him killed. An old friend was betrayed because Mace had a new one now. It reminds me of a criticism of Metternich, the nineteenth-century diplomat, that he changed his allies like cutlery between courses at a banquet.

I was angry with Mace, who, as always, has his own justification for his actions: 'We may not be able to see England's finest streaming across the fields of Waterloo, but we are at war, Harry. We cannot say any more, this we do not do. Post nine eleven, no one is off limits.'

But are we at war? This is 2004, not Orwell's 1984. There are hostile states and rogue elements who wish harm on our country. But when has this not been the case? Young men are not conscripted. Women and children do not sleep in their beds fearing bombs in the night.

If the Cold War was cold, this 'war' is positively freezing.

It's a rhetoric that suits certain factions in this country, of course. Politicians like an undercurrent of minor panic. It's helpful to some elements in the intelligence agencies as well.

It would be more helpful if all the elements in the intelligence agencies could work together. Look at the lack of inter-departmental communication that led to 9/11. Our relationships here are almost as fractured.

Last week, we had a team of MI6 officers attempting to trail Adam through the streets of London. Whose interests does that serve exactly? You'd have thought there were enough enemies in the world without creating our own.

It doesn't help that everything crosses the desk of Mace, the Chairman of the JIC. He owes all his loyalties to Six. You can see it in the way he deals with us — always through clenched teeth and an upturned nose. We are a provincial agency, glorified coppers with a limited outlook on the world. Whereas over the river, they can take a step back in their elegantly tailored suits and their ridiculous, expensive glasshouse of a building and see the broad span of world events. Our officers are based in London; our agents are in places like Birmingham and Leeds and Solihull. Theirs are in Addis Ababa and Beirut and Rio de Janeiro. They're playing the great game; we're playing parochial little games.

It's not a world view that does them, us or the public any favours.

[1 December 2004]

I just got a cryptic postcard from someone I assume must be Tom. He appears to have embarked on some kind of round-the-world trip. There was a hidden reference in the innocuous text to how nice it was to be using only one passport as he travelled.

No more boxes, then. Just Tom Quinn. On holiday.

I hope he's taking Christine with him, wherever she might be these days.

[2 December 2004]

The latest round of Middle East talks have been abruptly aborted following the kidnapping of Patricia Norton, the UN chief negotiator.

The last thing she said to Adam was that he should investigate David Swift, the neo-con newspaper mogul with extreme pro-Israel views. Swift is a member of the November Committee, whose slogan is 'Security through a greater Israel'. They would do

285

anything to stop the creation of a Palestinian state, including murder an excellent UN negotiator.

Elsewhere, Danny and Zoe are undercover in the Palestinian Freedom Campaign, investigating suspicions that it is being used as a front to channel funds to terrorist organisations.

Such is the nature of the Middle East — dirty funding, implacable opponents and extremes on either side. It is not an easy place for moderates.

Two things further complicate the operation.

One: what will the November Committee do next? We have discovered a list of prominent figures they would like 'removed'.

Two: my daughter, Catherine, is working at the Palestinian Freedom Campaign.

[20 December 2004]

I can't remember the last time I saw Catherine. Was it really eight years ago? Clambering on to the back of her boyfriend's bike outside Graham's birthday party. Tom, of course, saw her more recently — in Iraq.

Danny is undercover at the campaign and I've listened to transcripts of the two of them speaking together and try to picture what she must look like now. I've only seen fuzzy surveillance footage of her boarding a human-shield bus in London. She is a fully grown woman, almost the same age as her mother when we married.

The Palestinian Freedom Campaign is above board, we've discovered. But we believe the November Committee has an agent in there targeting the left-wing MP who runs it. Current intelligence points to Catherine.

What am I now? A father? Or the Head of MI5's Counter-Terrorism Department, Section D.

It doesn't make much sense. Catherine's emotions always triumphed over her intellect. I saw her a bit during her teenage years. She never hated me like Graham did. We might not be very close, but I know her instinctively well enough to know that she could never side with the likes of the November Committee. She went to Iraq, for God's sake. She's been helping out Palestinians in the West Bank. You could always rely on her to find the bird with the broken wing and nurse it.

[27 December 2004]

The mole inside the Palestinian Freedom Campaign was the left-wing MP's gay lover. His sister was killed by a Palestinian bomb in Israel. We managed to stop him before he took an eye for an eye.

Swift was set up in an elaborate honey-trap by Adam's wife, Fiona (an excellent temporary addition to the team). He has left the country and we won't be hearing from him again.

But these two successful outcomes pale into insignificance alongside the proof of Catherine's innocence.

There was an emotional reconciliation on a park bench this afternoon. She forgave me. She forgave me everything — Jane, Graham, Tom in Amman. Everything. It was a forgiveness I must have craved subconsciously for a long time as I almost broke down. And she must have longed to forgive, too, for it seemed to affect her almost as much as me. We live in emotional times. Yesterday, hundreds of thousands of people died in a tsunami that swept across the Indian Ocean. We've all realised the fragility of life, its viciously short timetables. How many people died on Boxing Day with regrets still in their hearts, unspoken words of forgiveness on their tongues?

I gave Catherine a small present: a copy of Yeat's poem, 'A Prayer for My Daughter', which I used to read out loud when she was sleeping as a baby.

Where my own words fail me, these two lines keep on turning around in my head:

Considering that, all hatred driven hence,
The soul recovers radical innocence.

2005

[1 January 2005]

Poor Danny and Zoe have just spent their New Year's Eve on a boat in the North Sea, playing scarecrow to a renegade scientist called Dr Newland who is attempting to sell biochemical material to rogue elements.

I'm not sure it was a good idea for me to put them working together. I've always operated on the principle that a bit of creative tension is a good thing for a team in the field. But there's creative tension and there's thoroughly counter-productive, dangerous, jealous, destructive tension. With these two, I wonder if it might be the latter.

My team probably think I'm a fuddy-duddy, that I have no heart, no soul and don't notice the things that go on under my nose. But it's obvious that Danny is still carrying a flame for Zoe. She, meanwhile, has met a photographer, a nice young man called Will North. He's obviously a bit troublesome as well. But if he wasn't, she wouldn't like him. It takes quite a man to date a female MI5 officer.

In any case, it appears to be leading to a significant

deterioration in the relationship between Danny and Zoe. This isn't helped by Zoe falling seasick on the boat. Our current intelligence on Dr Newland suggests that we might have to step this operation up a gear tomorrow.

[2 January 2005]

In the end, we had to step it up all the way. Adam gave (and I confirmed) a direct kill order for Danny to assassinate Newland. The boat was in international waters. It was our only chance and our only option. If he'd been allowed to disembark, the lethal materials would have been only moments away from getting into the wrong hands.

I don't question my judgement call for a moment.

My sympathies do go out to Danny, though. Your first kill is never easy. Adam told Danny how well he could remember his.

Personally, I can't be sure when exactly I first killed a man. Things were never quite so clear-cut in the army. There were skirmishes in Northern Ireland. Grenades and crossfire. Men were lost on both sides. Perhaps I threw one of the fatal grenades. Or pulled the relevant trigger. But it's impossible to know. Not unless you're there and looking them in the face.

The first time I knew for sure was with A Section in Northern Ireland. I've written about it here before: I shot two of McCann's henchmen as I escaped. I came home, had a fight with Jane and slept on the sofa. It didn't feel like a landmark at the time. I was immune to death by then.

But I've always liked that poem 'Five Ways to Kill a Man' by Edwin Brock. It reads like a recipe's instructions: nail him to a cross, run him through with a length of steel, blow gas at him, press a small switch in an aeroplane etc. 'For this you need . . .' But what I really like about it is that it shows the progression of warfare and assassination through history. If you wanted to kill someone in the good old days, you had to get up close and personal with them. See the whites of the eyes. And then push a metal blade through their ribs. Even in the Great War, soldiers found themselves shooting one another at point-blank range.

Now, the military fights with aerial bombardments and laser-guided weapons and unmanned drones and tanks that fire from the other side of the valley.

It's a metaphor for how MI5 fights most of the time as well. How many people have I killed? Directly – maybe a handful. How many deaths have I caused? Indirectly – I'd rather not think about it. Agents who've been left to their fate. Blind eyes turned. Lesser of two evils chosen. Attacks that weren't foiled.

We're in the business of death here. Too often we let others do our dirty work for us. We become immune to our own industry, the protective layers of lies that we place between our decisions and their consequences.

Danny is hurting right now. But it's good for him to have to face up to the real nature of his job.

Martin Luther King once said, 'A man who won't die for something is not fit to live.' It's an admirable statement. But I would turn it round and say, 'A man who won't kill for something is not fit to live.' Especially when that man is an MI5 officer.

It's just that we have to be very, very careful in defining what that 'something' is.

[5 January 2005]

Our friendly coroner has just delivered a verdict of accidental death in the case of Dr Newland – an overdose of insulin while under the influence of alcohol.

It's very useful having a coroner friendly to MI5. We make sure that all our suspicious cases are delivered direct to him. He's excellent at making murder appear like a car accident or an unfortunate fall from a top-floor flat or an overdose of paracetamol. All it takes is a little bit of make-up, elementary medical knowledge and zero scruples.

[14 February 2005]

Catherine sent me an email today – to my Hotmail address, of course – from the West Bank.

'Dear Daddy,' it began. 'My new film about displaced Palestinian orphans will soon have them swarming in the multiplexes . . .'

It's good to be back in touch with my immediate family, even if it's only twenty-five per cent of them. Catherine has promised to do what she can to put in a good word for me with Jane. In that naïve, childlike way of hers, she probably still holds out a hope of us getting back together. But I wouldn't want to. Jane has Robin now, in any case. But it would be nice to be on speaking terms, at least.

I've discovered that Graham rarely communicates with Jane, either. In a horrible sort of way, that makes me feel a little better.

[2 March 2005]

I held a disciplinary hearing with Ruth today. At the beginning of January, I'd become concerned that she was spending too much time listening to static surveillance tapes. There was a man called John Fortescue whom we'd been tasked to protect. Ruth seemed to take this task to extremes by staying up all hours listening in to his life.

I put Sam on to her to find out exactly what was going on. It turned out that Ruth had engineered a chance lunch meeting with Fortescue and then taken Malcolm to a scratch choir singalong requiem so she could 'bump' into him again. It had got completely out of hand and I had to step in before it got any worse.

Part of the problem, I think, is that our job turns us into very nosy people. It is our professional calling – to snoop, to ask questions, to find out things that others hope to keep secret. The temptation to transfer these skills to our private lives can sometimes be overwhelming. Is your neighbour annoying you with late parties? Apply your dirty-tricks training to them. Is your credit rating low? Just look at what Danny did.

This temptation is exacerbated, of course, when it comes to love. Who is that pretty girl you met on the Tube? Run her face through our database and find out. What's your former lover up to these days? Read her emails, intercept her post and find out. If we're not careful, we can turn into pretty horrendous human beings. Apply your training learned here against an innocent individual – a 'civilian', if you like – and they don't stand a chance.

[spooks]

I've seen it happen. This job attracts all sorts: loners, obsessive compulsives, the lot. Most of them manage to keep the more fringe elements of their personalities under wraps. Some of them don't. But in some ways, everyone who works here is a little unbalanced. Sane, level-headed people become accountants, not spies.

I'm not saying that's what happened to Ruth, of course. She was naïve, but it was more that she was lonely. I know how she feels. This job can leave little time for socialising sometimes. And it's difficult to make small talk with new people when most of our personal details are off limits. It defeated Jane and me, in the end. We spend our days having big talk — very big talk indeed. It can be hard to wind down in the evenings.

Anyway, Ruth put up a surprisingly combative performance in the disciplinary hearing today. She's always been a bit timid since she arrived here — so grateful to be seconded and then to be kept on permanently. This is her life. Without it, I think she'd go to pieces. She speaks her mind, certainly, but she has a very definite sense of deference.

Today, however, was different. She called me 'simple' and 'cowardly'. The disciplinary process was a 'shambles'. I, apparently, had 'lost my sense of proportion'.

And I must say, I rather liked it. I would never admit it to anyone, but I'm now a little jealous of that Fortescue bloke she was so smitten with. Perhaps I could arrange for a few dirty tricks to be played on him myself.

[2 April 2005]

The Pope died today — not unexpectedly, of course. It's not exactly an event that no one can say they saw coming. The obituaries had already been written, the TV documentaries recorded, the politicking begun among the leading cardinals.

But I do feel rather sorry for Prince Charles and Camilla, who've been forced to delay their wedding. It seems that nothing can go right for that couple. Yet I suppose that when you've been waiting for decades, a few more days won't matter quite so much.

[6 April 2005]

As you enter the CIA's headquarters you pass an inscription that reads: YOU SHALL KNOW THE TRUTH, AND THE TRUTH SHALL SET YOU FREE.

As dark ironies go, it's up there with *ARBEIT MACHT FREI* over the gates of Auschwitz.

Truth in the intelligence agencies — ours as well as the Americans' — is a highly elastic concept. We make it elastic. We play with it for our own ends. We just hope that we don't stretch it so far that it breaks and snaps back in our faces.

We're walking a fine line at the moment. Zoe is on trial as Officer X, charged with conspiracy to murder and involuntary manslaughter by an unlawful act. Strictly speaking, she's guilty.

A few weeks ago, she infiltrated the Turkish mafia and befriended a young man called Ozal. She then used his sexual jealousy to turn him into her weapon. The leader of this mafia was Emre Celenk. We've been trying to get at him for years. He'd been running many of Al Qaeda's business interests in Europe. Ozal was our way to him.

Zoe interpreted an escalation in the mission's objectives as a kill order. Ozal acted. Tragically, an undercover policeman was shot as well as Celenk.

In court, I've instructed Zoe to lie — Celenk's death can never be admitted as an operation goal — and she is holding up well under interrogation. Truth, here, has nothing to do with morality. It's a practical decision. The government wanted a chance to showcase its rusty, liberal credentials. Here it is. The policeman has a young widow. Shady spooks or brave copper's family? We always knew which side they'd be on.

Also, we'd never be able to explain our methods properly in public. A decent barrister would make mincemeat of an operation to take out a mafia leader, however convincing our own arguments. That does not mean our operations are wrong. I have faith in all of MI5's activities, but they could not stand up to tub-thumping, left-wing lawyers with the bit between their teeth. What can, in fact, these days?

There used to be a general acceptance in this country that everyone was doing their best. If doctors made a mistake, they were gently reprimanded, not sued. If politicians put a foot wrong, they resigned, with dignity. But now we live in a culture of denials, shrill 'investigations' by groups with vested interests, widespread media hysteria, idealists with no sense of reality and ruthless pragmatists with no sense of idealism.

In any case, we have assurances. Zoe will get no more than a rap on the knuckles and will be able to return to work. The police will feel that justice has been done. The media will have their story. The public will have their explanation. Everyone goes home happy.

[7 April 2005]

Zoe was given ten years by the judge and this has turned into all-out war.

I went to see the Attorney General this afternoon and he was immovable. I hope he remembers his pious bullshit the next time there's a terrorist outrage in this country. I lost my temper when he asked me to talk about it over a Scotch in the club. Is that all he thinks Zoe is worth to me? A bloody Scotch?

They gave us a political trial. Now we're going to get political on them. Reputations will go down with Zoe. I know where the bodies are buried and I'm going to disinter the corpses.

[8 April 2005]

I've forgotten more explosive state secrets than the Lubyanka has had overnight guests. So it was not mere bluster when I threatened a coup over Zoe's imprisonment: I genuinely believed I could deliver one. Almost thirty years in MI5 gives you access to a lot of information that important people would not like to see made public.

We have files on the cabinet with sufficient content to bring down the government. And not just the usual youthful flirtations with far-left socialism, either. Foreign business links. Affairs. Emails they thought they'd deleted. The lot.

We have sufficient dirt on every chief executive of every FTSE 100 company to crash the stock exchange overnight.

We could blackmail every national tabloid and broadsheet newspaper editor into printing whatever we liked.

We could reveal which member of the royal family is illegitimate.

Part of Section M's remit is to investigate every conspiracy theory in the public domain. It wouldn't take much to tweak their sane, rational (and frankly quite dull) conclusions and tell the public that the moon landings were faked, Elvis is alive, Salman Rushdie assassinated J.F. Kennedy and President Bush is descended from the direct bloodline of Jesus.

The Attorney General is a decent, family man. But he won't look that way after Malcolm has downloaded child pornography on to his hard drive and alerted the police.

I could go on. My point is that MI5 would be a dangerous sleeping beast to wake.

The Attorney General was made aware of the seriousness of my threats — I would have happily lost my job on a point of principle over Zoe's sentence — and has arranged a deal for Zoe.

It is something of a Pyrrhic victory, however. Zoe will have to assume the new name of Gina Hamilton, adopt Chilean identity and never see her friends and family again. Danny was instrumental in persuading her to accept the deal. It was a brave and noble thing for him to do. Part of him might have thought that she'd get out within ten years; that she'd change her mind and come to him then. But he acted selflessly.

Going to Chile was Zoe's only way out and Danny knew that. But it means that none of us will ever see her again.

We ask so much of our officers. We demand so much and give so little in return. And yet they seldom shirk their response. Over the years, Zoe has been shot at, set up, kidnapped and now rejected by the country she loved to protect. Yet she went without a hint of accusation to a new life under a new name in a foreign country.

[28 April 2005]

Tomorrow is Ruth's birthday. She hasn't told anyone about it – she's not that kind of person – but I looked it up in her personnel file.

I'm not sure if I should do anything about it. Would she be pleasantly surprised? Or embarrassed? And is it appropriate for me to be giving her a present? Why, in fact, am I thinking of giving her a present anyway? It's not as if I'm going to put it on expenses. I've never given Danny a birthday present. Or Malcolm. And I've known them a lot longer.

[29 April 2005]

I found out (subtly, from Sam) that Ruth's favourite film is *The Red Shoes*. So I gave her an album inspired by the film. I also gave her a book about cats. Both were hidden in her desk. I could see her discover them after lunch, her slight blushing visible from my office.

In the afternoon, we were all in the meeting room together and she shot me a furtive little smile. I smiled back.

[4 May 2005]

Zoe's now safely in Chile — I've just heard from Six's man in Santiago — but her former fiancée Will has been making a nuisance of himself, continually turning up at Danny's flat and pestering him for information on where she's gone. He'd read reports in the paper about Officer X and assumed it was her. Danny stupidly told him that a deal had been cut and she wasn't actually in prison.

I feel sorry for all of them. Danny has lost his flatmate and his colleague. Will has let slip the woman he was meant to marry. God only knows what is going through Gina Hamilton's mind at the moment.

But there really is nothing I can do about it. It was difficult enough securing a deal for Zoe as it was. I can't risk it all unravelling now. If I told Will that she was in Chile, there's no guarantee that things would work out. What if they broke up and he decided to sell the story? It's a tale that newspapers would pay thousands for. Zoe went on the condition of protection.

I know she trusted him. But it's a human failing she'll have to overcome.

[5 May 2005]

At least Zoe won't have to live underneath this government any more. They just won re-election today.

Electioneering is always a tedious time for civil servants, whether we work in the Department of Work and Pensions or MI5. Politicised trials aside, our work goes quiet. No one is sure if they're serving this master or the next. Even if the party in power is voted out, there is still a high chance of a reshuffle post victory.

The election period is particularly tedious for Five because politicians suddenly decide that there are hundreds of babies in their constituencies crying out to be kissed by unfamiliar, middle-aged legislators. Walkabouts become the curse of their protection officers. The less important ones, of course, can be left to fend for themselves. But cabinet ministers always want extra security at these times. It means delegating sulky officers to trudge around dreary town shopping centres, fending off eggs and punches from angry protesters (even from cabinet ministers themselves sometimes). Every venue needs to be security checked, every speaker vetted.

It's also an opportunity for all the political freaks to crawl out of the woodwork. One of the scariest moments is the counting hall after the ballots have closed and our junior officers sit and wonder which loony party might knock off the other.

[8 May 2005]

There are some worrying techno-freaks hacking into pharma-
ceutical companies, clearing bank accounts, diverting 999 calls
to chat lines and setting all traffic lights to green. Modern
technology makes life very easy until it all goes wrong. When
it's used against us – viz. 9/11 – we're buggered.

But is this a 9/11 scenario? Guy Facer, the new Security
and Intelligence Coordinator, certainly wants to blame it on
Muslim extremists. It suits the government in the current
climate to blame everything on Muslim extremists. The public
likes black and white, the goodies and the baddies. Train
delayed – blame the Muslims. Overcast skies – probably a form
of chemical attack initiated by bin Laden.

It doesn't help us one bit though. The Muslim community
quickly gets whiff of any such cover-up. It means that the next
time something serious happens and it does involve them, no one
believes us. We're stoking our own conspiracy theories by acting
like this.

[10 May 2005]

The culprit was one of our own. We'll cover it up, of course.
But it's not a good sign that so many intelligence officers keep
on going bad on us.

At least this one worked at GCHQ, not MI5. As I've written
before, I've never really liked GCHQ types – Ruth aside, of
course. They're too intellectual for their own good. Too
socially maladjusted. They spend all their time in darkened

302

rooms, wrestling with codes and foreign languages and bugs and chips and other strange concepts that have little anchorage in the real world. If they applied their expertise to the private sector, they could earn millions — especially now that IT skills are so highly prized.

Most of them seem to cope — perhaps because they're too timid to know any better. But Andrew Forrestal, an old friend of Ruth's from GCHQ, went wrong in the most spectacular fashion. One of his Cambridge friends had made a great deal of money out of a computer code (the technicalities of which meant nothing to me). Forrestal was jealous and wanted to release this code to everyone as a legacy of his work. Colin assured me this would be devastating — every computer system in the world could be hacked into.

Ruth was on to Forrestal. She's excellent at her job; I've never known anyone spot so many allusions and links that the rest of us would miss. 'God is in the details,' she's fond of saying, quoting Flaubert. She'll always find that personal touch, the reference to a long-dead Persian poet or a military cell that was prevalent in seventh-century Mesopotamia. It makes her great at her desk, but not so good in the field, unfortunately. I think she must have taken a liking to Forrestal because she agreed to go round to his for dinner. Thinking with her heart and not her head, no doubt, but at least this time she'd met a man properly and not through eavesdropping on his tape transcripts.

Still, no one else among us would have realised it was Forrestal. I don't think she did until she went to his and was kidnapped. And the outcome was a successful one: Forrestal's laptop has been destroyed. Forrestal himself is dead. Ruth is safe.

[1 June 2005]

The Director General is retiring at the end of the summer and they have asked me to apply for the position. It's not the kind of thing you can say 'No' to. When people ask you to do things at Thames House, it's more of a rhetorical question than anything else.

Question: 'Would you like to go undercover with a violent, terrorist gang and not see your wife and children for a few months?'

Correct answer: 'Yes, delighted.'

Incorrect answer: 'Let me think about it and get back to you. But I must admit my knee-jerk response is, no, I'd rather not.'

Question: 'The DG is retiring at the end of the summer and we were wondering whether you'd like to apply for the vacancy, Harry.'

Correct answer: 'Of course, I'd love to. Thank you for giving me this unique opportunity.'

Incorrect answer: 'You must be joking. Sit on the seventh floor in splendid isolation, brown-nosing politicians and getting gout over long lunches. I'd rather . . . etc., etc.'

I've taken Ruth into my confidence and she's agreed to help prepare me for the interview. I have to turn in a decent performance. I can't have the bigwigs thinking that I don't run Section D properly. But it can't be too good a performance. This is not a job I want to leave.

The last time I prepared for an interview like this with someone else was with Jane, back in 1978.

Ruth is very organised, dividing my revision time into four main areas: state of readiness of the service; my character; operational experience; and nature of the present threat and how far we go to combat it. I feel a little bit like a schoolchild preparing for his O levels again.

She seems very worried that I'd let the power go to my head if I became DG. 'Hypothetically,' she asked, 'you wouldn't forget about us, would you, when you're pacing the thickly carpeted floor of your new office?'

Fortunately, I think that's a very hypothetical question indeed.

[2 June 2005]

More pressingly for my immediate duties as Head of Section D, Adam and Danny are currently interrogating a mercenary called Morgan.

It's a fine line between what they're doing and torture. I certainly wouldn't want UN observers in Morgan's cell at the moment. They might have one or two awkward things to say about the Geneva Convention.

We've tried all the obvious channels. We've put pressure on the three Fs — finances, friends and family. We've offered him money. Nothing. Then we cleared his bank accounts. Nothing. We threatened to destroy his reputation. Still, nothing. We're now working on family.

Adam is an effective interrogator; more so than Danny, who

is not quite convincing enough to scare Morgan. Adam, on the other hand, is even scaring Danny, who's not sure himself how far he'll go. I've read Adam's file. He suffered horribly under interrogation in Yemen. But I've got faith in him here. He's not exacting some kind of weird, protracted revenge. He's just adapting what he learned about himself. He knows how big the stakes are.

As ever, it's a means-and-ends debate. Ruth has just uncovered a piece of intelligence from Morgan's bank accounts, which show deposits from a major oil company. Fiona discovered that they intend to use Morgan's missile to 'remove' a rival company from the bidding process for a multibillion-pound oil-pipeline-route deal.

We can't let this happen. Morgan is a tough nut. It's not as if we've just picked someone off the street and harmed them. He is a mercenary, operating illegally for an oil company. Lives will be lost if he goes ahead.

This is the future, I suppose. Once upon a time, countries fought each other. Knights led their serfs into battle behind heraldic shields and under the King's banner. People died for their homelands. Now it's corporations fighting among themselves, legally and illegally. But no one wants to sacrifice their life for a bank or a law firm or an oil company. So they're paying mercenaries huge sums of money to do their dirty work for them. The prize isn't glory any more. It's money.

[3 June 2005]

Adam broke Morgan.

We used his ill daughter on him in the end. It was a low thing to do, but she remained unaware of what was going on. It was the only thing we had left on Morgan that we hadn't used.

I also had my interview for the DG's position. It went OK. I probably overstepped the mark in some of my comments and it was sufficient for them not to give me the job. It's gone to a political type instead. The usual desk type. School friend of Mace's. Good luck to him.

I'm happy to be back down on the right floor again.

I'm even happier that Fiona has agreed to join the team full-time. She and Adam are an excellent couple, both personally and professionally. My new Archie and Amanda. And the others like her too.

[2 July 2005]

Simultaneous 'Live 8' concerts took place around the world today as overpaid pop stars attempted to emotionally blackmail people into caring about Africa. I know we should try not to be cynical about this. There is no hidden agenda here, no great uncovered evil. The motives are laudable. These people are trying to do good, not bad.

But it is difficult to accept being preached at. And it is even harder not to question whether that poor continent might deserve better than a bunch of concert revellers texting their mates who weren't canny enough to get tickets.

[4 July 2005]

Invading Iraq was always going to come back and bite us. It was just a question of when and how. And how often.

Yesterday, Danny became the first obvious victim on domestic soil of British government foreign policy. He and Fiona were kidnapped by Iraqis demanding the withdrawal of our troops. Danny was shot dead.

'We do not negotiate with terrorists.' That is always the line, isn't it? Well, it's completely untrue. We always negotiate with terrorists. Or at least we always used to. Look at the IRA: as I've said before, we had back channels to them for years. A better line would be, 'We do not negotiate with terrorists openly.' Or, more accurately, 'We cannot be seen to negotiate with terrorists.'

The problem with Iraq and Al Qaeda (and they *are* separate issues) is that we haven't kept the back channels of communication open. It's all very well spouting pious rubbish in public about not negotiating with terrorists, but you have to have some sort of way of contacting these people. *Know thyself; know thine enemy.* Otherwise, what do you do when someone is kidnapped? How can you respond to their demands if you have no counter-demands and no way of exerting your own pressure?

It doesn't have to be a capitulation. But the Home Secretary closed down all these avenues. Danny and Fiona weren't civilians, he told me, as if this somehow made the moral dilemma less acute. I'd say it was the opposite. We had an even greater duty to save their lives. Not pulling troops out of Iraq, of course. That *would* be capitulation. But there's always something else you can offer.

Sadly, in this job, we don't get to deal with the nice guys. But that doesn't mean that you can't deal with them full stop. You can always make a bloody deal. There's always a way out.

The Home Secretary's pig-headedness cost me the life of one of my best officers. Fiona, who was rescued by Adam, told me Danny died a good death, that he looked it in the face, broad-shouldered, square-jawed, and told it he was ready. I wouldn't have expected anything less of him. Danny is, was, a great man. But a good death is a poor consolation for a short life.

There is another, worrying, aspect to these kidnappings. In a recorded statement, the Iraqi kidnapper said, 'Let this be a warning that we will take hostages wherever we choose.'

If he means that, it's a terrifying prospect. We've all seen the footage of British and American hostages paraded in orange jumpsuits in Iraq. But what if sympathisers started doing it over here as well? They've got fifty million potential victims to choose from and a twenty-four-hour media to fuel the panic.

[7 July 2005]

Danny was Five's first victim of our Iraq policy. Today, fifty-six people died as three bombs exploded on the London underground and a fourth on a bus.

Politicians will never link Iraq and today's events. Few will be brave enough to state it publicly. But I will spell it out here: our ill-advised foreign policy has radicalised British Muslim youth.

Of course, the semantic tightrope is rather more precarious than that. Might suicide attacks have occurred here had we not invaded Iraq? Yes, of course. But there is a simpler line of questioning: did invading Iraq make us safer? No. Has it made us more vulnerable? Yes. Did we have to do it, then? No.

Fifty-six of my countrymen. And for what?

It's different when these things happen abroad. Abroad, you try to understand. You empathise. You sympathise with the causes, with what must have happened to drive these people to desperate measures. But here, at home, there is nothing but anger. Anger and incomprehension. Anger and revenge. And fear.

That's the public reaction. But we don't have the luxury to indulge those emotions. What we feel is shame. Remorse. Self-anger. And a sense of complete exhaustion. We've tried. My God, we've tried our best. But it's finally come to roost here as well.

New York, Bali, Istanbul, Casablanca, Madrid. Now London.

[2 August 2005]

I've noted this before, that you can get the measure of a man by noting how he acts in extremis. I think you can also get the measure of a nation as well. Its character. Its values. Its identity.

Londoners haven't turned in on each other. They've carried on with their daily lives, quietly, robustly and with good humour.

Websites always spring up after this kind of atrocity. One is called www.werenotafraid.com. It features pictures sent in by contributors – of themselves, their pets, digitised cartoons, their families – all holding up the slogan, WE'RE NOT AFRAID.

It's an uplifting sign of solidarity, albeit a little cheesy, which is why there's another website Colin showed me that I rather prefer – www.iamfuckingterrified.com.

'I am fucking terrified,' says the speech bubble next to a large bear made up to look like a Beefeater.

'Get me on the first flight out of here,' says a group of pigeons in Trafalgar Square.

'Join the fucking queue,' says a drinks vendor underneath.

Insensitive? I don't think so. It's honest, at least. And sometimes we need irony to help us react to this kind of event. Blitz spirit. Gallows humour. It's a very British thing.

[16 August 2005]

I've had to relocate Sam Buxton to GCHQ. She reacted badly to Danny's death and has barely come off sedatives since. We need tougher souls for these tough times.

[28 August 2005]

As if the current state of mild panic isn't enough, a nihilist American terror group called Shining Dawn is trying to set off bombs in London. The Grid is swamped with visitors – some welcome, some not. I've just asked Zafar Younis to stay with us on a permanent basis. He's a little bit full of himself for my liking, uses the word 'cool' rather too much and thinks of himself as something of a hit with the ladies, but he's an excellent officer, nonetheless. I think he'll grow on me.

The CIA are also swarming all over the place, attempting to lend us some of their expertise on Shining Dawn. It hasn't been much help so far.

And then there is Juliet Shaw, back from Tehran, Beirut, Moscow, Washington and my Parisian bed to make life difficult for me again. It was quite a shock to see her again. I thought we'd simply continue to observe each other's careers at a distance. The birdlike quality of her face has softened. There are a few lines around the eyes. More expensive suits. Elegant where she was once pretty. But she's still Juliet: bossy, driven, ambitious and bloody sexy.

[29 August 2005]

There's something else about Juliet that hasn't changed: she's still horribly ruthless. Upset that her security clearance wasn't sufficiently high, she tried to blackmail me about Operation Omega. People have long memories in the security services. Omega was almost thirty years ago.

I have offered my resignation to the Home Secretary once the Shining Dawn operation is over. I refuse to live under the cloud of exposure for the rest of my career.

Her blackmail threat led Adam and me to suspect her of leaking information on our current operation against Shining Dawn. Someone, somewhere, is leaking and she appeared to be the prime target.

When we confronted her this afternoon, she was extremely

angry, especially as she had been up all night identifying Shining Dawn's bomb-maker. Stung, she embarrassed me in front of Adam by mentioning our affair. Perhaps I'd asked for it. Loyal officers don't take kindly to being accused of treason.

[30 August 2005]

A successful outcome to the Shining Dawn operation. It's a relief to have completed an operation without losing yet another officer.

We weren't far off it at one point though. Adam suicidally decided to stay with a waitress — a nice young girl called Tash — who was strapped to a bomb, instead of making a run for it himself. It was the right call in the end. We managed to get the code out of one of the Shining Dawn agents and defuse the bomb.

I could see why Adam took a liking to Tash. She embodies many of the virtues, as well as the vices, of her generation. She was plucky, witty and good company. But there is no sense of society any more in this country. No duty among the young. No responsibilities to go with the rights that everyone demands. No concept that you give back what you receive.

I'm also pleased that everything is straight again with Juliet. She was excellent at interrogating our Shining Dawn agent.

This evening, I had a chat with the Home Secretary. They want to appoint Juliet National Security Coordinator and I was asked if I had any problem with the appointment. I confirmed that I had none. I am looking forward to working with her. As a close friend of the Prime Minister's, she was the obvious choice. God knows why she's so keen on the current occupant of Number Ten. I wouldn't want to save this one's life.

But I do like the current Home Secretary. It's rare we get a politician we can actually work with at Five. Most of them think we're a nuisance to be endured until they can call on us for their own ends. They're suspicious — probably rightly so. We had incriminating student files on the last three. And they keep on swapping jobs so quickly.

This one seems to understand us. And he appears to like me, which is particularly useful. Operation Omega has been swept under the carpet again, as far as that means anything at Thames House. It's a bulging carpet here, full of intrigue and skeletons. Not everything gets lost under there for good.

[12 September 2005]

England drew the final Test match to win the Ashes today. I was there at the ground, where I spotted at least forty other senior civil servants and politicians skiving from the office.

A wonderful day. Drank a little too much to celebrate and sent another tongue-in-cheek message to my counterpart in Australia.

[14 September 2005]

If only all our elected representatives could be trusted in the same way as the Home Secretary.

We're dealing with a particularly nasty piece of work

called William Sampson MP at the moment. He's in the mould of far-right politicians every where – egomaniacal, personable, good-looking, demagogic and utterly mad. It's just the right/wrong time for him as well. Recent terror attacks have made the country fearful. Immigrants are experiencing backlashes. Multiculturalism is collapsing all around us.

Sampson is attempting to exploit these trends by renouncing the Conservative Party and joining the far-right British Way instead. To this end, he has resigned his seat in order to re-fight it in a by-election.

We've seen this sort of thing before, of course. But in the current climate it's more scary. And Sampson is a professional.

But, two can play at this game. If he wants to use the democratic process in order to destroy it, then we'll destroy it in order to save it. He can expect a very dirty fight indeed.

[15 September 2005]

Zaf is earning his spurs with a first-rate dirty-tricks campaign against Sampson. So far, he's faked polls, printed spurious leaflets, messed up his Internet shopping and turned off his water supply.

My favourite trick, however, was when Zaf painted his door blue and then posed as a council official to fine him for 'aesthetic anarchy'.

Later, he rang Sampson at home: 'This is the establishment calling. How do you feel now we've added a little colour to your life?'

Zaf is a devious one. I'm just glad he's on our side.

[16 September 2005]

The other problem with far-right parties is that their public figures are rarely representative of their actual policies. I'm sure the Nazis could be very charming if you put them next to a pretty girl at a dinner party and kept the conversation away from politics. It's the grassroots you have to worry about. What's going on behind the chiselled smiles and the attempts to couch racism within the parameters of 'rational debate'?

Adam is undercover as a party member, where he has struck up a bond with Keith Moran, the leader of the British Way outside parliament.

We're embracing the old concept: divide and rule. Exploit internal rivalries. We used to do it regularly in Northern Ireland as well. If you can't get at your enemies directly, use others to get at them. There's nothing like stirring a little jealousy as a motivating factor.

Zaf on dirty tricks, Fiona running rings around Sampson as a 'lobbyist', Adam stoking up resentment among the foot soldiers? The British Way don't stand a chance.

[24 September 2005]

A successful outcome, although we were disappointed to lose one of our agents who was acting as a lookout for Adam. Killing her was a very, very stupid thing for the British Way to do. If they'd left her alone, we might have been content with a successful operation and left it at that. As it is, we'll now make all their lives difficult for a long time. MI5 doesn't forget easily, especially when it concerns our own.

It was good to see Ruth have a brief sortie into the field as well. I was rather worried about her after the Shining Dawn operation. She fell asleep while guarding Professor Curtis at a safe house and Danny's death affected her more than most. But she did well on this op. Adam tells me that he distracted Moran in the woods while she thumped him over the head with a branch.

Apparently, she asked Adam whether she could hit Moran again, brandishing the branch triumphantly above her head.

I wish I'd been there to see it.

[8 October 2005]

I'm just back from an interesting trip to Israel after taking up an invitation from its domestic security agency, Shin Bet, to see how they protect the country against suicide bombers. The events of July this year made us all realise how woefully unprepared we were for attacks of this nature. The poor Israelis have had years of experience.

I learned a lot from them, but it's not a vision of Britain that I'd particularly like to see in the future: scanners at bus and train stations, a militarised society, checks in every shopping centre and restaurant.

I've spent time in Israel before — eight months on a kibbutz after school. So it was good to go back and see what has changed. Israel used to be a young country, full of youthful vigour, idealists, poet-soldiers, its kibbutzim filled with Western hippies. Now it's battle-scarred, weary, like an alcoholic that occasionally lashes out at random. It's lost the goodwill support of the world that it used to enjoy, too.

It was a sad trip in many ways. But I did get the chance to see Catherine in the West Bank. My Israeli minders didn't like it one bit. Why on earth did I want to go to Jenin? they asked. It wasn't so much suspicion as disbelief.

But Catherine has a nice young French diplomat as a boyfriend out there and he offered to drive me from Jerusalem out to the West Bank. I could see why Catherine liked him. He was charming, witty, warm and utterly biased against Israel. When we came to the checkpoints, he'd wind the window down, put on a tape of loud Quranic music and refuse to speak anything except Arabic to the Jewish soldiers. Catherine told me that the Republic of Ireland had played a football match in Tel Aviv against Israel the week before. Fabian had gone in the only green T-shirt he could find. The slogan across the front read, FREE PALESTINE.

I had a great time with the two of them. Catherine's film is still 'work in progress' but she showed me areas of the occupied territories that I would never have seen otherwise.

How many people really understand the situation in that part of the Middle East? This tiny plot of promised land that has been promised to so many *by* so many. God. The British. The Jordanians. And the false prophets who've pretended to care while kicking it around like another political football. Nasser. Saddam Hussein. The Gulf States.

It's impossible to return home and not find British politics horribly parochial in comparison.

[11 October 2005]

The first time, I think, in my career that I've been right and Juliet was wrong. But it wasn't a very satisfying victory.

We'd bugged the London hotel suite of Prince Hakim, a playboy member of a Gulf royal family whom we believed to be involved with smuggling routes into this country.

Adam and Zaf then intercepted a known terrorist, Mohammed Yazdi. We thought we'd turned him. It's the greatest form of flattery — to be desired by your enemies. He demanded to interrogate the prince whom he claimed was masterminding his terrorist cell.

I had an awful feeling about this, a sense in my bones that something terrible would happen if we allowed Yazdi and Prince Hakim in the same room together. My instincts have rarely failed me.

Juliet thought otherwise. She overruled me.

Yazdi stabbed the prince with his glasses in the neck and killed him. Yazdi's objection was to the decadent ways of the oil-rich Gulf kingdoms, the sheikhs who preach abstinence at home, practise sharia law and then come here in the summer, shave their beards, drink alcohol and sleep with prostitutes. He objected to our alliance with these regimes, the blind eye we turn to their oppressive domestic structures in return for a free flow of oil and support against more militant Islam.

Of course, I knew nothing of this when Juliet overruled me and allowed the fatal interview to take place. I just thought I knew it.

As we cleared up the mess, both physical and political,

Juliet said to me that neither of us should ever resign. 'Let's make that a ground rule between us.'

It's a ground rule that suits me fine — she's my superior after all. But I'm not sure I trust her to keep to it.

Still, if she ever brings up Operation Omega again I now have something almost as good on her. I'm sure a certain King somewhere would be very interested to know how and why his son, Prince Hakim, really died. One more thing for Thames House's bulging carpet, then.

[1 November 2005]

It was my fifty-second birthday today. I found four bottles of thirteen-year-old malt hidden in the top drawer of my desk and the letters R, U, T and H written on them.

[7 November 2005]

My old friend Clive McTaggart has just been found dead. It was disguised to look like suicide but a journalist who was there that day caught a glimpse of his murderers.

I'm very upset about this. Clive was a very good man in poor health. He had started writing his memoirs in his retirement and someone had decided that they were worth killing him for. God knows what drove him to this. Boredom, maybe. Or perhaps he had something to say. We all think we have something to say.

I can't let his death go unanswered. Clive had more integrity that anyone I've ever known. But it terrifies me seeing him killed in that way. Who knew he was writing his memoirs? Why wasn't Clive more careful? If only he'd taken the kind of precautions that I have. And what exactly was he writing that was so explosive?

[20 November 2005]

Juliet was behind this nonsense. Her and a nasty little ferret called Roy Woodring, another intelligence officer. I broke into his house last week. That scared him a bit – to come back and find me sitting in his drawing room with a whisky. I want him to crawl under a rock somewhere and ensure that our paths never cross again.

Clive's book apparently contained explosive secrets on MI5's operations. That was the rationale of Juliet and Woodring. She had no sympathy for 'cowards who can't meet their maker without taking everyone else down with them'.

Well, maybe. But I have no sympathy for gung-ho National Security Coordinators who can't do these things through the proper channels. Clive was in ill health. He'd served his country well. He didn't need to be taken out in this way. Whatever happened to stealing a book and destroying it?

It's virtually impossible to block a publication these days anyway. Even the DGs are publishing their memoirs. And look at our various renegade officers. They've got away with it, haven't they?

[25 November 2005]

The only good thing to come out of the Clive affair is that we've secured the services of an excellent new officer called Jo Portman. She used to work as a freelance journalist but her quick wits helped us track the people targeting my men after she met Adam undercover during the Clive operation. My only fear is that it won't be long before Zaf is inviting her to share a flat with him for 'the sake of convenience'.

Journalists and spies aren't so very different really. We both try to find things out that others would rather not know. We both have sources that need protecting. We're both distrusted by the general public. We both have an interesting relationship with alcohol.

Still, the whole team was lucky to find Jo, as they'd been wading through application forms for weeks. Times have changed, rather, since I was in charge of recruitment. Nowadays, we have a website. Even MI6 launched a website last month. Anyone can apply. And anyone *does* apply. Occasionally, there are pearls among the dung, but mainly it's just dung.

It also gives our vetting people a constant headache. Al Qaeda sympathisers now have an easy way of attempting to infiltrate MI5. We have also become the employer of choice for every egomaniac, fantasist and weirdo university graduate. Each time something happens in the press that involves us — a near miss, a plot foiled, a new James Bond film etc. — our applications double. These applicants are the maddest of them all. Our oldest was in her nineties. Our youngest, eleven.

No doubt it also won't be long until we have equal opportunities legislation clamping down on us.

[30 November 2005]

French surgeons have just carried out the first successful human face transplant. Colin quipped in this morning's news round-up that this will be useful for disguising undercover MI5 officers one day — a joke that Malcolm found amusing out of all proportion with its obvious comic value.

[8 December 2005]

Are we any better than anyone else?

That's the question we often ask ourselves here. We take lives. We destroy lives. We often lie, cheat and manipulate to do so. I sometimes wonder how many of the ten commandments we break on a daily basis at Thames House. As we all know, the only one that really counts here is the eleventh.

Our aims are worthy — good God, we could not look ourselves in the mirror if they were not — but our means are often very, very dirty. You have to break an egg to make an omelette, but sometimes it feels like we're on a rampage around a battery chicken farm.

Today, however, we did a good thing. Special Branch had wrongly imprisoned a man in a case of false identity. It's the kind of story the left-wing press and human rights lawyers love: evil police state bang up guy because he's a Muslim etc., etc.

I have to admit, it looks pretty bad on paper.

But when we found out their mistake, we acted honourably. The man's family was in danger. We rescued them. The man himself had been blackmailed into an assassination. We could have shot him. Zaf talked him down instead.

And now we have arranged for the Irish government to give them new names, a new life and enough money for them never to have to work again.

I don't mean to blow our own trumpet. I'm not saying we're whiter than white. But I'd like to hear of the Syrian secret servicer — or even the CIA, for that matter — righting a wrong in this way.

I don't like propaganda; I prefer shades of grey to black and white. My country or yours? Christianity or Islam? My god or yours? My imaginary friend versus your imaginary friend?

Not every side can be right. But you have to believe in what you're fighting for. You can't descend into self-loathing.

I didn't choose to live in this country; I was born here. But had I not been, I still think I'd have been envious of its citizens. For there are certain inalienable truths I like to hold on to — a belief in liberty, liberalism, free speech, democracy, rights and responsibilities, individuality, security — which I find expressed in the British character, its institutions and its ways of doing things.

It's not nationalism. It's barely even patriotism. But it's a quiet, gentle pride in something worth preserving.

It deserves preserving. It deserves protecting.

2006

[4 January 2006]

Fiona was shot dead yesterday by her former husband, Farook Sukkarieh, having deliberately put herself into a situation where she knew she'd have to confront him. Adam subsequently shot Sukkarieh dead.

It pains me so much to lose another excellent officer. The only (very small) consolation is that Fiona died at peace, having exorcised some of her demons. I don't think she could have carried on living much longer with the fear of Sukkarieh hanging over her. And at least he didn't succeed in taking her back to Syria with him. It doesn't bear thinking about how badly he could have treated her. Once they were out of the country, I'm not sure how much we could have done to get her back. We'd certainly have lost Adam to a long, fruitless hunt.

But it's Adam I'm really worried about now. There are many ways of dealing with grief. It hangs over a man like a dark curtain. I remember what it was like when my mother died. You can embrace that grief – think about it all the time, carry it with you, nurture it, suckle it until you slowly learn to live with it and it dissipates, slow day by slow, torturous night. Or you can ignore it altogether – pretend it doesn't exist, carry on with a normality that will never be normal again until it comes back, a thousand times stronger, and destroys a man. You can postpone mourning, but you can't cancel it completely.

Something suggests to me that Adam won't be very good at it. The problem is that he's too much of a coper. He'll see it as a sign of weakness to admit any human frailty. He's meant to be above all that – in control of his emotions, superior to the ebbs and flows that characterise normal human responses.

If ever a couple embodied Aristophanes' speech from Plato's *Symposium*, it was Adam and Fiona. I used to love that passage: 'Do you desire to be wholly one; always day and night to be in one another's company? For if this is what you desire, I am ready to melt you into one and let you grow together, so that being two you shall become one, and while you live a common life as if you were a single man, and after your death in the world below still be one departed soul instead of two.'

I fear for Adam. And I fear for his son, Wes, and what he is going to be told about his mother.

[2 February 2006]

A row over Danish cartoons mocking the prophet Mohammed has escalated to ridiculous proportions. Today the Danish Prime Minister went on Arabic television to apologise for the offence caused while still attempting to defend freedom of expression.

The whole world is a tinderbox at the moment. Both sides are trying to push their luck as far as they can. Muslim troublemakers are making political hay while the sun shines. Belligerent Westerners are lauding the values of free speech at any cost. But of course it has a cost. There is no such thing as truly free speech, even here.

Our world is too integrated and too divided. Too integrated for this sort of thing to go unnoticed. Too divided to sort it out adequately when it does.

[8 February 2006]

I've had to send Adam down to Tring to talk to Diana Jewell, the head of psychology.

He's been a pest here on the Grid since Fiona died. I tried to give him some routine surveillance work to keep his mind off things — I didn't feel I could trust him on bigger ops for the time being — and he accused me of asking him to 'perform slops'. When I refused him permission to join in on Operation Songbird, he kept on showing up out of the blue, walking into surveillance vans and begging Ruth to give him progress reports.

We can't have Adam messing up Songbird; it's sensitive enough as it is. The government is attempting to sell off the NHS to a Russian billionaire, Oleg Korsakov — the third richest man in the world. We believe his intentions are dishonourable, that he only wants it so he can asset-strip it.

In effect, what we're doing here amounts to treaso working against the democratically elected government day. But our reasoning is that it would be treason to to go ahead. There are degrees of treason, afte absence of anything approaching mass Christian in this country, the NHS comes pretty close to God in the eyes of most Britons. Of course, it's criticised, loathed, cajoled, mocked and loved in equal measure. But you allow its destruction at your considerable peril.

'Healthcare free at the point of delivery' – it's hardly *liberté, égalité, fraternité* – but it's still an *a priori* policy for any serious political party.

But how to get to Korsakov? I think the answer might lie in the man we had Adam 'performing slops' on – Hugo Ross, a Communist who's just been released from prison.

[10 February 2006]

Ross and I go back a long way. When I returned from Operation Omega to Five in London, I used to go and visit him in prison once a week. There has always been something admirable about the man. He wasn't a dilettante Communist. He believed in it. And he had a twinkly humour and a sense of style that was atypical of most British Communist traitors.

I used to look forward to our weekly chats. He took it upon himself to try to turn me. We had some heated but friendly debates. He used to tell me with a wry smile that I would be the first against the wall when the revolution came to London. I told him that when the Iron Curtain came down, we'd let him out with egg all over his face.

It is refreshing now to see someone who has stayed true to his beliefs. Ross has the right pedigree to get into Korsakov's ˙r circle and he is agreeing to work with us after seeing the to which Korsakov has 'betrayed' Mother Russia.

Billionaire moguls? Health Service asset-stripping? This was not what the glorious revolution was meant to be about.

Ironically, it is I who have ended up turning him.

[11 February 2006]

The US Vice President accidentally shot a 'friend' of his today on a ranch in Texas. Unfortunately, it wasn't the friend we'd all hoped it was.

[15 February 2006]

Adam checked himself out of Tring to help at the end of Songbird, and it was his quick thinking while Zaf and Ross were in a meeting with Korsakov that extracted the latter's confession as to his true plans for the NHS.

While it is good to have my officers firing on all cylinders again, I was upset to lose Ross now. Old adversaries come to fill a special place in the cold heart of an intelligence officer. It is rare that they turn into friends as well.

I don't think this is the last we'll hear of Korsakov, either. No doubt he'll pop up soon with another British plaything into which he can plough his millions.

[11 March 2006]

Slobodan Milosevic died today from a heart attack in his prison cell in The Hague. Four years after his trial started, this wasn't the kind of swift international justice his prosecutors had hoped for. It makes the decision to try Saddam Hussein in his native Iraq seem more sensible.

[16 March 2006]

I spoke to Fiona's parents today. It had taken Adam a long time to get round to telling them and Wes what had happened. They've taken it very well, with that old-fashioned British reserve that accepts that bad things sometimes happen to good people. It was in marked contrast to the reaction of Helen's family.

[24 March 2006]

The American President decides to invade Iraq; we jump up and down asking to be taken along for the ride. And a ride is exactly what we have been taken for.

Now the Americans are picking up British subjects on British soil and deporting them at will. God knows what happens to them once they're on American soil. Or, more likely, a torture chamber in a third country. The CIA have always acted like the big kid in the playground; now they're treating other countries as an extension of their playground. It's really beginning to get on my nerves.

I sometimes wonder who is running this country. It's certainly not the Prime Minister.

Today, the CIA extradited their third British citizen to Guantanamo Bay without alerting me first. I refuse to allow this to continue. The next time, I'll put my foot down. Just when exactly did this country become a US colony?

[10 April 2006]

I put my foot down and then promptly shot myself in it.

Yesterday, we intercepted a British citizen of Iranian origin called Louis Khurvin. Irish mother, Iranian father – just my favourite combination.

The Americans were trying to deport him; we decided he was no risk and placed him under low-grade category-four surveillance. He escaped, shooting two MI5 surveillance officers.

Juliet has suspended me, the treacherous little whelp. You can't support someone in their decision – like she did – and then jump backwards and pretend you had nothing to do with it when it all goes wrong.

So, I'm sitting at home with my dog, Scarlet, watching daytime television while a bunch of talentless goons keep watch on me from outside. The most annoying thing is that I've given ammunition to the Americans. I hate to see them get one over on me. I know I've made a mistake here, but my instincts are also telling me that there's something else going on.

At least by staying at home I appear to be at less risk of dying of bird flu – the latest media sensation that's going to bring about Armageddon.

[15 April 2006]

I've been touched by the loyalty of my team during my suspension. Ruth keeps on sending me food parcels. Zaf has sent me a bundle of DVDs. The man has slightly dubious taste (fortunately, I don't have a DVD player so I won't be tempted to watch them).

They've also managed to keep me in the loop on operational procedures. Ruth met me on a night bus to pass on a file on David Pollard — a debt collector they suspect of working as a CIA deniable. I hope I didn't imagine it, but I thought I might have detected a frisson of interest from Ruth. There was definitely a moment on that bus. A touch of the hand. A hint of scent in the air. But can I be sure? And what would I do about it anyway?

There was less of a frisson in the air, fortunately, when I managed to meet Adam at the dog track. I've surprised myself being out in the field again like this. I've found it exciting — slipping notes to the newsagents, evading my surveillance teams, talking to Adam at the kennels so no one could eavesdrop on our conversation. It's good to return to the shop floor every now and again.

[22 April 2006]

Pollard *was* a CIA deniable — running Khurvin in an attempt to draw this country into a war against Iran. Our team neutralised him today as he was about to shoot down a plane near Heathrow. We came within minutes of getting embroiled in another costly and unnecessary war in the Middle East.

The sweetest victory of all has been over the CIA. Pollard has been retained in British custody and they've been told they'll have to apply through the official channels to have him extradited. Next time, I hope they put their own house in order before messing around in ours. It's a good biblical lesson for their evangelical President: take the log out of your own eye before removing your friend's.

It's good to be back on the team. I'll have to make sure someone's feeding and walking Scarlet again though, after sacking his previous handler. Perhaps I could lend him to Adam's son, Wes, for a bit. I think they'd get on well.

[29 April 2006]

Ruth's birthday. I hid a series of clues in this morning's intelligence briefing which, put together, led her to the back of the water cooler where there was an old edition of Ovid.

[1 May 2006]

Six have just placed recruitment adverts in *The Times* and the *Economist*. We've been teasing them mercilessly about this.

[2 May 2006]

The twenty-ninth attempt on my life was by another former MI5 officer — Angela Wells. She'd got some mad Diana conspiracy into her head that we'd killed the People's Princess and held us all to ransom until we produced the 'proof' for her. Unfortunately, she'd got confused between events and *contingent* events. We did not assassinate the mother of the future King of England, despite what the *Daily Express* and others maintain. She died in a car crash.

I'm not sure what it is about Diana that touches people in such ridiculous ways. Her ability to turn otherwise sane people mad is highly distressing.

It's a generic problem with conspiracy theories. They help people come to terms with unpalatable truths. Islamic extremists fly planes into the Twin Towers: blame it on Mossad. A young, beautiful woman dies in her prime: MI5/6 must have done it.

It drove Angela mad. It also killed her. She committed suicide yesterday after we'd foolishly stuck to our code and let her walk out of the Grid. Death was probably the best thing for her and we were about to initiate a kill order anyway. You can't go around planting bombs in the Royal Protection Bunker and expect to get away with it. She would have had a horrible time in prison.

She shot Adam before jumping and he's just come out of major surgery in hospital. He's a tough old nut and his body has endured a lot. The doctors tell me he'll be fine, but it's going to be a long, painful journey back to full recovery.

[9 May 2006]

The World Cup starts next month and the media is in its usual frenzy of excitement about how far we are going to go. Somehow I doubt we'll get any further than the second round with this group of preening charlatans. Meanwhile, we have the unenviable job of ensuring crowd safety in pubs and public places during the bigger, televised games. Drunken, massed football fans make a good target for extremists.

[2 June 2006]

Incredibly, it only took Adam four weeks to return to work. The doctors thought it would take him at least twice that long.

God knows, we need him at the moment. The country is almost ungovernable. Fuel depots are being bombed everywhere. This morning, a man on the bus started weeping 'tears of blood', raising fears of biological warfare. The media – and one media mogul in particular – is stoking the flames. An anti-terror bill is going through parliament. The message DJAKARTA IS COMING is appearing on walls everywhere. And, just for good measure, there are threats on the PM's son as well.

Are all these events linked? That is the question we're working on at the moment. Adam doesn't think it has the hallmarks of a classic Al Qaeda attack. But if it's not them, then who?

[3 June 2006]

Colin was found murdered today, and it has affected us all very badly. Staff shortages are partly to blame. But I also blame myself. Colin was a highly valued operator behind the scenes. He should never have been in a dangerous situation in the field.

Malcolm, in particular, is finding it difficult to cope. They were very close, those two, as thick as thieves, babbling away in a language that the rest of us barely understood.

Malcolm flipped in a meeting this morning, calling me a 'pompous old fool'. Adam stepped in and defused the situation. We have to keep what remains of the team together.

[6 June 2006]

This has escalated into a full-blown coup attempt, involving MI6 officer Ros Meyers, her father, who is a former Ambassador to Moscow, the media mogul, Millington, and Michael Collingwood, my counterpart at MI6.

They are attempting to introduce 'special measures to protect democracy', an Orwellian concept if ever I've heard one. It's the wet dream of every intelligent, élitist, demagogue everywhere: sweep away the troublesome paraphernalia of democracy – elections, a free media etc. – and run the country as an oligarchy with a cabal of people you can trust.

The measures are terrifying, and terrifyingly close to implementation after being smuggled through in a Trojan horse of a Home Office bill: compulsory detention orders; monitoring of the media; judicial appointment by ministers; executive orders without parliament etc., etc. That way lies madness.

They tried to get me on board. 'Why do you fetishise democracy so much?' they asked.

The answer is that I don't fetishise democracy; it is a flawed system of government for a flawed human society. But show me a better system. Brave people have died to protect it. They died for a reason. People campaigned for centuries because they cared. That is why it's worth protecting and that is why I won't join this horrid coup.

Churchill had it right: 'Democracy is the worst form of government except for all those others that have been tried.'

This has just got deadly serious. Today, a bomb almost killed Juliet in Parliament Square. She will probably not walk again.

[30 June 2006]

The coup threat has been neutralised, but the successful outcome had little to do with me. I was one of the first victims of what could have been the new order: arrested in Parliament Square and banged up in a detention centre with a smorgasbord of civil liberties protesters and anyone else thought likely to threaten the Brave New World.

The team worked brilliantly in my absence, but it was the British public themselves who provided the most reason for cheer.

The government likes to rail against apathy, but I have nothing against it. Low turnout at the ballot box doesn't bother me. One bunch of charlatans or another – what does it matter where you put the tick in the box? I've served with all political parties and there's little to distinguish between them, especially when it comes to security matters. You can talk all sorts of sanctimonious rubbish about liberty while in opposition. My experience is that it is us reining them in, and not the other way round, once they're in government. It's been written before: power corrupts, and absolute power corrupts absolutely.

What the British public showed last week was a very different sort of political awareness. The mass protest they staged — aided by Internet bloggers everywhere — wasn't about petty party politics or score-settling. It was about preserving the status quo, a system of government and a set of beliefs that we've come to take for granted in this country.

'For evil to flourish, it is only sufficient for good people to do nothing.' There were a lot of good people in Britain yesterday.

We'll leave Millington alone — we've got him over a barrel for a future occasion. But Juliet wants the book thrown at Meyers. Paralysis has, understandably, brought out the hawk in her. It's also brought out a brutally direct honesty that I haven't seen before.

'Are you in love with Ruth?' she asked when I visited her in hospital.

The question took me by surprise. Not because I haven't asked myself the same question, but because it came from Juliet of all people.

'Don't let this opportunity pass you by,' she said.

[6 July 2006]

We had to wait until today to hold a memorial service for Colin. There was no time during the coup crisis.

I sat next to Ruth and lent her my handkerchief during Malcolm's reading. Maybe Juliet was right: I shouldn't let this pass me by.

[12 July 2006]

I don't like the situation in the Middle East one bit at the moment. Israeli troops invaded Lebanon today in response to Hezbollah kidnapping two of their soldiers and killing three others.

It seems a disproportionate response on the face of it. This kind of thing occurs the whole time on the border. Most of the retaliation takes place below the radar. Prisoners are quietly exchanged as often as gunfire.

There's been a ferocious urgency about Israel's response, which is worrying. There's speculation that the new PM is anxious to make up for his lack of military credentials in a country where the army means everything. Israel is also anxious to neutralise the Iranian-sponsored threat on its northern border.

I'm worried about Catherine. She's in Gaza now and experience shows that there's nothing that Israel welcomes more than a diversion elsewhere to allow it to do what it likes in that narrow strip. It's not so much that the world will turn a blind eye than the fact that its eyes can't be everywhere at once.

I emailed her today: 'Do not under any circumstances stay in Gaza. Please.'

[14 July 2006]

I've just come back from a date with Ruth, whistling all the way home. I haven't felt this happy since we discovered the French

Ambassador and the Foreign Secretary involved in an intimate tête-à-tête.

The date went well, I think. I'm so rusty at this sort of thing. For all the years that we've worked together, it was the first time we didn't talk about work the whole time. We had a lot in common. She let me pay at the end. I hope she whistled on her way home, too.

[15 July 2006]

Adam authorised the shooting dead of a terrorist in central London today. It was a successful end to Operation Waterfall, but a nail-biting one. We got the right man but, at best, I think Adam was only seventy per cent sure in his decision. Was that enough to risk shooting an innocent?

Again, I'm reminded of the IRA's words: 'We only have to be lucky once. You will have to be lucky always.'

The concept of luck now works on more levels than they intended. Today, we got lucky with our judgement call. But what if we'd been unlucky? What if we had shot an innocent man? The public would be scared, communities would turn against us. We'd re-examine our motives and our practices and think twice about shooting to kill the next time. That next time might be for real.

This is what the public doesn't realise. Our calls are life and death and all we have to go on is a balance of probabilities. Sometimes, we're lucky. More often than not it's a case of being damned if we do and damned if we don't.

[16 July 2006]

Ruth told me today that she can't have dinner with me again because people are laughing at us.

I didn't know whether to laugh along with them or cry. We put up with a lot in our jobs. People sniggering behind our backs should be the least of our worries. Are they jealous of the boss dating a colleague? Or scorning? I really don't care.

I thought I could talk her round. I still think I could talk her round. We both know there's something there. So why are we holding back?

[18 July 2006]

Catherine finally emailed back: 'Don't worry, I've done what you said. I haven't stayed in Gaza. I've gone to Beirut to help out. Fabian's with me too.'

The stupid, little girl. But what can I do about it? She's not so little any more. She has Fabian. There's no Tom to send out to bundle her to the safety of Amman.

[25 July 2006]

I've just returned from an exhausting African trade conference. Nothing is ever as it seems at these places — clandestine talks between American arms traders and Japanese representatives, bugs everywhere, orphaned, vengeful waitresses, ambitious British Foreign Secretaries who don't care two jots about Africa. It's all a far cry from long-haired pop stars organising concerts in Hyde Park where young management consultants wave their wristbands in the air to U2 and then go back into the office to screw over some more Third World countries.

It was a successful, but messy, outcome in the end. The Foreign Secretary threatened us so we silenced him with a recorded transcript saying it was all about PR. Suppressed MI6 intelligence showed that the leader of West Monrassa was planning genocide having secured the moral capital of a trade agreement. We allowed an assassin to take him down.

It was a very difficult call. We are officers of the state, required to implement state policy, however abhorrent. We are not supposed to make moral or political judgements. We're certainly not supposed to play God. But should we play with the Devil? Knowing what we knew, I think we had no choice in the end but to take the course of action we did.

[26 July 2006]

Our new recruit, Ros Meyers, is an excellent addition to Section D. Combining Zoe's charm, Fiona's steel and Tessa's ambition, she's already been a huge asset in our last two operations.

But I worry about her personal life after her father was sent down for twenty years for his role in the coup plot. In fact, I'm beginning to worry about the personal lives of everyone on the team. Adam still hasn't really come to terms with Fiona's death. Zaf is increasingly flamboyant in his private life. Jo is Jo.

And Ruth and I. Well, Ruth and I . . . it barely started,

but it hasn't burned out either. I'm not sure if we can continue to work under this escalating tension. It needs an outlet, a fire escape, a release valve. Either way, it needs to come to some sort of conclusion. Or I fear for what will happen.

[1 August 2006]

Another email from Catherine. She is working with the Red Crescent in Southern Lebanon. I prayed today, for the first time in forty years, to a god I've never believed in.

[4 August 2006]

Ruth is in trouble and all my protective instincts have surfaced to try to sort it out.

Yesterday morning, a man asked Ruth for change for a £10 note at a Tube station. He then jumped in front of a train. She was convinced it was a drop of some sort but the note has revealed nothing.

The man who jumped was called Mick Maudsley; he was head of security at the prison where seven terror suspects were killed in a fire. Special Branch's report on the incident reads like a cover-up from start to finish.

What is this? Is someone condoning the murder of terror suspects to avoid the awkward business of bringing them to trial? Are we sleep-walking into vigilantism? Or is it worse?

[6 August 2006]

It was worse; much worse. This was all part of an elaborate sting operation by Mace. The seven suspects were removed before the fire so their deaths could be faked and they could be tortured at will. Overnight, they became non-persons.

Mace's logic is that it has worked. It's the same old means-versus-ends debate. Torture someone and stop a second terror attack with the information they give you. But can you still be proud of the kind of regime you're protecting?

Mace believes you can and that is why he set up Ruth for the murder of Maudsley. CCTV footage has been faked to make it look as if she pushed him on the platform. My choice is stark and simple: save Ruth and join Mace's little club of torturers. Or stand up for my principles and watch her burn with them.

He'd forgotten the third option, of course, which was to sacrifice myself. So I did. I threatened Mace over lunch and attacked him with a jagged glass. It was one of the most satisfying things I've ever done. The police were called and I was arrested on suspicion of the murder of Maudsley.

[7 August 2006]

I hadn't counted on Ruth deciding to sacrifice herself for the sake of me. Adam came to collect me from prison today and briefed me that Ruth had set herself up, faking a photo of her receiving orders from Mace to extradite these seven prisoners and perform 'special interrogation measures' on them.

The Defence Secretary has already resigned. Mace's own

position looks increasingly untenable. The seven have been found in Egypt.

And Ruth? Dear Ruth. I've just identified a dead body as hers. It wasn't. Zaf has arranged safe passage for her to France and I'm going to see her tomorrow before she leaves for the last time.

[10 August 2006]

I met Ruth. We kissed. I never said the thing I wanted to say. The words hung, unspoken, in that autumn morning by the Thames. Let's leave it as something wonderful that was never said. Those were her words as we kissed and parted.

There will be no Will and Zoe ending for us. No postcards of gratitude back to dead colleagues in London. No second chances. No grand tour together, drinking white burgundy and joking about surveillance teams watching her purse. No luck, no joy, no future, just the pain of something left undone, a journey never started, a life choice that left us with no choice at all.

I loved her. I loved that silly, stubborn mule. That's what I wanted to say. I still love her.

But there is never time for anything in this job. Our farewells are rushed, our mourning cut short, our grief always truncated by the next reality.

Ruth turned and boarded her boat. I returned to the office and found a message from our man in Beirut. Catherine has been badly injured by unexploded Israeli ordinance and he's not sure where she is. The last he'd heard, she was being cared for by Hezbollah doctors. I am on the next plane to Lebanon.

[5 September 2006]

I always thought that the idea of 'a man possessed' was a cliché. But it's an accurate cliché when it describes a man trying to find his injured daughter in a foreign country.

I broke every rule in the book. A snotty little journalist in Beirut, Helen Nicholas, wouldn't share her information on Hezbollah's whereabouts so I slapped her. In Baalbek, the Hezbollah capital, I shouted at everyone in a yellow T-shirt I could find. I even ran into a mosque without removing my shoes and was almost lynched.

And then, gloriously, finally, I found her, transferred to a hospital in Beirut, Fabian at her bedside. I gave her my blood. Her limbs were saved.

I'd left a messy trail behind me. But none of it mattered any more. Catherine and Fabian were sitting beside me on a plane back to London. And there to meet us – with a smile for me as well as the others – was Jane.

[10 November 2006]

I was burgled again while I was away. Nothing was taken – it looked like a professional job, as if they were looking for something specific. And all I can think about is Clive. The idea of my diaries falling into the wrong hands terrifies me. But who would want them? Mace? Could he know about them? He'd certainly want to destroy what appears here if he could.

In any case, I think I might take a break from writing. Events are just events. There's no meaning in them. Some of them we direct. Others put us at their mercy.

In my bleaker moments, I wonder why I've destroyed everyone I've touched in my life. Graham, damaged. Archie, Amanda, Danny, Colin, Clive and Fiona, dead. Ruth, exiled.

But then I remember the look on Catherine's face, mirrored briefly in Jane's at the airport. I remember the lives we've saved, the debt I owe to friends fallen in the course of duty. Coups thwarted, terrorists brought to justice, rogue elements neutralised, enduring values upheld, fights worth fighting.

I look up from my keyboard and I see Ruth's cat, curled up between Scarlet's paws by the fire and I know that not everything has been in vain.

I'll write again one day, I'm sure. I'll certainly read this again — maybe in my dotage with a wry smile of recollection. Or perhaps someone else in my family is reading this now, long after my death, with a little more understanding of what it was like to have lived, worked and suffered for MI5.

For now, though, I'll go back to my job, dispassionately and professionally, as I always have done. There will be the same old terror plots, some predictable, many with new and terrifying twists. We'll do our best to stop them. Sometimes, we'll be lucky. Occasionally, we'll fail.

Life carries on. Work carries on. I'll carry on.

It's all I know to do.